THE EFFECTS OF EU CITIZENSHIP

Economic, Social and Political Rights
in a Time of Constitutional Change

THE EFFECTS OF EU CITIZENSHIP

Economic, Social and Political Rights in a Time of Constitutional Change

Flora Goudappel

T·M·C·ASSER PRESS

ISBN 978-90-6704-278-9

PRINTED IN THE NETHERLANDS

FOREWORD

When the Court of Justice of the European Union decided in more and more cases on EU citizenship, this became a 'hot topic' in EU law. Several of these cases, like the famous *Chen* case, were even controversial and seemed to bring cases under EU law which would have been national cases before. This did not only raise questions on what EU citizenship meant but also what the influence of membership of the EU in a Member State has become on traditional ideas of citizenship. In this book, I have tried to discuss developments in 'traditional' citizenship within the structure of the European Union. It is therefore not meant to contain complete in-depth descriptions of all elements involved in EU law, like the free movement of persons, but rather a focus on the elements which deviate from or are in congruence with theories on citizenship rights.

While writing this book, the Treaty of Lisbon was signed and eventually ratified by all Member States. The references to Treaty provisions are therefore double: both to the Treaty of Amsterdam and to the Treaty of Lisbon. When applicable the new situation under the Treaty of Lisbon is discussed separately. In all other parts, the relevant case-law and legislation has been developed under the Treaty of Amsterdam and therefore mainly refers to this.

While writing this book, I received support from many people. Philip van Tongeren, Marjolijn Bastiaans and Antoinette Wessels of T.M.C. Asser Press deserve more than only thanks for their continuous extreme patience with me and their never-ending support. I am grateful to the staff of the T.M.C. Asser Institute in The Hague for not only supporting me but giving me an office in which I could write without being disturbed. This was a luxury which I have cherished every day I spent there.

My colleagues of the European Union law department at the Erasmus School of Law in Rotterdam, especially Fabian Amtenbrink and Helena Raulus, have been willing sparring partners for my ideas. Without them, I would not have been able to finish formulating the ideas laid down in this book. Sytske Kooijman has been most helpful with language suggestions. Mehrnoush Golafshan, Masuma Shahid, Eva Hendricks, Caroline Peters and Alex Verhoeff helped me finding the relevant information and I thank them for their efforts. Finally, I want to thank Roel de Lange for helping me with a good title for the book.

Rotterdam/Curaçao, December 2009   Flora GOUDAPPEL

TABLE OF CONTENTS

LIST OF ABBREVIATIONS

A-G   Advocate-General
Am. J. Comp. L.   American Journal of Comparative Law
Ariz. J. Int'l & Comp. Law   Arizona Journal of International and Comparative Law

CFI   Court of First Instance
Colum. J. Eur. L.   Columbia Journal of European Law
Comp. Lab. L. & Pol'y J.   Comparative Labor Law Journal & Policy Journal

E. L. Rev.   European Law Review
EBLR   European Business Law Review
EC   European Community
ECHR   European Court of Human Rights
ECJ   European Court of Justice
ECR   European Court Reviews
EioP   European Integration online Papers
Emory L.J.   Emory Law Journal
EU   European Union

Fordham Int'l L. J.   Fordham International Law Journal

Guild Prac.   Guild Practice

Harv. L. Rev.   Harvard Law Review

Ind. Int'l & Comp. L. Rev.   Indiana International & Comparative Law Review
Ind. J. Global Leg. Stud.   Indiana Journal of Global Legal Studies

Loy. L. Rev.   Loyola Law Review

OJ   Official Journal of the European Communities

PNR   passenger name records

SEW   Sociaal Economische Wetgeving
SIS   Schengen Information System
Stan. L. Rev.   Stanford Law Review

TEC   Treaty Establishing a European Community
TEU   Treaty Establishing a European Union
TEU-L   Treaty Establishing a European Union, as amended
                             by the Treaty of Lisbon
Tex. Int'l L. J.   Texas International Law Journal
TFEU-L   Treaty on the Functioning of the European Union

UK   United Kingdom
UN   United Nations
USA   United States of America

Va. J. Int'l L.   Virginia Journal of International Law
VIS   Visa Information System

Chapter 1

INTRODUCTION

Chapter 1

INTRODUCTION

Many of the developments in European law the last decades concern the position of the citizen in the European Union. Direct influences on this position come from case-law of the European Court of Justice (ECJ) in which the notion of 'EU citizen' is being defined and refined, while indirect influence can be found in the immigration paragraph of the EC Treaty and the developments in the fight against terrorism. In combination with the changes on all these issues as they are foreseen in the Treaty of Lisbon, all developments taken together lead to a new position of the citizen in the Member States of the European Union under the influence of European law.

A special feature of the notion of EU citizenship is that it has been given form and substance through different means simultaneously: not only by means of the texts of the Treaties, but also through secondary legislation and the case-law of the ECJ. Firstly, the rights (and duties) given to EU citizenship are listed in the EC Treaty and need to be seen in addition to citizenship rights in the national systems of the Member States, according to the second sentence of Article 17 sub 1 TEC (Art. 20 TFEU-L).[1] The meaning of the rights of an EU citizen and the scope of the notion of EU citizenship can therefore only be understood by means of a thorough discussion of what citizenship means or should mean, both within a national system and in general. This needs to be placed alongside the contents of EU citizenship and its legal limitations.

The development of EU citizenship in legislation and case-law has led to different categories of citizens within the EU: those with rights which are

---

[1] The new numbering after the coming into force of the Treaty of Lisbon will be given in between brackets in this book, with '-L' after it to indicate that it is a provision in the Treaty of Lisbon.

F. Goudappel, The Effects of EU Citizenship
© 2010, T·M·C·ASSER PRESS, *The Hague, The Netherlands and the Author*

complementary to the nationality of the Member States, those from old Member States and those from new Member States, third-country nationals with only the right of residence. It appears that the EU citizens who have made use of the possibilities of free movement have thus obtained several new and additional rights that EU citizens who have not made us of them do not possess. In order to understand and evaluate the differences between the categories, the contents of each of them needs to be studied in detail.

A simultaneous but opposite development concerns the limitations to these citizenship rights in the course of the ongoing fight against terrorism. In several cases before the ECJ and in literature and the media, questions have been raised concerning judicial protection, access to justice, the right to privacy and other basic rights which have been balanced out against the urge to fight terrorism. In order to paint a complete picture of the position of a citizen in the EU, all developments and limitations need to be taken into consideration, although the description of each element will be limited to the involvement of citizenship issues. As a result, it will be possible to establish whether EU citizenship is an asset, a bonus or leads to an unwanted form of inequality between citizens or even forces Member States to limit their national citizenship rights.

1.1   EXPLORING THE PROBLEM

The legal notion of 'EU citizenship' was first formally proposed by the Spanish delegation to the Intergovernmental Conference preparing the Treaty of Maastricht in 1990. Spain proposed a separate title in the new Treaty on EU citizenship, specifying the rights and duties of EU citizens, including fundamental rights protection, equal opportunities, the right to move and reside freely, the right to take part in the political life, the right to diplomatic protection in third countries, as well as provisions on the way in which citizenship could be obtained and the creation of a special Mediator in all Member States for problems following from this.[2] The proposal was taken seriously but was not accepted in this form; most rights were either indirectly given (like the

---

[2] Spanish Delegation, Intergovernmental Conference on Political Union, European Citizenship, 21 February 1991 (based on a proposal of November 1990), as reproduced in F. Laursen and S. Van Hoonacker (eds.), *Institutional Reforms, New Policies and International Identity of the European Community* (Maastricht 1992) pp. 325-328.

right to fundamental right protection) or are now scattered in the Treaty texts compared to the original idea of the Spanish government.[3]

After this, the Treaty of Maastricht introduced the concept of EU citizenship, although it was unclear for a long time what this could and would entail.[4] Article 8 of the EC Treaty in the Maastricht version contained the following text:

'Article 8
1. Citizenship of the Union is hereby established. Every person holding the nationality of a Member State shall be a citizen of the Union.
2. Citizens of the Union shall enjoy the rights conferred by this Treaty and shall be subject to the duties imposed thereby.'

To this, a list of rights was added: right to free movement (Art. 8a), right to vote (Art. 8b), right to diplomatic protection (Art. 8c), and the right to petition (Art. 8d). It remained unclear what the scope of these new provisions was, and it was one of the reasons for a 'no' in a national referendum in Denmark on the Treaty of Maastricht.[5] For an explanation of what was meant by the original text in the Treaty of Maastricht, a special European Council Declaration was added to the Treaty of Maastricht after the Danish 'no':

'The provisions, of Part Two of the Treaty establishing the European Community relating to citizenship of the Union give nationals of the Member States additional rights and protection as specified in that Part. They do not in any way take the place of national citizenship. The question whether an individual possesses the nationality of a Member State will be settled solely by reference to the national law of the Member State concerned.'[6]

---

[3] J. Shaw, 'Citizenship of the Union: Towards Post-National Membership?', Jean Monnet Working Paper, 10 April 1994, Part I, Introduction, available at <www.jeanmonnetprogram.org/papers/97/97-06-.html> (accessed 13 May 2009).

[4] See for an overview of early literature on EU citizenship: D. Kostakopoulou, 'Ideas, Norms and European Citizenship: Explaining Institutional Change', 68(2) *The Modern Law Review* (2005) p. 233, footnotes 1 and 2.

[5] W. Song and V. Della Sala, 'Eurosceptics and Europhiles in Accord: The Creation of the European Ombudsman as an Institutional Isomorphism', 36(4) *Policy and Politics* (2008) p. 481.

[6] Edinburgh European Council, 11 and 12 December 1992. Conclusions of the Presidency, Part B, Annex 1, Decision of the Heads of State of Government, meeting within the European Council, concerning certain problems raised by Denmark on the Treaty on Euro-

Yet, the Danish government added a Declaration to the Treaty, in which it indicates specifically that 'Nothing in the Treaty on European Union implies or foresees an undertaking to create a citizenship of the Union in the sense of citizenship of a nation State.'[7] Moreover, any legislation concerning citizenship rights needed unanimity, according to this Declaration, and even national parliamentary approval. In the Treaty of Amsterdam, the text of the Declaration of the European Council was added to the provision in order to clear any doubts about the status of EU citizenship.

It can therefore be concluded that this new concept of EU citizenship was not meant to give rights to more citizens but rather to open future options for more rights for the nationals of the Member States.[8] Only later on, at first through the case-law of the ECJ, did the notion of EU citizenship gain independent importance in European Union law. Citizens of the Member States may thus derive rights from being an EU citizen.

Yet, the idea of 'citizenship' as a source of rights and duties is by no means a new one. Through the ages, this notion has been developed as a pivotal element in the relations between a state and its inhabitants. Giving EU citizenship the label 'citizenship' means that expectations are automatically created because citizenship is a traditional source of rights and duties in a state system.

This leads to the question whether EU citizenship fulfills the criteria set for citizenship in a state system or that it has led to a new idea about citizenship. It also leads to the question whether 'real' citizenship is possible in the European Union: which citizenship rights do the citizens of the Member States have in addition to their national citizenship right and what is the influence of the European Union on the citizenship rights of the nationals (and non-nationals) of the Member States? A comparison between what is expected to be part of citizenship rights and duties – based on theory and legislation – and the contents of EU citizenship will lead to an evaluation of

---

pean Union, Section A, Citizenship, *OJ* 1992 C 348, p. 1, <http://europa.eu/abc/treaties/archives/en/entr21.htm> (last visited on 13 May 2009).

[7] Ibid., Annex 3, Unilateral Declarations of Denmark, to be associated to the Danish Act of Ratification of the Treaty on European Union and of which the eleven other Member States will take cognizance, Declaration on Citizenship of the Union, Para. 1, Edinburgh European Council, 11 and 12 December 1992.

[8] Art. 8e of the Treaty of Maastricht laid down the possibility for the Council to adopt legislation 'to strengthen or to add to' these rights is laid down in Art. 8e of the Treaty of Maastricht, *OJ* 1992 C 191.

the effect of the introduction of EU citizenship on citizenship rights and duties of the inhabitants of the Member States of the European Union. Thus, it will be possible to evaluate what the effects of European Union law on the position of the citizens in the Member States is.

In this study, the meaning and implications of the double system for these citizens will therefore be the focal point: the national system of the Member States offers the nationality, from which EU citizenship follows. A double system of citizen's rights together with the European Union provisions means that different elements need to be studied side by side in order to obtain an overview of the position of a citizen in one of the Member States of the European Union. For whom does EU citizenship offer something additional to national citizenship or does it devaluate traditional national citizenship? Is it possible to say that EU citizenship equals national citizenship plus additional rights? Did the introduction of EU citizenship to the European system lead to a new impetus in free movement and possibilities for citizens of the Member States or did it lead to inequality between these citizens? And what can the influence of the Treaty of Lisbon be?

A distinction needs to be made for each of the elements involved between the persons who are entitled to citizenship rights and the scope of the rights involved. Both parts involve their own discussion and development while they are both necessary together for a full overview of the citizenship study in an EU context.

Legal basis

In order to begin answering the questions posed above, it needs to be established what the legal base of EU citizenship is. Article 17 of the EC Treaty (Art. 20 TFEU-L) maintains that European Union citizenship is established and that it does not replace national citizenship. This indicates that inhabitants of the Member States of the European Union (who have the nationality of one of the Member States) possess a double system of citizens' rights: national rights and EU rights, usually referred to as 'multiple citizenship'.[9] However, it is very difficult to assess what the implications are and may be of this provision. Is it an addition to the pre-existing free movement of per-

---

[9] E. Meehan, *European Citizenship* (London 1993). See also Kostakopoulou, op. cit., note 4, pp. 234-235.

sons or has it introduced a completely new concept? Moreover, the new Treaty of Lisbon[10] adds several existing provisions to the chapter on EU citizenship, like the provision on the prohibition of discrimination under the heading 'Non-Discrimination and Citizenship of the Union'.[11] An insight in what it means to be a citizen in one of the Member States of the European Union is thus needed but relatively complicated to obtain. Yet, it seems to be impossible for Article 17 TEC (Art. 20 TFEU-L) to be the only legal base for EU citizenship. Apart from the fact that Article 18 TEC (Art. 21 TFEU-L) offers a legal basis for secondary legislation concerning the right to free movement, there are many more specific legal bases to be found in the Treaties. Several of these more specific legal bases predate Article 17 TEC (Art. 20 TFEU-L), like the right to free movement of workers in Article 39 TEC (Art. 45 TFEU-L), Article 17 TEC (Art. 20 TFEU-L) and Article 18 TEC (Art. 21 TFEU-L) are therefore a *lex generalis* compared to more specific provisions in many places in the Treaties.

1.2   RELEVANT EUROPEAN LAW

From a European Union point of view, the subject of the position of the citizen in the European Union is first of all regulated by obligations for the Member States and rights for the citizens following from the EU Treaty and the EC Treaty. Directly applicable rights, like the prohibition of discrimination on the basis of nationality as laid down in Article 12 TEC (Art. 18 TFEU-L), form part of this system just like derived rights which follow from regulations, directives and framework decisions. According to many authors,[12] the notion of the prohibition of discrimination on the basis of nationality as laid down in Article 12 TEC (Art. 18 TFEU-L) forms the core of the system of the European internal market, especially for the free movement of per-

---

[10] Version: Consolidated Texts of the EU Treaties as Amended by the Treaty of Lisbon, as published by the Foreign and Commonwealth Office of the United Kingdom, January 2008, <www.sin-online.nl/webmail/exec/frgstaf/src/download.php?startMessage=76&passed_id= 33429&mailbox=INBOX&ent_id=2&passed_ent_id=0> (last visited on 28 February 2008).

[11] The heading of Part 2, before Art. 18 TEU, *OJ* C 191 of 29 July 1992.

[12] For instance P. Craig and G. de Búrca, *EU Law. Text, Cases and Materials*, 4th edn. (Oxford 2008) pp. 558-559; or C. Barnard, *The Substantive Law of the EU. The Four Freedoms*, 2nd edn. (Oxford 2007) pp. 254-256.

sons. As already was the situation in the Spanish government proposal for EU citizenship in 1990, the Treaty of Lisbon places this notion in the Title on EU citizenship, which indicates that it is crucial for a complete understanding of EU citizenship.[13] In conjunction with the text of Article 39 Paragraph 2 TEC (Art. 45 Para. 2 TFEU-L), this prohibition concentrates on the nationality of the Member States, excluding third-country nationals from its scope. Moreover, only with the introduction of the predecessor of Article 18 TEC in the Treaty of Maastricht did this prohibition gain its present scope, including non-economically active citizens.

However, as stated above, other Treaty provisions have a similar influence on the position of the citizen or may have in the future. Such directly applicable Treaty provisions include EU citizenship (Arts. 17 and 18 TEC – Arts. 20 and 21 TFEU-L), the free movement of workers (Art. 39 TEC ff – Art. 45 TFEU-L), the freedom of establishment (Art. 43 TEC ff – Art. 49 TFEU-L), and the free movement of services (Art. 49 TEC ff – Art. 56 TFEU-L), provisions which aim at economically active persons.

Much secondary legislation forms the core of EU citizenship rights in addition to this. Directives, regulations and framework decisions on economic rights and social rights, as well as on the position of third-country nationals and against terrorist activities have been adopted. The most prominent ones are the so-called Persons Directive,[14] the Directive on Family Reunification,[15] and the different adoptions of Security Council Resolutions containing blacklists of terrorists or financiers of terrorism.[16] The impact on national legislation and the case-law of the ECJ following from them mean that the influence of EU citizenship has increased. This is valid for both the meaning of the notion and its contents. The ECJ has also been very influen-

---

[13] A.A.M. Schrauwen, 'Naar een "fundamentele status"? Democratie en Europees na het Verdrag of Lissabon', *SEW* (2008) pp. 288-292.

[14] European Parliament and Council Directive 2004/38/EC of 29 April 2004 on the right of citizens of the Union and their family members to move and reside freely within the territory of the Member States amending Regulation (EEC) No. 1612/68 and repealing Directives 64/221/EEC, 68/360/EEC, 72/194/EEC, 73/148/EEC, 75/34/EEC, 75/35/EEC, 90/364/EEC, 90/365/EEC and 93/96/EEC, *OJ* PB L 158 of 30 April 2004, rectified in PB L 229 of 29 June 2004. See Annex III to this book for a full text.

[15] Council Directive 2003/86/EC of 22 September 2003 on the right to family reunification. *OJ* PB L 251 of 3 October 2003, pp. 12-18.

[16] Via Council Common Position 2001/931/CFSP of 27 December 2001 on the application of specific measures to combat terrorism *OJ* PB L 344 of 28 December 2001, pp. 93-96.

tial through its case-law. Not only did it widen the access to justice options for the citizen in its very early case-law by means of establishing direct effect,[17] it limited it on the other hand through a strict interpretation of the phrase 'directly and individually applicable' of Article 230 sub 4 TEC (Art. 263 TFEU-L).[18] Still, it brought many new cases under its umbrella via the EU citizenship notion, aiming at protection of the EU citizens, especially – but not exclusively – those who are economically active.[19] In addition, many of the key notions have been given form and substance by the ECJ, like the definition of a worker[20] and the scope of family reunification.[21]

1.2.1   The Treaty of Lisbon

The most important influence in the future will come from the coming into force of the Treaty of Lisbon. This means that changes concerning the rights and duties of citizens will either automatically follow from the Treaty text or will be made possible under the new Treaty. These influential changes may range from additions to the chapter on EU citizenship[22] to very specific measures concerning the freezing of funds while combating terrorism.[23] For instance, as is clear from the text of the Treaty of Lisbon, the European Council has tried to solve the legal problems concerning the fight against terrorism that have risen over the years: legal base, fundamental freedoms, pillar structure and cross-pillar issues. Yet, it cannot immediately be said that the problems concerning a legal stronghold for anti-terrorism measures in the Treaties are solved this way.

One of the most important changes to be introduced by the Treaty of Lisbon[24] is the end of the pillar structure as we know it. The matters of the Area of Freedom, Security and Justice as they are at present laid down in

---

[17]   ECJ, Case 26/62 *Van Gend & Loos* [1963] *ECR* 3.

[18]   ECJ, Case 25/62 *Plaumann* [1963] *ECR* 207.

[19]   For example ECJ, Case C-184/99 *Rudy Grzelczyk* [2001] *ECR* I-06193; or ECJ, Case C-200/02 *Zhu and Chen* [2004] *ECR* I-09925, as will be discussed in this book.

[20]   ECJ, Case 66/85 *Lawrie-Blum* [1986] *ECR* 02121.

[21]   ECJ, Case C-127/08 *Metock and Others* [2008] *ECR* I-06241.

[22]   As discussed in the previous paragraph.

[23]   Art. 75 of the TFEU (consolidated version) *OJ* C 115 of 9 May 2008.

[24]   Treaty of Lisbon amending the Treaty on European Union and the Treaty establishing the European Community, Brussels 3 December 2007, CIG 14/07 *OJ* C 306 of 17 December 2007.

Title VI EU and in Title IV TEC will be placed together and fall under the 'ordinary' legislative procedure, as Article 61H TFEU states, i.e. the communautarian procedure.[25] This means that the problems concerning access to justice and direct effect will be solved for present third-pillar legislation because the there will no difference between what is now a directive and a framework decision, both falling under the definition of a framework decision. This may also solve any direct problems arising from a combined legal base of the third and the first pillar.

The possibilities for the impact of this text on the rights and duties of citizens need specific attention because the present-day situation may change and the description of secondary legislation, its implementation, and case-law will be influenced accordingly.

1.2.2   Charter of fundamental rights of the European Union

A second important text in addition to the EU and EC Treaties is the EU Charter of Fundamental Rights. This Charter, which has been signed by all Member States but is non-binding,[26] is a commitment to the rights laid down in it by the signatories.[27] The ECJ has also accepted the texts of the Charter as indicating a commitment by the Member States, but only in combination with the binding provisions in the Treaties:

'According to settled case-law, the principle of effective judicial protection is a general principle of Community law stemming from the constitutional traditions common to the Member States, which has been enshrined in Articles 6 and 13 of the ECHR, this principle having furthermore been reaffirmed by Article 47 of the Charter of fundamental rights of the European Union, proclaimed on 7 December 2000 in Nice (...).'[28]

---

[25] J.H. Reestman and F.A.N.J. Goudappel, 'Het Verdrag of Lissabon en de Ruimte of Vrijheid, en Recht', *SEW* (2008) pp. 441-445.

[26] It is a 'solemn proclamation', see <www.europarl.europa.eu/charter/pdf/text_en.pdf> (last visited on 10 March 2008).

[27] As stated by the then president of European Parliament, Mrs Nicole Fontaine, <www.europarl.europa.eu/charter/default_en.htm#declarations> (last visited on 19 May 2009).

[28] ECJ, Joined Cases C-402/05 P and C-415/05 P *Kadi and Barakaat* [2008] *ECR* I-06351.

Thus, the formula of Article 6 Paragraph 2 TEU (Art. 6 TEU-L) has been taken as a basis,[29] in which both the European Convention of Human Rights and the constitutional traditions of the Member States are taken together, with the Charter as a 'reaffirmation'. The Commission, however, has taken a slightly different approach to valuating the Charter by in its legislative proposals by placing it at the same level as the European Convention on Human Rights[30] or by simply referring to the contents as rights to be upheld at the European level.[31] As a solution, the text was incorporated in the Constitutional Treaty in 2005, which meant that it would become a binding text. In the Treaty of Lisbon, a different solution has been sought: the following Declaration was added to the text:

> The Charter of Fundamental Rights of the European Union, which has legally binding force, confirms the fundamental rights guaranteed by the European Convention for the Protection of Human Rights and Fundamental Freedoms and as they result from the constitutional traditions common to the Member States.
> The Charter does not extend the field of application of Union law beyond the powers of the Union or establish any new power or task for the Union, or modify powers and tasks as defined by the Treaties.'[32]

This Declaration does not make the text binding in the way the Constitutional Treaty did, but in the approach the ECJ has taken so far, combining the

---

[29] 'The Union shall respect fundamental rights, as guaranteed by the European Convention for the Protection of Human Rights and Fundamental Freedoms signed in Rome on 4 November 1950 and as they result from the constitutional traditions common to the Member States, as general principles of Community law.'

[30] 'Measures concerning family reunification should be adopted in conformity with the obligation to protect the family and respect family life enshrined in many instruments of international law. This Directive respects the fundamental rights and observes the principles recognised in particular in Art. 8 of the European Convention for the Protection of Human Rights and Fundamental Freedoms and in the Charter of Fundamental Rights of the European Union.' Second recital in the Preamble of the Council Directive 2003/86/EC of 22 September 2003 on the right to family reunification *OJ* L 251 of 3 October 2003, pp. 12-18.

[31] 'The Regulation observes the fundamental rights and principles which are acknowledged in particular in the Charter of Fundamental Rights of the European Union', recital 15 in the preamble of the Council Regulation (EC) No. 343/2003 of 18 February 2003 *OJ* L 50 of 25 February 2003, pp. 1-10 establishing the criteria and mechanisms for determining the Member State responsible for examining an asylum application lodged in one of the Member States by a third-country national.

[32] Declaration concerning the Charter of Fundamental Rights of the European Union *OJ* C 364, 7 December 2000.

European Charter on Human Rights and the common constitutional traditions of the Member States.[33] It needs to be noted that several Member States
have limited the application of the Charter in Declarations added to the Treaty
of Lisbon.[34]

The contents of the Charter, however, go further than the European Convention on Human Rights. Although many provisions are similar, some others, like the freedom to conduct a business (Art. 16) and the right to asylum
(Art. 18) stem from existing European Union law. In addition, the rights of
the child (Art. 24) or the right to protection in the event of unjustified dismissal (Art. 30) originate in UN Conventions or the European Social Charter. All taken together, the rights laid down in the Charter reflect citizenship
rights which are valid for citizens residing in the European Union.

1.3   RESEARCH METHODS

In order to be able to evaluate what the European influence is on the position
of the citizen, this book will study the most important elements. Any evaluation of this position needs to begin with the basis for comparison, i.e., establishing what the notion of citizenship actually comprises from a more
traditional point of view. To this method of defining the notion will be added
the meaning of EU citizenship while the scope of EU citizenship will be
discussed separately. For the latter discussion, the tripartite approach will be
used which has been developed by Marshall.[35] Although this represents a
non-legal approach to understanding citizenship,[36] it provides a useful starting point for exploring the subject in a legal context.[37]

---

[33] M.L.H.K. Claes, 'Het Verdrag of en de Europese grondrechtenmozaek', *SEW* (2009)
pp. 162-168.

[34] Like Poland, the United Kingdom, Ireland or the Czech Republic have done in different ways.

[35] T.H. Marshall, *Citizenship and Social Class* (Cambridge 1950).

[36] See also Samantha Besson and André Utzinger, 'Introduction: Future Challenges of
European Citizenship – Facing a Wide-Open Pandora's Box', 13 *European Law Journal* (September 2007) pp. 573-590.

[37] See for instance Shaw, op. cit., note 3 for an early application of this approach on EU
citizenship.

The Marshall approach can be summarized as follows. Based on the development of citizenship in England in the 19th and early 20th century,[38] there were first civic rights, which gave rise to political rights, which led to the emergence of social rights. There are thus three sets of rights which together form citizenship. In the European sense, this means economic rights, political rights, and social rights. Each of them can be defined by means of their contents and their relationship with the other rights:

> 'The civil element is composed of the rights necessary for individual freedom – liberty of the person, freedom of speech, thought and faith, the right to own property and to conclude valid contracts, and the right to justice. (…) This shows us that the institutions most directly associated with civil rights are the courts of justice. By the political element I mean the right to participate in the exercise of political power, as a member of a body invested with political authority or as an elector of the member of such a body. The corresponding institutions are parliament and councils of local government. By the social element I mean the whole range (…). The institutions most closely connected with it are the educational system and the social services.'[39]

However, this development has not taken place as such a logical string of follow-ups in the European context: all three types of rights were at least partially present from the early days in the EEC Treaty, but have developed at a different speed. Also, the system cannot be transposed as such to modern day and to the European developments. Some of the elements are even overlapping, as Marshall himself also remarked.[40] Yet, the tripartite system – with some modification – still helps to give a good overview of the contents and scope of EU citizenship after the definition above.

However, concentrating on the rights of EU citizens only does not provide a full evaluation of the position of all citizens in the European Union. Separate attention needs to be paid to the position and rights of third-country nationals in the European Union. Not only do they possess indirect citizenship rights through attachment to an EU national,[41] they possess certain citizenship rights without distinction from EU nationals like human rights

---

[38] Marshall, op. cit., note 35, p. 10 ff.

[39] Marshall, op. cit., note 35, pp. 10-11.

[40] Marshall, op. cit., note 35, p. 21.

[41] See for instance ECJ, Case C-127/08 *Metock and Others* [2008] *ECR* I-06241; or ECJ, Case C-200/02 *Zhu and Chen* [2004] *ECR* I-09925.

protection, and partial citizenship rights in other cases.[42] Moreover, to the description of all rights which an EU national has been given through European Union law, a separate discussion needs to be added of the instances in which citizenship rights at both the European level and the national level were being challenged by European law, like several anti-terrorism cases[43] and third-pillar case at the ECJ have shown.[44] It needs to be noted that many of these rights need to be seen in combination with the rights a citizen – the own national or not – possesses at the national level. Not all citizenship rights are exclusively EU citizens' rights. Many are much broader than this, like human rights protection shows, which is given to all inhabitants, or free movement rights, which may be given to a larger group. The question is therefore whether this differs from the more traditional practice to give several citizenship rights to the own nationals and only limited citizenship rights to other inhabitants. The question to be answered for this is whether this represents an 'access-oriented' concept or rather a participatory or exclusionary process.[45]

A short overview of the rights of EU citizens

An inventarisation is needed of the rights and duties of EU citizens according to the Treaty texts before it will be possible to evaluate the concept. In the failed European Constitution, the rights and duties of the citizen were not changed but re-listed (although suggestions in such a direction were made at the Convention[46]), giving a good overview of the state of affairs. Article I-8 of the European Constitution (which thus summarizes the present-day Arts. 17-22 EC) read as follows:

---

[42] For instance Council Directive 2003/109/EC of 25 November 2003 *OJ* L 16 of 23 January 2004, pp. 44-53 concerning the status of third-country nationals who are long-term residents.

[43] A prominent example is the judgment of the Court of Justice in ECJ, Joined Cases C-402/05 P and C-415/05 P *Kadi & Barakaat* [2008] *ECR* I-06351.

[44] For the European arrest warrant this was the subject in ECJ, Case C-303/05 *Advocaten voor de Wereld VZW* v. *Leden of de Ministerraad* [2007] *ECR* I-03633.

[45] Shaw, op. cit., note 3, I. Introduction.

[46] For the suggestion to include third-country nationals who are long-term residents: Opinion of the European Economic and Social Committee on 'Access to European Union Citizenship', *OJ* C 208/19, 3 September 2003.

'1. Every national of a Member State shall be a citizen of the Union. Citizenship of the Union shall be additional to national citizenship: it shall not replace it.
2. Citizens of the Union shall enjoy the rights and be subject to the duties provided for in the Constitution. They shall have:
  – the right to move and reside freely within the territory of the Member States;
  – the right to vote and to stand as candidates in elections to the European Parliament and in municipal elections in their Member States of residence, under the same conditions as nationals of that State;
  – the right to enjoy, in the territory of a third country in which the Member State of which they are nationals is not represented, the protection of the diplomatic and consular authorities of any Member State on the same conditions as the nationals of that State;
  – the right to petition the European Parliament, to apply to the European Ombudsman, and to address the Institutions and advisory bodies of the Union in any of the Constitution's languages and to obtain a reply in the same language.
3. These rights shall be exercised in accordance with the conditions and limits defined by the Constitution and by the measures adopted to give it effect.'[47]

The above shows that EU citizenship contains more elements than traditional national citizenship. Some fundamental rights, like the right to petition, are mentioned specifically. Moreover, the rights and duties laid down in the Treaty texts include basic right protection, as Article 6 part. 2 TEU (Art. 6 TEU-L) states:

'The Union shall respect fundamental rights, as guaranteed by the European Convention for the Protection of Human Rights and Fundamental Freedoms signed in Rome on 4 November 1950 and as they result from the constitutional traditions common to the Member States, as general principles of Community law.'

---

[47] F. Goudappel, 'From National Citizenship to European Union Citizenship; The Reinvention of Citizenship?', *European Review of Public Law* (Spring 2007) pp. 21-45.

Chapter 2

A THEORY OF CITIZENSHIP

Chapter 2

A THEORY OF CITIZENSHIP

The notion of 'citizenship' is a traditional notion which has received new attention recently. The reason for this is that it has gained much importance in especially the European Union over the last decades. While 'citizenship' is traditionally associated with the state and with the relationship between the state and its inhabitants,[48] this more traditional perception changed with the introduction of the notion of 'European Union citizenship' in the Treaty of Maastricht in 1992. In this Treaty, citizenship was suddenly linked to both the state (through the Member States) and the international organization (the European Union) in its legal definition.[49] There is a close link to citizenship rights, fundamental rights and EU citizenship in the eyes of the Commission:

> 'The Union is an area of shared values, values which are incompatible with the crimes of totalitarian regimes. In the interests of reconciliation, the memory of crimes against humanity must be a collective memory, shared by us all. The Union must play the role of facilitator, respecting the approach that each State adopts. These values provide the basis for European citizenship and respect for them is an essential criterion for membership of the Union. European citizenship complements, but does not replace national citizenship. It confers rights and obligations specific to European citizens which must be given practical and effective expression.'[50]

---

[48] E. Guild, *The Legal Elements of European Identity; EU Citizenship and Migration Law* (The Hague 2004) pp. 1-18.

[49] For more details, see N.W. Barber, 'Citizenship, Nationalism and the European Union', in J. Ferrer and M. Iglesias (eds.), *Law Politics and Morality: European Perspectives I; Globalisation, Democracy, and Citizenship – Prospects for the European Union* (Berlin, Duncker & Humblot 2003) pp. 201-226.

[50] Communication from the Commission to the European Parliament and the Council; an area of freedom, security and justice serving the citizen, 10 June 2009, COM(2009)0262 final.

F. Goudappel, The Effects of EU Citizenship
© *2010, T·M·C·ASSER PRESS, The Hague, The Netherlands and the Author*

2.1   HISTORICAL APPROACH

In history, citizenship has always been an important issue for philosophers
and political thinkers alike: who will be awarded citizenship and what does
or should this citizenship entail?

Self-governance defines freedom as the rule of law among a community
of equals who are citizens of the polis and who have the right to rule and be
ruled. This ideal emerges in 5th-century Athens and is revived throughout
history in episodes such as the experience of self-governing city-states in the
Renaissance, the Paris commune of 1871, the anarchist and socialist com-
munes of the Russian Revolution, and the Spanish Civil War.[51]

Many of the ideas on citizenship stem from Aristotle's Politics, who iden-
tified the appropriate criteria for full membership in the community, at least
in Greek and Roman times. This definition excluded women, slaves, for-
eigners and those who had other duties like physical labour. The elite class
thus selected as citizens had duties which could be seen as a sacrifice, like
giving time and perhaps life (in times of war) to the city-state. The rights
included the right to vote, the right to sit as a judge, and the right to decide on
matters of state.[52] However, Aristotle's emphasis on the incompatibility of
citizenship with physical labour was already changed in the (late) middle
ages.[53] The citizen was a representative of the elite classes in society, excluding all other groups, by which economic conditions prevail and active citizenship is expected. This influence on the position of the citizen lasted until
the French Revolution, to be replaced by the modern notion of passive citizenship,[54] in which citizens are 'members of the community who are to be
protected and rewarded.'[55] For France, the birth of the modern citizen or

---

[51] S. Benhabib, 'Borders, Boundaries, and Citizenship; Democratic Citizenship and the
Crisis of Territoriality', *PSOnline*, <www.apsanet.org> (last visited 10 August 2006), October 2005, pp. 673-677.

[52] S. Vergnières, 'Les solutions aristotéliciennes à la crise de la démocratie athénienne au
IVe siècle aoft Jésus Christ', in L. Borot (ed.), *Civisme et citoyenneté: une longue histoire*
(Montpellier 1999) pp. 15-36.

[53] C.J. Nederman, 'Mechanics and Citizenship: The Reception of the Aristotelian Ida of
Citizenship in Late Medieval Europe', *Vivarium* (Leyden 2002) pp. 75-102.

[54] G. Bacot, 'Les citoyens passifs dans la Constitution de 1791', in E. Desmons (ed.),
Figures de la Citoyenneté (Paris 2006) pp. 51-84.

[55] P. Riesenberg, *Citizenship in the Western Tradition; Plato to Rousseau* (Chapel Hill
and London 1992) pp. xv-xxiv.

citoyen took place during the French Revolution in which the citizen's person, property and liberty were protected by means of the *Déclaration des Droits de l'Homme de du citoyen*.[56] The need for government, legal and military aid, as well as protection by the state are part of this approach.[57]

Because of the emphasis on the citizen in the history of the constitutional system of the United States of America (USA), many definitions tend to focus on the demands of a citizen in the US system. A good example of such an American definition is the following list of rights and duties: the right to travel throughout the state, the right to be domiciled anywhere in the USA, the right of suffrage, the right to qualify for public office, the right to serve as jurors, and the right to attend the public schools.[58] From this list, the right to serve as jurors is of course more relevant for the USA than for the European Union or for any of the legal systems not having a system of jury duty.

Originally, US citizenship was linked to state[59] citizenship or nationality, giving similar rights to these citizens in the other states.[60] The basis of American citizenship was laid down in the US Constitution, in Article IV, Section 2. Originally, this system made an exception for slaves and Indians. Especially the struggle of the Afro-American population in both the 19th century and the 1950s and 1960s for equal rights, and thus for full citizenship, attracted much attention. Only after amending the US Constitution and a series of subsequent cases in (federal) courts, we can nowadays say that there legally exists no distinction of that type.[61]

One of the most prominent basic elements of US citizenship has always been the free movement of citizens within the USA, while simultaneously limiting the freedom of movement from other states.[62] The basis of citizen-

---

[56] P. Riesenberg, *Citizenship in the Western Tradition; Plato to Rousseau* (Chapel Hill and London 1992) pp. 267-273.

[57] Riesenberg, op. cit., note 56, pp. xv-xxiv.

[58] C.J. Antieau, *The Intended Significance of the Fourteenth Amendment* (Buffalo, NY 1997).

[59] J.H. Kettner, *The Development of American Citizenship, 1608-1870* (Williamsburg 1978) pp. 336-338.

[60] Antieau, op. cit., note 58, pp. 11-13.

[61] Antieau, op. cit., note 58, pp. 5-10.

[62] A.P. van der Mei, 'Freedom of Movement for Indigents: A Comparative Analysis of American Constitutional Law and European Community Law', 19 *Ariz. J. Int'l & Comp. Law* (2002) p. 803.

ship is the US nationality. For contents, US citizenship has always focused most prominently on civil rights.[63] Or it at least 'implies equality, justice and autonomy'.[64] Yet, over the decades, the notion of citizenship has developed towards additional requirements mostly linked to the welfare state.[65] This includes at least

> 'federal and state government employment, private employment, eligibility for specific professions, protection of labour laws and nondiscrimination laws, public benefit programs, public education, land ownership, jury service, access to courts, eligibility for military service, conscription, and tax liability.'[66]

It needs to be noted here that, while immigration legislation is in general regulated at the federal level, welfare citizenship and residency requirements are regulated at state level.[67]

2.2   CITIZENSHIP IN PHILOSOPHY AND THEORY

It has often been said that traditional citizenship in the USA involves the following rights and duties: the right to travel throughout the state, the right to be domiciled anywhere in the USA, the right of suffrage, the right to qualify for public office, the right to serve as jurors, and the right to attend the public schools.[68] Of this list, the right to serve as jurors cannot be considered part of citizenship in each nation-state, but is more part of the Anglo-American legal tradition. Originally, US citizenship was linked to state[69] citizenship or nationality, giving similar rights to these citizens in the other states.[70] Nowa-

---

[63] See for instance P.J. Spiro, 'Book Review: The Citizenship Dilemma', 51 *Stan. L. Rev.* (1999) p. 597.

[64] K. Faulks, *Citizenship* (London and New York 2000) p. 13.

[65] P.H. Schuck, 'Citizenship in Federal Systems', 48 *Am. J. Comp. L.* (2000) p. 195; Van der Mei, op. cit., note 62, p. 803.

[66] S.H. Legomsky, 'Why Citizenship?', 35 *Va. J. Int'l L* (1994) p. 279.

[67] H. Motomura, 'Comment: Immigration and Alienage, Federalism and Proposition 187', 35 *Va. J. Int'l L.* (1994) pp. 201 ff.

[68] C.J. Antieau, *The Intended Significance of the Fourteenth Amendment* (Buffalo, NY 1997).

[69] J.H. Kettner, *The Development of American Citizenship, 1608-1870* (Williamsburg 1978) pp. 336-338.

[70] Antieau, op. cit., note 58, pp. 11-13.

days, it is linked to the nationality of the whole federation of the USA. This was not originally the case for all inhabitants of the USA or at least for all those born in the USA. The American discussions concerning citizenship do not necessarily focus on the different elements establishing citizenship nowadays but on necessity of citizenship: is a dual citizenship necessary within the USA?[71] What are the requirements and uses of naturalization?[72]

The basis of American citizenship was laid down in the US Constitution, in Article IV, Section 2. Originally, this system made an exception for slaves and Indians. Especially the struggle of the Afro-American population in both the 19th century and the 1950s and 1960s for equal rights, and thus for full citizenship, attracted much attention. Only after amending the US Constitution and a series of subsequent cases in (federal) courts, we can nowadays say that there legally exists no distinction of that type.[73]

One of the most prominent basic elements of US citizenship has always been the free movement of citizens within the USA, while simultaneously limiting the freedom of movement from other states.[74] The basis of citizenship is the US nationality. For contents, US citizenship has always focused most prominently on civil rights.[75] Or it at least 'implies equality, justice and autonomy'.[76] Yet, over the decades, the notion of citizenship has developed towards additional requirements mostly linked to the welfare state.[77] This includes at least

'federal and state government employment, private employment, eligibility for specific professions, protection of labor laws and nondiscrimination laws, public benefit programs, public education, land ownership, jury service, access to courts, eligibility for military service, conscription, and tax liability.'[78]

---

[71] Y. Zilbershats, 'Reconsidering the Concept of Citizenship', 36 *Tex. Int'l L. J.* (2001) p. 689.

[72] S.H. Legomsky, 'Why Citizenship?', 35 *Va. J. Int'l L.* (1994) p. 279.

[73] Antieau, op. cit., note 58, pp. 5-10.

[74] Van der Mei, op. cit., note 62, p. 803.

[75] See for instance P.J. Spiro, 'Book Review: The Citizenship Dilemma', 51 *Stan. L. Rev.* (1999) p. 597.

[76] Faulks, op. cit., note 64, p. 13.

[77] P.H. Schuck, Citizenship in Federal Systems, 48 *Am. J. Comp. L.* (2000) p. 195; Van der Mei, op. cit., note 62, p. 803.

[78] Legomsky, op. cit., note 72.

It needs to be noted here that, while immigration legislation is in general regulated at the federal level, welfare citizenship and residency requirements are regulated at state level.[79]

This development concerning the contents of citizenship, sometimes referred to as social citizenship,[80] is not the only development: recently, the 'automatic' link between US nationality and citizenship has changed. Because of the growing population in the USA of immigrants, most notable Mexicans, the call to grant them more civil rights grew stronger and stronger. This has resulted in legislation giving non-national or dual national inhabitants at least part of citizenship.[81] This means that there are at least two types of citizenship in the US legal context: full citizenship for nationals and partial citizenship for a specific group of non-nationals and for dual nationals. For the latter category, this means an improvement in the situation, namely from not having any citizenship rights and duties to having some of them. In addition, a third category of citizenship is the one of non-citizens who do not fall within any of the two other categories.

Yet, inequality between citizens was not the starting point of the system, but the close link between nationality and citizenship led to this result. Options to eliminate this inequality vary from an introduction of more possibilities for dual citizenship to a denationalized citizenship,[82] which would enable the federal and state governments to protect a broader group of inhabitants.[83]

2.3   NATIONALITY VERSUS CITIZENSHIP

For theory and history, it is never clear whether 'citizenship' and 'nationality' are one and the same notion or different notions. Any distinction between the two appears to be a recent phenomenon.[84] For many theoreticians, the two are 'analytically distinct'. It identifies nationality with cultural ele-

---

[79] H. Motomura, 'Comment: Immigration and Alienage, Federalism and Proposition 187', 35 *Va. J. Int'l L.* (1994) pp. 201 ff.

[80] Spiro, op. cit., note 75.

[81] P.J. Spiro, 'Dual Nationality and the Meaning of Citizenship', 46 *Emory L.J.* (1997) p. 1411.

[82] H. Klug, 'Contextual Citizenship', 7 *Ind. J. Global Leg. Stud.* (2000) p. 567.

[83] See also F. Goudappel and S. Romein, 'Evolving Legal Personality: The Case of EU Citizenship', *Ius Gentium* (Spring 2005) pp. 1-34.

[84] D. Colas, *Citoyenneté et nationalité* (Paris 2004) p. 41.

ments and citizenship with political ones.[85] Yet, 'it is difficult to imagine modern citizenship divorced from statehood or the "national principle".'[86]

In some constitutional systems, like the Dutch constitutional system, only the notion of nationality is present, while in other constitutional systems, like the French, citizenship is the core element. In several legal systems, the meaning of the two words coincides, most notably in several new Member States. Such legal systems concentrate on citizens rather than nationals, which means that everyone in possession of citizenship is considered to be a national of that state. This has led to some problems when acceding to the European Union. Latvia, for instance, has not given citizenship to their inhabitants or residents of Russian origin, referring to them as non-nationals.[87] An opposite approach has been applied by Hungary, which gave citizenship to persons of Hungarian origin living in the boundaries of the former Hungarian state. For those living in other EU Member States, this is not a problem where EU citizenship rights are concerned. However, for those living in the non-Member States Ukraine and Romania, it does give rise to difficulties.[88] In this respect, it is perhaps better to make a distinction between citizenship/nationality on the one hand and residents on the other because that is the distinction which causes the most problems and is the most frequently used one in practice.

The link with nationality turns out to be very crucial in constitutional thinking since most discussions on citizenship in Western Europe are part of nationality issues; many countries emphasize the rights and duties given to nationals with much more limited rights for non-nationals.[89] Citizenship can therefore be considered to contain two aspects,[90] namely a functional aspect and a non-functional one. The nonfunctional aspect concerns a sense of cultural identity and community. This aspect is very difficult, if not impossible,

---

[85] D. McCrone and R. Kiely, 'Nationalism and Citizenship', *Sociology* (2000) pp. 19-34.

[86] C. Shore, 'Whither European Citizenship? Eros and Civilization Revisited', *European Journal of Social Theory* (2004) p. 31.

[87] N. Reich, 'The Constitutional Relevance of Citizenship and Free Movement in an Enlarged Union', 11 *European Law Journal* (November 2005) pp. 691-693.

[88] Reich, op. cit., note 87, pp. 696-697.

[89] The problems concerning dual nationality will largely remain outside the scope of this book.

[90] As described in a note: 'The Functionality of Citizenship', 110 *Harv. L. Rev.* (June 1997) pp. 1814 ff.

to establish in a legal context. Yet, because it represents the legal relationship between the individual and the state, the functional aspect is about an individual's membership of a political community. It excludes those who are not part of this political community, thus those who usually do not have the nationality of the state in which they reside.

In daily life, a very important aspect of citizenship is not only formed by the question which rights and duties a citizen has, but by the award of citizenship. Who can obtain citizenship and how can one obtain it? And who will be awarded which citizenship rights? Citizenship as the equivalent of nationality[91] can be awarded at birth either via *ius soli* or *ius sanguinis* according to the rules of public international law.[92] Changing nationality or obtaining multiple nationality and thus obtaining full citizenship of a different nation-state depends on the rules of the individual nation-states. In the Netherlands, for instance, it first needs to be noted that most of its contents are linked to the Dutch nationality.[93] Simultaneously, several of these rights and duties are given to third-country nationals as well as to Dutch and EU nationals. In basis, the third-country nationals enjoy the same basic rights laid down in the national Constitution, usually formulated as 'everyone has the right to ...'. Yet, these rights tend to be limited by law, especially immigration legislation, limiting possibilities to stay in the country. On the other hand, third-country nationals were given the right to vote in municipal elections after a five year legal stay in the country, a right not limited to the nationals of the other Member States of the European Union. Yet, it is also possible to be awarded citizenship rights by another nation-state than the one you're a national of.

2.4   EU CITIZENSHIP

The introduction of the new European Union citizenship raises many questions non-legal questions like: is the development of EU citizenship equal to

---

[91] See the paragraph on citizenship and nationality below.

[92] P. Malaczuk, *Akehurst's Modern Introduction to International Law*, 7th revised edn. (London and New York 1997) p. 264.

[93] Th. Holterman, *Vreemdelingenrecht: toelating en verblijf of vreemdelingen in Nederland* (Deventer 2002).

the development of a European identity?[94] The implications of EU citizenship are therefore multiple.

As the text of Article 17 TEC (Art. 20 TFEU-L) shows, there is a close link between citizenship and nationality[95] from the EU point of view:

> '1. Citizenship of the Union is hereby established. Every person holding the nationality of a Member State shall be a citizen of the Union. Citizenship of the Union shall complement and not replace national citizenship.
> 2. Citizens of the Union shall enjoy the rights conferred by this Treaty and shall be subject to the duties imposed thereby.'

There are many explanations for this relationship. 'Nationality' is for instance often seen as the international law aspect, while 'citizenship' refers to its implications in national law.[96] Or EU citizenship is considered to be parasitic upon national citizenship (or nationality).[97] It has been noted that:

> '(…) it is obvious that 'nationality' refers to the formal link between a person and a state, irrespective of how this link is called under national law, whereas "citizenship of the Union" refers to the newly created status in Community law.'[98]

The least that can be said is that the basis is nationality of the Member States (and not citizenship of the Member States because that may vary from Member State to Member State). It thus intends to offer an addition to 'traditional' nationality although the use of the term 'national citizenship' can be confusing. Nationality as a basis for awarding – perhaps extra – citizenship rights does not coincide with the practice at the national level in many Member States, as is clear from the example of the Netherlands described above.

EU citizenship has now been mentioned several times as being different from state citizenship and as a prime example of the changing nature of citi-

---

[94] J. Bhabha, *Belonging in Europe: Citizenship and Post-national Rights* (UNESCO 1999) p. 16.

[95] The Declaration on Nationality of a Member State (protocol added by the Treaty of Maastricht) states that each Member State decides who will be awarded the nationality of that Member State.

[96] S.H. Legomski, 'Comment: Why Citizenship?', 35 *Va. J. Int'l L.* (1994) pp. 279 ff.

[97] K. Rostek and G. Davies, 'The Impact of Union Citizenship on National Citizenship Policies', *EIoP* (4 July 2006).

[98] G-R. de Groot, 'Towards a European Nationality Law – Vers un droit européen de nationalité', inaugural lecture, 13 November 2003, Maastricht (2003) p. 6.

zenship. It is now possible to evaluate EU citizenship in light of the more theoretical aspects of citizenship and nationality. EU citizenship originates from the Treaty of Maastricht and was introduced by the Commission on the initiative of Spain.[99] In the first years of its inclusion in the EC Treaty, the by some expected importance of EU citizenship was limited.[100] Of course, the European Community, later accompanied by the European Union in this respect, already provided many rights and duties to nationals of the Member States, rights and duties which would traditionally be given at the national level.

The rights and duties of EU citizens were laid down in the EC Treaty (Arts. 18-22). In the replaced European Constitution, the rights and duties of the citizen were not changed but re-listed (although suggestions in such a direction were made at the Convention[101]), giving a good overview of the state of affairs. Article I-8 of the European Constitution read as follows:

'1. Every national of a Member State shall be a citizen of the Union. Citizenship of the Union shall be additional to national citizenship: it shall not replace it.
2. Citizens of the Union shall enjoy the rights and be subject to the duties provided for in the Constitution. They shall have:
– the right to move and reside freely within the territory of the Member States;
– the right to vote and to stand as candidates in elections to the European Parliament and in municipal elections in their Member States of residence, under the same conditions as nationals of that State;
– the right to enjoy, in the territory of a third country in which the Member State of which they are nationals is not represented, the protection of the diplomatic and consular authorities of any Member State on the same conditions as the nationals of that State;
– the right to petition the European Parliament, to apply to the European Ombudsman, and to address the Institutions and advisory bodies of the Union in any of the Constitution's languages and to obtain a reply in the same language.

---

[99] As reported by civil serofts closely associated with the negotiation process.
[100] As described in 1999, for instance, in Bhabha, op. cit., note 94, p. 16, and T. Kostako-poulou, 'Nested "Old" and "New" Citizenships in the European Union: Bringing out the Complexity', 5 *Colum. J. Eur. L.* (1999) pp. 389 ff.
[101] Suggestion to include third-country nationals who are long-term residents: Opinion of the European Economic and Social Committee on 'Access to European Union Citizenship', *OJ* C 208/19, 3 September 2003.

3. These rights shall be exercised in accordance with the conditions and limits defined by the Constitution and by the measures adopted to give it effect.'

This is summarized by the Commission as: 'By establishing citizenship of the Union, the Union placed the individual at the heart of its activities.'[102] And by the Court of Justice: 'Citizenship of the Union is destined to be the fundamental status of nationals of the Member States.'[103] The Court of Justice comments on citizenship in the *Garcia Avello* case:[104] 'Citizenship of the Union, established by article 17 ECT, is not, however, intended to extend the scope ratione materiae of the Treaty also to internal situations which have no link with Community law.' Still, such a link is easily created. In this particular case, the system of family names in Spain had to be respected by Belgium in order not to block the possibilities of free movement of workers:

First, with regard to the principle of the immutability of surnames as a means designed to prevent risks of confusion as to identity or parentage of persons, although that principle undoubtedly helps to facilitate recognition of the identity of persons and their parentage, it is still not indispensable to the point that it could not adapt itself to a practice of allowing children who are nationals of one Member State and who also hold the nationality of another Member State to take a surname which is composed of elements other than those provided for by the law of the first Member State and which has, moreover, been entered in an official register of the second Member State. Furthermore, it is common ground that, by reason in particular of the scale of migration within the Union, different national systems for the attribution of surnames coexist in the same Member State, with the result that parentage cannot necessarily be assessed within the social life of a Member State solely on the basis of the criterion of the system applicable to nationals of that latter State. In addition, far from creating confusion as to the parentage of the children, a system allowing elements of the surnames of the two parents to be handed down may, on the contrary, contribute to reinforcing recognition of that connection with the two parents.

---

[102] Report from the Commission, *Fourth Report on Citizenship of the Union* (1 May 2001 – 30 April 2004), Brussels, 26 October 2004, COM(2004)695 final. Also stated in the Preamble to the EU Charter on Fundamental Rights, 2000, *OJ* C 364 1, 7 December 2000.

[103] ECJ, Case C-148/02 *Garcia Avello* [2003] *ECR* I-11613.

[104] ECJ, Case C-148/02 *Garcia Avello* [2003] *ECR* I-11613.

Second, with regard to the objective of integration pursued by the practice in issue, suffice it to point out that, in view of the coexistence in the Member States of different systems for the attribution of surnames applicable to those there resident, a practice such as that in issue in the main proceedings is neither necessary nor even appropriate for promoting the integration within Belgium of the nationals of other Member States.

In itself the notion of EU citizenship does not confer new rights on the nationals of the Member States.[105] As Habermas[106] already stated, it is not necessary to have all powers represented at the highest, i.e. European, level, which citizens traditionally possess at a national level, as long as the total package of the two levels combined represents the general rights and duties of citizenship. Yet, the Court of Justice has enlarged the scope of the notion in its case-law, bringing groups of inhabitants under the umbrella of EU citizenship who would otherwise have fallen outside the scope of EU law.

It exceeds the scope of this study to go into details for each right attached to EU citizenship. Yet, several elements deserve to be highlighted and explained. It needs to be noted first that the free movement of persons, and the free movement of workers and services in particular, is at the heart of the citizenship rights.[107] This is sometimes described as 'market citizenship'.[108] One element not listed in Article 18 TEC (Art. 21 TFEU-L) and further is the importance of basic rights protection. The importance of basic rights is clear from the Preamble to the EU Charter on Fundamental Rights and from the examples described above for the award of citizenship. Especially the right to family life (as laid down in the European Convention on Human Rights) has been important for interpreting and applying the right to free movement. Basic rights have to be applied on all inhabitants of the Member States by the Member States (and thus at the national level) while the citizen's rights are mostly aimed at the nationals of the Member States.[109]

---

[105] A. Schrauwen, 'Sink or Swim Together? Developments in European Citizenship', *Fordham Int'l L. J.* (2000) pp. 778 ff.

[106] J. Habermas, 'Why Europe Needs a Constitution', 11 *New Left Review* (September-October 2001), <www.newleftreview.net/?page=article&view=2343> (last visited 21 August 2006).

[107] M. Jeffery, 'The Free Movement of Persons within the European Union: Moving from Employment Rights to Fundamental Rights?', 23 *Comp. Lab. L. & Pol'y J.* (2005) pp. 211 ff.

[108] P. Hansen, '"European Citizenship", or Where Neoliberalism Meets Ethno-Culturalism; Analysing the European Union's Citizenship Discourse', *European Societies* (2000) p. 147.

[109] R.W. Davis, 'Citizenship of the Union ... Rights for All?', 27 *E.L. Rev.* (2002) pp. 121-137.

It is not automatic for every national of a Member State to profit from all citizenship rights. As already mentioned above, the EC Treaty already places limits on it by emphasizing the role of the economically active in the free movement of workers and only giving secondary free movement rights to the non-economically active.[110] When one is economically active and thus has the right to free movement can be deduced from both the new Directive on the free movement of workers,[111] and case-law of the Court of Justice like the *Trojani* case:[112]

Moreover, neither the *sui generis* nature of the employment relationship under national law, nor the level of productivity of the person concerned, the origin of the funds from which the remuneration is paid or the limited amount of the remuneration can have any consequence in regard to whether or not the person is a worker for the purposes of Community law (see Case 53/81 *Levin* [1982] *ECR* 1035, Para. 16; Case 344/87 *Bettray* [1989] *ECR* 1621, Paras. 15 and 16; and Case C-188/00 *Kurz* [2002] *ECR* I-10691, Para. 32).

In the present case, as is apparent from the decision-making the reference, Mr Trojani performs, for the Salvation Army and under its direction, various jobs for approximately thirty hours a week, as part of a personal reintegration programme, in return for which he receives benefits in kind and some pocket money.

In the *Bidar* case,[113] the Court of Justice judged in a case in which grants for students in higher education are concerned. The Court decided that:

'Moreover, there is nothing in the text of the Treaty to suggest that students who are citizen of the Union, when they move to another Member State to study there, lose the rights which the Treaty confers on citizens of the Union (Grzelczyk, paragraph 35). (…)

---

[110] See in this respect also A. Schrauwen, 'Sink or Swim Together? Developments in European Citizenship', 23 *Fordham Int'l L. J.* (2000) pp. 778 ff.; and M. Jeffery, 'The Free movement of Persons within the European Union: Moving from Employment Rights to Fundamental Rights?', 23 *Comp. Lab. L. & Pol'y J.*(2005) pp. 211 ff.

[111] Directive 2004/38 or 29 April 2004 on the right of citizens of the Union and their family members to move and reside freely within the territory of the Member States, *OJ* L 158, 30 April 2004, pp. 77-123. See also J.W. de Zwaan, 'European Citizenship: Origin, Contents and Perspectives', in D. Curtin, A.E. Kellermann and S. Blockmans (eds.), *The EU Constitution: The Best Way Forward?* (The Hague 2005) pp. 245-264.

[112] ECJ, Case C-456/02 *Trojani* [2004] *ECR* I-07573.

[113] ECJ, Case C-209/03 *Bidar* [2005] *ECR* I-02119.

On the other hand, the existence of a certain degree of integration may be regarded as established by a finding that the student in question has resided in the
host Member State for a certain length of time. (…)'

The first paragraph of Article 12 EC must be interpreted as precluding national legislation which grants students the right to assistance covering their
maintenance costs only if they are settled in the host Member State, while
precluding a national of another Member State from obtaining the status of
settled person as a student even if that national is lawfully resident and has
received a substantial part of his secondary education in the host Member
State and has consequently established a genuine link with the society of that
State.

From this case, and previous cases on (higher) education,[114] can be concluded that EU citizenship has extended beyond a supportive competence
like education by linking it to non-discrimination and to free movement of
persons, while limiting it with the requirement of the 'genuine link'. This
genuine link played an important role in the *Collins* case[115] as well. Contrary
to the *Bidar* case, the genuine link was lacking for Mr Collins, an Irish national who applied for an unemployment benefit in the United Kingdom (UK)
after having worked there many years ago:

'It may be regarded as legitimate for a Member State to grant such an allowance
only after it has been possible to establish that a genuine link exists between the
person seeking work and the employment market of that State.'

The existence of such a link may be determined, in particular, by establishing that the person concerned has, for a reasonable period, in fact genuinely
sought work in the Member State in question.

In the *D'Hoop* case,[116] the Court of Justice also discussed linkage with
citizenship rights, in casu the right to move from Member State to Member
State. Ms D'Hoop was a Belgian national who had optioned her diploma of
completion of secondary education in France and subsequently moved back
to Belgium. She applied for a tideover allowance but was refused this be-

---

[114] For example: ECJ, Case C-184/99 *Rudy Grzelczyk* [2001] *ECR* I-06193; or ECJ, Case
C-337/97 Meeusen [2001] *ECR* I-03289.
[115] ECJ, Case C-138/02 *Collins* [2004] *ECR* I-02703.
[116] ECJ, Case C-224/98 *D'Hoop* [2002] *ECR* I-06191.

cause she did not possess such a diploma from a Belgium education institution:

However, a single condition concerning the place where the diploma of completion of secondary education was obtained is too general and exclusive in nature. It unduly favours an element which is not necessarily representative of the real and effective degree of connection between the applicant for the tideover allowance and the geographic employment market, to the exclusion of all other representative elements. It therefore goes beyond what is necessary to attain the objective pursued.

An third interesting element of EU citizenship which needs special attention is treatment of third-country nationals. For them, the general rule is of course that they do not have similar rights as the EU citizens: the rules for the free movement of persons do not apply to them, for instance. The national rules for aliens apply to this group of inhabitants, and the protection of their basic rights or limited right of suffrage stems for national law as well. The third-country nationals even run the risk of deportation, which the nationals of the Member States do not.[117] Yet, for third-country nationals who are long-term residents there is a new Council directive, which gives them free movement, just like EU citizens.[118] In addition, those married to a national of a Member State who has used his or her free movements rights, have secondary citizenship rights, as described above.

This leaves the in-between category of citizens of the New Member States. The Treaty of Accession gives them some of the EU citizens' rights as listed in Article 18 TEC and further (Art. 21 TFEU-L), but not all: the free movement of workers is limited.[119] They have been awarded the right to vote for The European Parliament and other rights, but they have only limited free movement rights under the Temporary Provisions of the Treaty of Accession.

In summary, it can be said that EU citizenship has apparently led to the creation of multiple categories of citizens, all with a different set of rights and duties:

---

[117] Bhabha, op. cit., note 94, p. 19.

[118] Council directive 2003/109/EC, *OJ* L 16, 23 January 2004, pp. 44-53 of 25 November 2003 concerning the status of third-country nationals who are long-term residents.

[119] See the many releoft Joint Declarations to the Final Act to the Treaty of Accession to the European Union 2003, *OJ* L 236, 23 September 2003.

1. nationals of an (old) EU Member State who have used their right to free movement;
2. nationals of an (old) EU Member State who have the possibility to use the options under free movement but have not yet done so;
3. nationals of a new EU Member State (limited possibilities for free movement);
4. legal third-country nationals married to an EU citizen who is living in another Member State;
5. legal third-country nationals not married to an EU citizen who is living in another Member State, with less than five years of residence in a Member State;
6. legal third-country nationals not married to an EU citizen who is living in another Member State, with more than five years of residence in a Member State.

The ideal EU citizen is, apparently, a cross-border worker.[120] This means that for many legal inhabitants of a Member State, citizenship and the accompanying rights and duties depend on the rules and regulations of that particular Member State. For others, EU citizenship offers additional rights and duties, although not similar for each.

---

[120] C. Shore, 'Whither European Citizenship? Eros and Civilization Revisited', 7 *European Journal of Social Theory* (2004), p. 37.

Chapter 3

ECONOMIC RIGHTS

Chapter 3

ECONOMIC RIGHTS

3.1 INTRODUCTION

Marshall's theory on citizenship explains that the first step in creating full citizenship is the creation of civil rights, which he specifies from the experience in eighteenth and nineteenth century England as economic rights via the principle of individual economic rights.[121] The right to free labour became a basic element of citizenship. In European Union terms, the equivalent is the economic right to free labour, even the right to do this labour anywhere in the European Union without restrictions, i.e. free movement of persons who are economically active.

From the description in the preceding chapter of the concept of EU citizenship and the rights attached to it, is cleat that the ideal EU citizen is, apparently, a transnational worker.[122] This means that for many legal inhabitants of a Member State, citizenship and the accompanying rights and duties depend on the rules and regulations of that particular Member State because they do not obtain any of the rights attached to the exercise of free movement rights until they decide to work in another Member State. For the ones who did, EU citizenship offers additional rights and duties, although not the same rights for each member of this group.

Economic rights for EU citizens are mostly given form and substance under the traditional free movement rights in the EC Treaty. Because the EC Treaty focuses on economic possibilities and market integration for the citizen,[123] it can easily be considered to be economic rights, although more and

---

[121] T.H. Marshall, *Citizenship and Social Class* (Cambridge 1950) p. 17 ff.
[122] Shore, op. cit., note 120, p. 37.
[123] M. Bell, *Anti-Discrimination Law and the European Union* (Oxford 2002) pp. 6-11.

F. Goudappel, The Effects of EU Citizenship
© 2010, T·M·C·ASSER PRESS, The Hague, The Netherlands and the Author

more social rights follow from these freedoms as well.[124] The emphasis in the EC Treaty lies on the free movement of workers, the freedom of establishment for the self-employed, and the free movement of services, since EU citizens can freely move to another Member State on the basis of each of these three possibilities.

The free movement of persons has existed since the foundation of the European Community in 1951, when it was conferred to workers and other economically active persons.[125] Regulation 1612/68 was in addition the basis for family members to obtain a kind of parasitic right to free movement. In 1986, the Single European Act set out to create a Europe without internal frontiers. It extended the right of residence in another Member State to persons who are not workers, provided they have sufficient resources and social insurance cover. In 1990 further steps were taken in order to create a more or less general right of residence. A package of three Directives came into force with respect to students, workers who have ceased their professional activities and a left-over category.[126]

Quintessential for the scope of the economic rights for EU citizens is the so-called Persons Directive.[127] The purpose of this recent directive is to harmonize free movement rights at both the national and the European level: 'With a view to remedying this sector-by-sector, piecemeal approach to the right of free movement and residence and facilitating the exercise of this right, there needs to be a single legislative act.'[128] The Persons Directive therefore lays down the basic rules for the group of persons involved and the rights they possess: it concerns Union citizens and their family members whether these latter are Union citizens or not. They possess the right of free movement, the right of residence, the right of entry, stay and exit, along with the equal treatment rights laid down in other secondary legislation.

In order to understand what the economic rights entail, the group of EU citizens needs to be determined first who possess the economic rights. This

---

[124] See the Chapter 4 for an indepth analysis of the social rights.

[125] Goudappel and Romein, op. cit., note 83.

[126] Directives 90/364-366, *OJ* L 180, 13 July 1990, pp. 26-31.

[127] European Parliament and Council Directive 2004/38/EC of 29 April 2004 on the right of citizens of the Union and their family members to move and reside freely within the territory of the Member States, *OJ* L 204, 4 August 2007, pp. 28-28 amending Regulation (EEC) No. 1612/68 and repealing Directives 64/221/EEC, 68/360/EEC, 72/194/EEC, 73/148/EEC, 75/34/EEC, 75/35/EEC, 90/364/EEC, 90/365/EEC and 93/96/EEC.

includes a discussion of which family members can come along with the EU citizen to another Member State. After this, is will be possible to study the economic rights which the EU citizens possess. These rights can be divided into two groups: the primary rights, i.e. the free movement rights, and the secondary or derived rights, which follow after the free movement rights have been exercised.

3.2   WHO HAS ECONOMIC RIGHTS?

As the headings of the respective chapters in the EC Treaty indicate, the rights aim at those who are economically active: the workers and the self-employed.[129] The Persons Directive covers rights for all EU citizens, although the recitals to the directive leave room for more rights for workers and self-employed persons:

> 'Certain advantages specific to Union citizens who are workers or self-employed persons and to their family members, which may allow these persons to acquire a right of permanent residence before they have resided five years in the host Member State, should be maintained, as these constitute acquired rights, conferred by Commission Regulation (EEC) No 1251/70 of 29 June 1970 on the right of workers to remain in the territory of a Member State after having been employed in that State and Council Directive 75/34/EEC of 17 December 1974 concerning the right of nationals of a Member State to remain in the territory of another Member State after having pursued therein an activity in a self-employed capacity.'[130]

For the free movement of workers – and in the next paragraphs for the freedom of establishment and the free movement of services – the limits are twofold: the answers to the question to whom the rights of free movement have been given and to the question what these rights entail from the point of view of economic rights. The category of persons who fall under the free movement possibilities is thereby determined by the nationality principle and by the concept of the 'worker'.

---

[128] Recital 4 to Directive 2004/38/EC.
[129] See also R.C.A. White, 'The Citizen's Right to Free Movement', 16 *EBLR* (2005) p. 547.
[130] Recital 19 to Directive 2004/38/EC.

1.   *Worker*

The scope of the concept of the 'worker' has been described often, mostly based on the case-law of the ECJ. The following description will follow the usual line of reasoning, but will be specifically aimed at establishing the width of the economic rights of the citizen. The free movement of workers is laid down in Article 39 TEC (Art. 45 TFEU-L), which does not give a definition of the term but gives the rights attached to it. The second paragraph of Article 39 TEC (Art. 45 TFEU-L), however, states that the right to free movement of workers is limited to the nationals of the Member States, so therefore to EU citizens.

Only relatively late in the development of the internal market did the ECJ formulate a definition of a 'worker, in the *Lawrie-Blum* case:

> 'That [i.e., the concept of a worker; *FG*] concept must be defined in accordance with objective criteria which distinguish the employment relationship by reference to the rights and duties of the persons concerned. The essential feature of an employment relationship, however, is that for a certain period of time a person performs services for and under the direction of another person in return for which he receives remuneration.'[131]

The *Lawrie-Blum* case has thus been the focal point for the notion of 'worker'. Yet, there are several reasons why this case is more than a milestone in the definition of the concept. Firstly, the case would most likely be part of education law under national law instead of under employees' law. The financing of an internship period could fall under the free movement of workers because of the German choices for financing. Other ways of setting up a system for such internships would not lead to the free movement of workers. In addition, the options under European law in 1986 were different than the options at present; EU citizenship was not yet created, although the ECJ refers to the notion of 'favoured EEC citizen' under Dutch law in the *Levin* case.[132] National legislation had apparently referred to a similar notion which was an implementation of Directive 64/221/EEC, in which 'citizenship' as such was not necessary. Under the present Treaty and consequent case-law of the ECJ, the *Lawrie-Blum* case could perhaps be brought under EU citizen-

---

[131]   ECJ, Case 66/85 *Lawrie-Blum* [1986] *ECR* 02121.
[132]   ECJ, Case 53/81 *Levin* [1982] *ECR* 01035.

ship, like it was done for Mr Bidar,[133] in which a student grant was given to the student not on the basis of his relatives being workers under the EC Treaty, but on the basis of his own 'genuine link' with the UK as a 'settled person'.

The Lawrie-Blum definition, however, separates the workers from establishment and service providers, as well as from non-economically active citizens. The definition contains an exhaustive list of elements which need to be fulfilled in order to be considered a worker. The situation in the *Lawrie-Blum* case also shows that not all of the employment relationship is regulated by European law. The German authorities made their own choice for the way in which they organized the training and examination of prospective teachers at a gymnasium, which included a preparatory service leading to the second state examination during which the candidate was a trainee teacher with the status of temporary civil servant. The choices for this system made by the German authorities led to a system in which the candidates were workers according the European law, for which Germany was not allowed to make any distinction based on nationality. Other Member States may have decided on other systems of training teachers which do not lead to the status of 'worker':

As regards those undergoing a traineeship, the Court has held that the fact that the traineeship may be regarded as practical preparation directly related to the actual pursuit of the occupation in point is not a bar to the application of Article 48 of the Treaty if the training period is completed under the conditions of genuine and effective activity as an employed person.[134]

Before the *Lawrie-Blum* case, the only decision by the ECJ on the status of 'worker' concerned the scope of application of Article 39 TEC (Art. 45 TFEU-L). In the *Levin* case, the ECJ stated that:

'The concepts of "worker" and "activity as an employed person" define the field of application of one of the fundamental freedoms guaranteed by the Treaty and, as such, may not be interpreted restrictively.'[135]

As a result, the ECJ has since then applied the definition to many different situations. In the *Meeusen* case,[136] the ECJ stressed that there needs to be a

---

[133] ECJ, Case C-209/03 *Bidar* [2005] *ECR* I-02119.
[134] ECJ, Case C-109/04 *Kranemann* [2005] *ECR* I-02421.
[135] ECJ, Case 53/81 *Levin* [1982] *ECR* 01035.
[136] ECJ, Case C-337/97 *Meeusen* [1999] *ECR* I-03289.

relationship of subordination between the migrant worker and the employer, but that the job involved does not need to be fulltime employment, yet: 'Any person who pursues activities which are effective and genuine, to the exclusion of activities on such a small scale as to be regarded as purely marginal and ancillary, must be regarded as a "worker".'

In the *Trojani* case,[137] the ECJ applied the definition on a work situation which did not fulfill the traditional criteria for an employment relationship because Mr Trojani

'was given accommodation in a Salvation Army hostel from 8 January 2002, where in return for board and lodging and some pocket money he does various jobs for about 30 hours a week as part of a personal socio-occupational reintegration programme.'

Another element of the definition of a 'worker' which has been decisive in determining which citizens can use the right to free movement of workers is the necessity of 'a genuine and effective economic activity'.[138] In the *Steymann* case,[139] it was concluded that religious communities could also perform genuine and effective economic activities, and that providing for the material needs of the workers involved and some pocket money can be considered 'remuneration' as the definition requires. If it, on the other hand, merely concerns activities which aim at rehabilitating persons who are 'unable to take up employment under normal conditions',[140] it does not fulfill the criteria set.

Not all workers fulfilling the criteria of the Lawrie-Blum definition are workers under European law, though. Article 39 Paragraph 4 TEC (Art. 45 TFEU-L) offers the Member States the possibility to make an exception for positions representing the state: 'The provisions of this Article shall not apply to employment in the public service.' Although the wording of this paragraph might suggest otherwise, this is limited to specific types of employment in the public service. The exception means that Member States can block free movement rights for these specific jobs and only allow the own nation-

---

[137] ECJ, Case C-456/02 *Trojani* [2004] *ECR* I-07573.

[138] C. Barnard, *The Substantive Law of the EU; The Four Freedoms*, 2nd edn. (Oxford 2007) pp. 287-288.

[139] ECJ, Case 196/87 *Steymann* [1988] *ECR* 06159.

[140] ECJ, Case 344/87 *Bettray* [1989] *ECR* 01621.

als to perform the duties involved. It is up to the Member States to decide which positions fall in this category.[141] The European norms for this national decision are that the position represents 'a specific bond of allegiance and mutuality of rights and duties between State and employee.'[142]

Moreover, a second exception is laid down in Article 39 Paragraph 3 EC (Art. 45 TFEU-L), which states that the free movement rights can only be exercised 'subject to limitations justified on grounds of public policy, public security or public health'. Contrary to the exception in the fourth paragraph of Article 39 EC (Art. 45 TFEU-L), this exception refers to the specific person instead of the specific function. This particular exception has been given a wider scope than only the free movement of workers in Article 27 of the Persons Directive, with the details in the second paragraph:

> 'Measures taken on grounds of public policy or public security shall comply with the principle of proportionality and shall be based exclusively on the personal conduct of the individual concerned. Previous criminal convictions shall not in themselves constitute grounds for taking such measures. The personal conduct of the individual concerned must represent a genuine, present and sufficiently serious threat affecting one of the fundamental interests of society. Justifications that are isolated from the particulars of the case or that rely on considerations of general prevention shall not be accepted.'

The person, or rather the conduct of the person, must have given rise to the application of the exception. There has been extensive case-law of the ECJ on the width of the application of this exception. Of course, there cannot be discrimination between the own nationals and the nationals of other Member States when applying this exception, as the ruling of the ECJ in the case of *Adoui and Cornuaille*[143] shows:

> 'It should be noted in that regard that reliance by a national authority upon the concept of public policy presupposes, as the court held in its judgment of 27 October 1977 in case 30/77 Bouchereau (1977) ECR 1999, the existence of "a genuine and sufficiently serious threat affecting one of the fundamental interests of society". Although community law does not impose upon the member states a

---

[141] N. Beenen, *Citzenship, Nationality and Access to Public Service Employment* (Groningen 2001).
[142] Craig and De Búrca, op. cit., note 12, p. 766.
[143] ECJ, Joined Cases 115 and 116/81 *Adoui and Cornuaille* [1982] *ECR* 01665.

uniform scale of values as regards the assessment of conduct which may be considered as contrary to public policy, it should nevertheless be stated that conduct may not be considered as being of a sufficiently serious nature to justify restrictions on the admission to or residence within the territory of a member state of a national of another member state in a case where the former member state does not adopt, with respect to the same conduct on the part of its own nationals repressive measures or other genuine and effective measures intended to combat such conduct.'

Thus, there is some discretion in application for the Member States, but within boundaries.[144] This discretion is shown in cases like the *Olazabal* case, in which the ECJ decided that the prohibition of discrimination on the basis of nationality does not mean 'identical measures' but may also mean more limited measures for the own nationals. It would of course otherwise be impossible to exercise this power for the Member States since it would mean expulsion of own nationals in order to have identical measures in place.

In the recent *Jipa* case,[145] another aspect of the exception on grounds of public policy or public security was decided upon by the ECJ: a situation in which the Member State of origin limits the right of exit for his own national on the basis of an earlier expulsion by another Member State:

'The answer to the questions referred must therefore be that Article 18 EC and Article 27 of Directive 2004/38 do not preclude national legislation that allows the right of a national of a Member State to travel to another Member State to be restricted, in particular on the ground that he has previously been repatriated from the latter Member State on account of his "illegal residence" there, provided that the personal conduct of that national constitutes a genuine, present and sufficiently serious threat to one of the fundamental interests of society and that the restrictive measure envisaged is appropriate to ensure the achievement of the objective it pursues and does not go beyond what is necessary to attain it. It is for the national court to establish whether that is so in the case before it.'

2.   *Establishment and services*

Where the ECJ was relatively late in giving a definition of the concept of 'worker', it has never provided a definition of the group of citizens falling in

---

[144] Craig and De Búrca, op. cit., note 12, p. 784.
[145] ECJ, Case C-33/07 *Jipa* [2008] *ECR* I-05157.

the category of 'establishment' or 'self-employed',[146] necessary for establishing the scope of free movement rights for other economically active citizens. It is only given when there is doubt about the choice between establishment and services in the *Gebhard* case:[147]

> 'The possibility for a national of a Member State to exercise his right of establishment, and the conditions for his exercise of that right, must be determined in the light of the activities which he intends to pursue on the territory of the host Member State.'

This can only be so if the situation is the opposite of services: 'The temporary nature of the activities in question has to be determined in the light of its duration, regularity, periodicity and continuity.' The text of the EC Treaty does not give a definition of this category either; Article 43 EC (Art. 49 TFEU-L) only states that freedom of establishment exists. Secondary legislation does not help in solving this problem: the Persons Directive, for instance, does not mention this at all.

The only element which has received attention relates to the mutual recognition of diplomas as laid down in Article 47 EC (Art. 53 TFEU-L). In order to give citizens the option to benefit from the right of establishment, the Member States must recognize diplomas issued by other Member States. A system is therefore set up in which either directives are adopted regulating professions or in which the Member States need to decide case by case how to deal with a certain diploma. A general directive on the recognition of professional qualifications[148] has established a basic system which was in the past ruled by many specific directives. Article 4 of the Directive contains this basic system:

> '1. The recognition of professional qualifications by the host Member State allows the beneficiary to gain access in that Member State to the same profession as that for which he is qualified in the home Member State and to pursue it in the host Member State under the same conditions as its nationals.

---

[146] J. Fairhurst, *Law of the European Union*, 6th edn. (Harlow 2007) pp. 403-404.
[147] ECJ, Case C-55/94 *Gebhard* [1995] *ECR* I-04165.
[148] Directive 2005/36/EC of the European Parliament and of the Council of 7 September 2005 on the recognition of professional qualifications.

2. For the purposes of this Directive, the profession which the applicant wishes to pursue in the host Member State is the same as that for which he is qualified in his home Member State if the activities covered are comparable.'

This system has led to extensive case-law by the ECJ. In the case of Mr Peros, for instance, the implementation by Greece of the forerunner of the general directive[149] was disputed because Greece required a further adaptation or exam before the diploma could be recognized. The ECJ, however, stated that the recognition of diplomas was unconditional. In a similar Greek case, the case of Ms Aslanidou,[150] the Greek authorities had decided not to recognize a German diploma for occupational therapist

'on the ground that the qualification relied on by her was not a higher-education diploma since, in order to be eligible for a place at the German institution in question, a basic training of eight to 10 years, and not 12 years, was required, so that the conditions laid down by Directive 89/48 were not satisfied.'

This in fact indicates that the Greek authorities not only evaluated the curriculum for the diploma in question but also the German education system in general, which was, as expected, not allowed by the ECJ.

In several other (earlier) cases, other qualifications were disputed for which no European system was yet developed. Most prominent among these is the law degree which is difficult to compare by nature because it studies national systems which automatically disqualifies for the law degree of another Member State. Yet, prior to the adoption of a specific directive for lawyers, there were several options to be able to be a lawyer in another Member State, all of which have been given by the ECJ. The landmark case was Ms Vlassopoulou's,[151] in which she already worked as a legal advisor in Germany with a Greek law degree (and a German doctoral exam). Germany refused to allow her to practice as a lawyer. The ECJ decided that the Member State has the obligation

---

[149] Council Directive 89/48/EEC of 21 December 1988 *OJ* L 19, 24 January 1989, pp. 16-23 on a general system for the recognition of higher-education diplomas awarded on completion of professional education and training of at least three years' duration.

[150] ECJ, Case C-142/04 *Aslanidou* [2005] *ECR* I-07181.

[151] ECJ, Case C-340/89 *Vlassopoulou* [1991] *ECR* I-02663.

'to examine to what extent the knowledge and qualifications attested by the diploma obtained by the person concerned in his country of origin correspond to those required by the rules of the host State. That examination must be carried out in accordance with a procedure which is in conformity with the requirements of Community law concerning the effective protection of the fundamental rights conferred by the Treaty on Community subjects. It follows that any decision taken must be capable of being made the subject of judicial proceedings in which its legality under Community law can be reviewed and that the person concerned must be able to ascertain the reasons for the decision taken in his regard.'

If those diplomas correspond only partially, the national authorities in question are entitled to require the person concerned to prove that he has acquired the knowledge and qualifications which are lacking. In this regard the said authorities must assess whether the knowledge acquired in the host Member State, either during a course of study or by way of practical experience, is sufficient in order to prove possession of the knowledge which is lacking.

Another famous case on a similar problem is Mr Gebhard's case,[152] which has become important for several reasons. For the element of diploma recognition in order to be able to use the right of establishment, 'Member States must take account of the equivalence of diplomas and, if necessary, proceed to a comparison of the knowledge and qualifications required by their national rules and those of the person concerned.' In addition, the *Morgenbesser* case[153] shows that this system even applies in case not all the professional obligations have been fulfilled in the Member State of origin.

The general directive on professional qualifications shows that Article 47 TEC (Art. 53 TFEU-L) not only applies to the freedom of establishment but also to the free movement of services although the provision is primarily placed in the Chapter on freedom of establishment; by means of Article 55 TEC (Art. 62 TFEU-L), Article 47 TEC (Art. 53 TFEU-L) also applies to free movement of services. This is a special category when one studies it from the point of view of free movement rights for citizens. It covers more than citizens' rights; not only the right to provide and receive services is involved because it is a left-over category as the definition in Article 50 TEC (Art. 57 TFEU-L) shows: 'Services shall be considered to be "services" within the meaning of this Treaty where they are normally provided for remunera-

---

[152] ECJ, Case C-55/94 *Gebhard* [1995] *ECR* I-04165.
[153] ECJ, Case C-313/01 *Morgenbesser* [2003] *ECR* I-13467.

tion, in so far as they are not governed by the provisions relating to freedom of movement for goods, capital and persons.'

Apart from the fact that, evidently, a cross-border element must be involved, the most important element in this definition turns out to be 'normally provided for remuneration'. This indicates that the text is meant to preclude that gratuitous services fall outside the free movement rules.[154] In addition, it indicates an economic link, it being part of economic free movement rights, which is necessary for a citizen to fall within the scope of the relevant Treaty provisions. The *Deliège* case[155] shows that sports can fall within this category, provided that it is not an employment relation as in the free movement of workers and that 'the activity is genuine and effective and not such as to be regarded as purely marginal and ancillary'. The situation in the *Grogan* case,[156] however, shows that not all activities are services: whereas medical termination of pregnancy itself may constitute an economic activity, distributing information about it by student associations is not.

Different activities are therefore considered to be services. The text of Article 50 TEC (Art. 57 TFEU-L) already contains a non-exhaustive list, which shows that at least the professions are services. Practice shows that services can mean that either the provider or the receiver moves, or both, or neither. The non-exhaustive list of professions in the Treaty text shows that it basic idea was that the service provider would move while the service receiver did not. However, the *Carpenter* case[157] shows that being a service provider could also be done without moving and have consequences involving citizenship rights:

'As is apparent from paragraph 14 of this judgment, a significant proportion of Mr Carpenter's business consists of providing services, for remuneration, to advertisers established in other Member States. Such services come within the meaning of "services" in Article 49 EC both in so far as the provider travels for that purpose to the Member State of the recipient and in so far as he provides cross-border services without leaving the Member State in which he is established.'

Yet, the economic rights mostly concern the rights of the service providers, although receiving a service may also constitute economic rights. Buying

---

[154] Barnard, op. cit., note 138, p. 360.
[155] ECJ, Joined Cases C-51/96 and C-191/97 *Deliège* [2000] *ECR* I-02549.
[156] ECJ, Case 159/90 *SPUC* v. *Grogan* [1991] *ECR* I-04685.
[157] ECJ, Case C-60/00 *Carpenter* [2002] *ECR* I-06279.

something over the internet from another Member State, for instance, primarily means that receiving a service has an economic, a market, dimension, although receiving the purchase may involve the free movement of goods. It is also possible that a service provider employs workers. In order to make this possible the so-called Services Directive[158] harmonizes the necessary elements; it focuses on the activities rather than on the persons involved:

'Art. 2:
1. This Directive shall apply to services supplied by providers established in a Member State.
2. This Directive shall not apply to the following activities: (...)

Art. 4:
1. 'service' means any self-employed economic activity, normally provided for remuneration, as referred to in Article 50 of the Treaty;
2. 'provider' means any natural person who is a national of a Member State, or any legal person as referred to in Article 48 of the Treaty and established in a Member State, who offers or provides a service; (...)'

The exceptions for workers on grounds of public policy and public security are also valid for self-employed persons and service-providers because Article 27 of the Persons Directive, in which this exception has been given form and substance, applies to all categories, even including the non-economically active citizens. The exception on the basis of a function in public service, on the other hand, is only laid down in Article 39 Paragraph 4 TEC (Art. 45 TFEU-L), and is thus limited in application to workers.

3.   *Not yet economically active persons*

Several groups of persons within the European Union possess economic free movement rights without falling in one of the categories above and without a direct link to free movement rights under EU citizenship. This concerns persons who are not yet economically active, but who do have a link to the labour market, now or in the future. In this category, both students and persons who ask for social benefits as an interim measure between school and labour market.

---

[158] Directive 2006/123/EC of the European Parliament and of the Council of 12 December 2006 *OJ* L 376, 27 December 2006, pp. 36-68 on services in the internal market.

Although the category of students has already been discussed in the previous chapter under general free movement rights of EU citizens who are not economically active, this category needs separate attention here as part of the economic citizens' rights because of the close connection between free movement of students and free movement of workers in practice. The ECJ took several of the most important decisions on the concept of 'worker' in cases in which in fact students were involved.

In the *Lawrie-Blum* case, it was shown that the financing of an internship period could fall under the free movement of workers because of the German choices for financing. Other ways of setting up a system for such internships would not lead to the free movement of workers. However, the options under European law in 1986 were different than the options at present; EU citizenship was not yet created, although the ECJ refers to the notion of 'favoured EEC citizen' under Dutch law in the *Levin* case.[159] National legislation had apparently referred to a similar notion which was an implementation of Directive 64/221/EEC, in which 'citizenship' as such was not necessary. Under the present Treaty and consequent case-law of the Court of Justice, the *Lawrie-Blum* case could perhaps be brought under EU citizenship, like it was done for Mr Bidar,[160] in which a student grant was given to the student not on the basis of his relatives being workers under the EC Treaty, but on the basis of his own 'genuine link' with the UK as a 'settled person'. Yet, the *Kranemann* case discussed above shows that the line of reasoning in *Lawrie-Blum* would probably have been maintained.

This means that the category of students is important for establishing the scope of the group of persons who possess economic free movement rights under European law. It is very well possible that, in time, one person changes category. In the *Payir* case,[161] for instance, it was established that Turkish nationals entering the UK as students or au-pairs under the Association Agreement with Turkey, became workers with independent rights once they became employed even for a limited number of hours per week. Because the Association Agreement allows students and au-pairs to work, these persons became workers under European law. In a much earlier case,[162] the ECJ had

---

[159] ECJ, Case 53/81 *Levin* [1982] *ECR* 01035 under 4.
[160] ECJ, Case C-209/03 *Bidar* [2005] *ECR* I-02119.
[161] ECJ, Case C-294/06 *Payir et al.* [2008] *ECR* I-00203.
[162] ECJ, Case C-357/89 *Raulin* [1992] *ECR* I-01027.

decided on how many hours of work would constitute the status of 'worker' in a case in which Ms Raulin was a worker first and then became a student:

'The conditions of employment of a person employed under a contract which provides no guarantee as to the number of hours to be worked, with the result that the person concerned works only a very limited number of days per week or hours per day, obliges the employer to pay the employed person and to grant that person social advantages only in so far as he has actually worked, and does not oblige the employed person to heed the employer's call for him to work.'

The Persons Directive does not contain a definition of a student but gives free movement rights to those who are enrolled in an educational institution and are not a burden on the social assistance system of the host Member State.[163] The problem of Ms Raulin is now covered by the same directive, stating that

'For the purposes of paragraph 1(a), a Union citizen who is no longer a worker or self-employed person shall retain the status of worker or self-employed person in the following circumstances: (d) he/she embarks on vocational training. Unless he/she is involuntarily unemployed, the retention of the status of worker shall require the training to be related to the previous employment.'[164]

In this way, students in the strict sense of the word may also be workers or become workers. The status of 'worker' is thus relatively easily obtained for students. Only those students who are not or have not been employed fall outside the scope of the economic rights and can therefore claim the non-economic citizenship right to move and reside freely within the territory of the Member States.

The above can be summarized in terms of citizenship rights: the Persons Directive gives students who are also EU nationals citizenship rights, but limited to the conditions set in this directive itself. These citizenship rights are based on the very general provisions of Article 12 TEC (Art. 18 TFEU-L) and Article 18 TEC (Art. 21 TFEU-L); they do not follow from economic free movement rights as such. This means that only by means of secondary

---

[163] Art. 7 Para. 1(c) of Directive 2004/38/EC, *OJ* L 158 of 30 April 2004, pp. 77-123.
[164] Art. 7 Para. 3 of Directive 2004/38/EC.

legislation can students obtain citizenship rights, rights which they would not have been able to obtain directly under the Treaties.

A second category of not yet economically active persons consists of job-seekers. The underlying rule is that persons falling in this category cannot be an unreasonable burden on the social assistance system of the host Member State[165] unless they built up social welfare under the system of the host Member State. This is especially true for those going to another Member State seeking a job. For them, the general rules of the Persons Directive apply, which give them the right to stay in the host Member State for up to three months without any formalities, as Article 6 of the Persons Directive states. The citizenship rights end with this and are therefore limited. If the job-seeker has become involuntarily unemployed after at least one year of work, this limitation ceases to exist. Yet, basically, such a job-seeker has similar citizenship rights as a worker for those three months:

> 'Nationals of a Member State seeking employment in another Member State thus fall within the scope of Article 48 of the Treaty and, therefore, enjoy the right laid down in Article 48(2) to equal treatment.'[166]

An exception to this system may exist at the moment someone moves to another Member State after finishing studies. In such a situation, depending on the national legislation of the host Member State, the right to social assistance may exist as well. In the *D'Hoop* case,[167] in which it concerned a refusal to grant a tide-over allowances for young people seeking first employment to a national of the host Member State simply because the applicant completed her secondary education in another Member State. Ms D'Hoop, a Belgian national, had returned to Belgium after having finished her secondary education in France. The ECJ decided that:

> 'However, a single condition concerning the place where the diploma of completion of secondary education was obtained is too general and exclusive in nature. It unduly favours an element which is not necessarily representative of the real and effective degree of connection between the applicant for the tideover allowance and the geographic employment market, to the exclusion of all other repre-

---

[165] Recital 10 to Directive 2004/38/EC.
[166] ECJ, Case C-138/02 *Collins* [2004] *ECR* I-02703. Art. 48 EC (old) is now Art. 39 EC.
[167] ECJ, Case C-224/98 *D'Hoop* [2002] *ECR* I-06191.

sentative elements. It therefore goes beyond what is necessary to attain the objective pursued.

Such inequality of treatment is contrary to the principles which underpin the status of citizen of the Union, that is, the guarantee of the same treatment in law in the exercise of the citizen's freedom to move.'

On the basis of this reason only, the Belgian government was not allowed to refuse this grant to Ms D'Hoop. Under such circumstances, the citizenship rights of Ms D'Hoop are larger than those described above for job-seekers. In other situations, however, this is not so. Mr Collins, for instance,[168] could not show such a 'real and effective degree of connection' with the allowance requested, and therefore fell outside this category. Mr Grzelczyk[169] claimed more rights than the nationals of the host Member State had, and this right to social benefits was limited by the ECJ:

'That interpretation does not, however, prevent a Member State from taking the view that a student who has recourse to social assistance no longer fulfils the conditions of his right of residence or from taking measures, within the limits imposed by Community law, either to withdraw his residence permit or not to renew it.

Nevertheless, in no case may such measures become the automatic consequence of a student who is a national of another Member State having recourse to the host Member State's social assistance system.'

Thus, the category of not yet economically active persons is limited by the ECJ. Only place of residence as a decisive factor is not allowed in this way.[170]

4.   *Citizens of new Member States*

The descriptions above are not all immediately applicable to citizens of new Member States: to the respective Accession Treaties, Annexes have been added which give options for the old Member States to temporarily withhold free movement rights to the citizens of the new Member States. Annexes VI

---

[168] ECJ, Case C-138/02 *Collins* [2004] *ECR* I-02703.

[169] ECJ, Case C-184/99 *Rudy Grzelczyk* [2001] *ECR* I-06193.

[170] P. van Nuffelen and N. Cambien, 'De vrijheid of economisch niet-actieve EU-burgers om binnen de EU te reizen, te verblijven en te studeren', *SEW* (April 2009) p. 149.

and VII to the Accession Treaty of Bulgaria and Romania, for instance,[171] give the individual Member States such options for a maximum period of five years.[172] The transitional arrangements thus concluded in the form of bilateral agreements between the individual old Member States and a new Member State. Several old Member States decided not to introduce such restrictions. It needs to be noted that these transitional arrangements concern mostly work permits and therefore the free movement of workers; the free movement of services and the freedom of establishment usually fall outside their scope. The restrictions to be taken can take different forms, ranging from limiting the number of working permits per year like Spain has done, limiting the number of work permits for certain professions like Luxembourg has done for agriculture, hotel and catering and certain areas of finance, or only issuing work permits when no suitable workers are available in the old Member States like the Netherlands has done for Bulgarian and Romanian workers.[173] The United Kingdom, Ireland and Sweden did not

---

[171] Treaty between the Kingdom of Belgium, the Czech Republic, the Kingdom of Denmark, the Federal Republic of Germany, the Republic of Estonia, the Hellenic Republic, the Kingdom of Spain, the French Republic, Ireland, the Italian Republic, the Republic of Cyprus, the Republic of Latvia, the Republic of Lithuania, the Grand Duchy of Luxembourg, the Republic of Hungary, the Republic of Malta, the Kingdom of the Netherlands, the Republic of Austria, the Republic of Poland, the Portuguese Republic, the Republic of Slovenia, the Slovak Republic, the Republic of Finland, the Kingdom of Sweden, the United Kingdom of Great Britain and Northern Ireland (Member States of the European Union) and the Republic of Bulgaria and Romania, concerning the accession of the Republic of Bulgaria and Romania to the European Union, Annex VI: List referred to in Art. 20 of the Protocol: transitional measures, Bulgaria, and Annex VII: List referred to in Art. 20 of the Protocol: transitional measures, Romania, 25 April 2005. Similar Annexes were added to the Treaty between the Kingdom of Belgium, the Kingdom of Denmark, the Federal Republic of Germany, the Hellenic Republic, the Kingdom of Spain, the French Republic, Ireland, the Italian Republic, the Grand Duchy of Luxembourg, the Kingdom of the Netherlands, the Republic of Austria, the Portuguese Republic, the Republic of Finland, the Kingdom of Sweden, the United Kingdom of Great Britain and Northern Ireland (Member States of the European Union) and the Czech Republic, the Republic of Estonia, the Republic of Cyprus, the Republic of Latvia, the Republic of Lithuania, the Republic of Hungary, the Republic of Malta, the Republic of Poland, the Republic of Slovenia, the Slovak Republic, concerning the accession of the Czech Republic, the Republic of Estonia, the Republic of Cyprus, the Republic of Latvia, the Republic of Lithuania, the Republic of Hungary, the Republic of Malta, the Republic of Poland, the Republic of Slovenia and the Slovak Republic to the European Union of 23 September 2003.

[172] Art. 2 of both annexes for Bulgaria and Romania.

[173] Information taken from the BBC website 'EU free movement of labour map', <http://news.bbc.co.uk/2/hi/europe/3513889.stm> (last visited on 2 July 2009).

place any restrictions at all at the free movement of workers while countries like the Netherlands have removed the restrictions for the Member States which acceded in 2004 after several years.

This means that, on top of falling in the categories of workers as discussed above, the economic rights of workers from the new Member States may vary depending on both the old Member State they want to move to and the type of work they want to do. Even this may change in time because of the time limits on the transitional measures.

3.3   THE ECONOMIC RIGHTS INVOLVED

Why is it then important for an EU citizen to possess the economic free movement right? The rights following from this status are broader than those following from the right to move and reside freely within the territory of the Member States. Whether it concerns workers or those providing the service or receiving it, the citizenship rights involved remain the same: the economic right of entry and access to services, and the right to equal treatment.

Primary and secondary rights can be distinguished in the economic rights. Primary rights are the rights which are laid down in the Treaty texts: free movement rights, the rights to non-discrimination, and equal treatment rights. Secondary rights are derived rights like the right to bring your family members when you move to another Member State, whether this family member is an EU citizen or a third-country national. Such rights are not laid down in the Treaty texts but follow from the rights laid down in there.

3.4   INTERMEZZO: THE IMPORTANCE OF THE ECONOMIC FREE
MOVEMENT RIGHTS

Free movement is considered to be a fundamental economic right[174] in the European Union system[175] by the institutions, which means that the relation-

---

[174] Social and political fundamental rights following from European law will be discussed in the following chapters.

[175] Following from both Art. 2 of the EC Treaty, *OJ* C 321E of 29 December 2006 (see also ECJ, Case C-265/95 *Spanish strawberries* [1997] *ECR* I-06959) and the current EU Charter of Fundamental Rights, *OJ* C 303 of 14 December 2007.

ship between free movement of persons and 'other' fundamental rights needs further attention before the contents of this free movement right can be discussed. How is free movement in balance with other fundamental rights in the European Union legal order? And a different question: is it enough to exercise free movement rights to receive a European Union fundamental right protection? The latter may work in two directions. On the one hand, fundamental rights may enhance the free movement possibilities, as in the *Carpenter* case.[176] Economic rights may thus give rights to third-country nationals. On the other hand, fundamental rights could restrict free movement rights, as in the *Viking Line* case.[177]

First, attention needs to be paid to the 'importance' of free movement as a fundamental economic right, balanced against other fundamental rights. The most prominent examples lay not in the free movement of persons but in the free movement of goods. In the so-called *Spanish Strawberries* case,[178] the Court of Justice refers to the free movement of goods as a 'fundamental freedom' and as a 'fundamental principle', which needs to be balanced against the rights of individuals, and needs to be upheld by the (authorities of) the Member States. In a later case, the *Schmidberger* case,[179] the Court of Justice came to a different conclusion because of differences in the facts: prior permission was asked and given of the national authorities and

> 'the obstacle to the free movement of goods resulting from that demonstration was limited by comparison with both the geographic scale and the intrinsic seriousness of the disruption caused in the case giving rise to the judgment in *Commission* v *France*, cited above.'

The ECJ therefore decided that the outcome of a clash of a fundamental right with a free movement right depends on the seriousness of the breach and the role of the national authorities.

For free movement of persons, on the contrary, the ECJ can be said to either consider the free movement right as a fundamental right, or to consider fundamental rights as a strengthening of the free movement right. The

---

[176] ECJ, Case C-60/00 *Carpenter* [2002] *ECR* I-06279.
[177] ECJ, Case C-438/05 *Viking Line* [2007] *ECR* I-10779.
[178] ECJ, Case C-265/95 *Spanish strawberries* [1997] *ECR* I-06959.
[179] ECJ, Case C-112/00 *Schmidberger* [2003] *ECR* I-05659.

prime example is the right to family life, as laid down in Article 8 ECHR. In the *Carpenter* case,[180] the ECJ found that

'It is clear that the separation of Mr and Mrs Carpenter would be detrimental to their family life and, therefore, to the conditions under which Mr Carpenter exercises a fundamental freedom. That freedom could not be fully effective if Mr Carpenter were to be deterred from exercising it by obstacles raised in his country of origin to the entry and residence of his spouse (see, to that effect, Singh, cited above, paragraph 23).

40. A Member State may invoke reasons of public interest to justify a national measure which is likely to obstruct the exercise of the freedom to provide services only if that measure is compatible with the fundamental rights whose observance the Court ensures (see, to that effect, Case C-260/89 ERT [1991] ECR I-2925, paragraph 43, and Case C-368/95 Familiapress [1997] ECR I-3689, paragraph 24).

41. The decision to deport Mrs Carpenter constitutes an interference with the exercise by Mr Carpenter of his right to respect for his family life within the meaning of Article 8 of the Convention for the Protection of Human Rights and Fundamental Freedoms, signed at Rome on 4 November 1950 (hereinafter the Convention), which is among the fundamental rights which, according to the Court's settled case-law, restated by the Preamble to the Single European Act and by Article 6(2) EU, are protected in Community law.'

In this way, the free movement of persons can be considered to be a fundamental economic right, containing the elements laid down in the EC Treaty.

3.5 WHICH ECONOMIC RIGHTS?

3.5.1 Free movement rights

The free movement rights lie therefore at the heart of the economic rights to be exercised by the persons listed above. As an economic right, the free movement right is more specific than 'only' the rights of entry, residence, and exit, as they exist for EU citizens in general. The economic right focuses on the right to work, the right of access to work, and the right of equal treat-

---

[180] ECJ, Case C-60/00 *Carpenter* [2002] *ECR* I-06279.

ment concerning work compared to the workers of the host Member State, i.e. on the contents of the work relation.

These economic rights are primary rights and follow directly from the text of Article 39 of the EC Treaty (Art. 45 TFEU-L), as well as of Article 43 TEC (Art.49 TFEU-L) for the self-employed and Articles 49 and 50 TEC (Arts. 56 and 57 TFEU-L) for service providers. They can be divided into non-discrimination rights, which includes both direct and indirect discrimination on the basis of nationality, equal treatment rights, the right to equal social advantages, and derived rights, which focus on the right to bring family members along because the exercise of free movement rights would otherwise be very difficult.

3.5.2   Non-discrimination rights

The non-discrimination rights follow from the second and third paragraph of Article 39 TEC (Art. 45 TFEU-L):

'2. Such freedom of movement shall entail the abolition of any discrimination based on nationality between workers of the Member States as regards employment, remuneration and other conditions of work and employment.
3. It shall entail the right, subject to limitations justified on grounds of public policy, public security or public health:
(a) to accept offers of employment actually made;
(b) to move freely within the territory of Member States for this purpose;
(c) to stay in a Member State for the purpose of employment in accordance with the provisions governing the employment of nationals of that State laid down by law, regulation or administrative action;
(d) to remain in the territory of a Member State after having been employed in that State, subject to conditions which shall be embodied in implementing regulations to be drawn up by the Commission.'

A similar system is set up for the self-employed in Article 43 TEC (Art. 49 TFEU-L). The ECJ has defined what is meant by the principle of non-discrimination in this regard, and it is similar to what is a regular interpretation at the national level:

'It is in this regard settled case-law that the principle of non-discrimination requires that comparable situations must not be treated differently and that different situations must not be treated in the same way (see, inter alia, Case C-354/95

National Farmers' Union and Others [1997] *ECR* I-4559, paragraph 61). Such treatment may be justified only if it is based on objective considerations independent of the nationality of the persons concerned and is proportionate to the objective being legitimately pursued (see, inter alia, D'Hoop, paragraph 36).'[181]

From the case-law of the ECJ also follows that the provisions mentioned above not only mean that Member States are prohibited from making it impossible or more difficult for a worker or self-employed from another Member State to work in the host Member State, but also from making it less attractive to do so:

'Article 43 EC requires the elimination of restrictions on freedom of establishment. All measures which prohibit, impede or render less attractive the exercise of this freedom must be regarded as constituting such restrictions.'[182]

Or:

'According to settled case-law, any national measure which, although applicable without discrimination on grounds of nationality, is liable to hamper or to render less attractive the exercise by a national of a Member State of the freedom of movement of workers, is an obstacle to that fundamental freedom guaranteed by the Treaty.'[183]

The limitations for actions by the Member States are therefore rather large. Following from this, the basis of these rights has already been laid down in Regulation 1612/68,[184] which, however only concerns free movement of workers. The preamble to Regulation 1612/68 states:

'Whereas freedom of movement constitutes a fundamental right of workers and their families; whereas mobility of labour within the Community must be one of the means by which the worker is guaranteed the possibility of improving his living and working conditions and promoting his social advancement, while helping to satisfy the requirements of the economies of the Member States; whereas

---

[181] ECJ, Case C-148/02 *Garcia Avello* [2003] *ECR* I-11613.
[182] ECJ, Case C-153/02 *Neri* [2003] *ECR* I-13555.
[183] ECJ, Case C-285/01 *Burbaud* [2003] *ECR* I-08219.
[184] Council Regulation (EEC) No. 1612/68 of 15 October 1968 *OJ* L 257, 19 October 1968, pp. 2-12 on the free movement of workers within the Community, lastly partially amended by the Persons Directive.

the right of all workers in the Member States to pursue the activity of their choice within the Community should be affirmed;
(…)
Whereas the right of freedom of movement, in order that it may be exercised, by objective standards, in freedom and dignity, requires that equality of treatment shall be ensured in fact and in law in respect of all matters relating to the actual pursuit of activities as employed persons and to eligibility for housing, and also that obstacles to the mobility of workers shall be eliminated, in particular as regards the worker's right to be joined by his family and the conditions for the integration of that family into the host country;'

The economic free movement right thus emphasizes mobility of labour, living and working conditions, and the right to bring family members along. For access to work, this means both the right to apply for the vacancy and the right to accept the position. National legislation which prescribes that the highest position on Belgian sea ships can only be occupied by Belgian nationals, for instance, is therefore precluded.[185] Where this concerns direct discrimination, indirectly discriminatory national legislation is also precluded, especially when it is based on the place of residence.[186] The prime example can be found in the *Angonese* case,[187] in which Mr Angonese was denied access to a position at a bank in Bolzano for which he had to be bilingual. In order to show that he was in fact bilingual, he needed a certificate which could only be obtained by Bolzano residents:

'Article 48 of the EC Treaty (now, after amendment, Article 39 EC) precludes an employer from requiring persons applying to take part in a recruitment competition to provide evidence of their linguistic knowledge exclusively by means of one particular diploma issued only in one particular province of a Member State.
That requirement puts nationals of the other Member States at a disadvantage, since persons not resident in that province have little chance of acquiring the diploma, a certificate of bilingualism, and it will be difficult, or even impossible, for them to gain access to the employment in question. The requirement is not justified by any objective factors unrelated to the nationality of the persons concerned and in proportion to the aim legitimately pursued. In that regard, even

---

[185] ECJ, Case C-37/93 *Commission* v. *Belgium* [1993] *ECR* I-06295.
[186] K.J.M. Mortelmans and R.H. van Ooik, *Europees recht en Nederlandse studiefinanciering* (Deventer 2003) pp. 100-105.
[187] ECJ, Case C-281/98 *Angones* [2000] *ECR* I-04139.

though requiring an applicant for a post to have a certain level of linguistic knowledge may be legitimate and possession of a diploma such as the certificate may constitute a criterion for assessing that knowledge, the fact that it is impossible to submit proof of the required linguistic knowledge by any other means, in particular by equivalent qualifications obtained in other Member States, must be considered disproportionate in relation to the aim in view.

It follows that, where an employer makes a person's admission to a recruitment competition subject to a requirement to provide evidence of his linguistic knowledge exclusively by means of one particular diploma, such as the Certificate, issued only in one particular province of a Member State, that requirement constitutes discrimination on grounds of nationality contrary to Article 48 of the EC Treaty.'

This line of reasoning shows that this form of indirect discrimination for access to work cannot be applied without a proportionality test. A comparable yet different line of reasoning is followed by the ECJ in the *Groener* case,[188] which does not primarily concern the place of residence but the language as the centre of discussion. In the *Groener* case, Ms Groener was refused the position of art teacher at a school in Ireland at which Gaelic is the first language because she did not pass the Gaelic language test:

'20. The importance of education for the implementation of such a policy must be recognized. Teachers have an essential role to play, not only through the teaching which they provide but also by their participation in the daily life of the school and the privileged relationship which they have with their pupils. In those circumstances, it is not unreasonable to require them to have some knowledge of the first national language.

21. It follows that the requirement imposed on teachers to have an adequate knowledge of such a language must, provided that the level of knowledge required is not disproportionate in relation to the objective pursued, be regarded as a condition corresponding to the knowledge required by reason of the nature of the post to be filled within the meaning of the last subparagraph of Article 3(1) of Regulation No 1612/68.

22. It must also be pointed out that where the national provisions provide for the possibility of exemption from that linguistic requirement where no other fully qualified candidate has applied for the post to be filled, Community law requires that power to grant exemptions to be exercised by the Minister in a non-discriminatory manner.

---

[188] ECJ, Case C-379/87 *Groener* [1989] *ECR* 03967.

23. Moreover, the principle of non-discrimination precludes the imposition of any requirement that the linguistic knowledge in question must have been acquired within the national territory. It also implies that the nationals of other Member States should have an opportunity to retake the oral examination, in the event of their having previously failed it, when they again apply for a post of assistant lecturer or lecturer.'

In this situation, the ECJ applied to different tests: aside from the proportionality test, the role and function of the profession is taken into consideration. This means that, for instance, a Dutch law school can require command of the Dutch language for a lecturer in Dutch private law because that is necessary to understand and work with the topic, but can be more flexible for a lecturer in European Union law, for which the command of a language like English can also be sufficient. The language requirement is therefore not precluded as such but depends on the situation, contrary to the place of residence requirement as described above, which is always precluded.[189]

Indirect discrimination can take place through secondary conditions of employment as well, as the *Van Lent* case shows.[190] In this case, the ECJ explained that the Belgian national requirement that the car of a Belgian national residing in Belgium has to be registered in Belgium can, under specific circumstances be discriminatory. In this particular case, Mr Van Lent worked for a Luxembourg company in Luxembourg and drove a Luxembourg lease car as part of his secondary conditions of employment:

> 'Such a measure, which has the effect of preventing a worker from benefiting from certain advantages, in particular, the provision of a vehicle, may deter him from leaving his country of origin in order to exercise his right to free movement.
> (…)
> In that regard, it is sufficient to observe that, since the vehicle cannot be registered in Belgium, the objectives of the obligation to register cannot be achieved. It follows that the restriction on freedom of movement for workers cannot be justified.'

While this particular condition of employment was given by the employer but precluded by the national legislation of a Member State, there are more ways in which Member States breach the obligation to equal treatment for

---

[189] Mortelmans and Van Ooik, op. cit., note 186, p. 101.
[190] ECJ, Case C-232/01 *Van Lent* [2003] *ECR* I-11525.

social advantages and benefits in employment, which can mean many elements of the employment relationship:

> 'Accordingly the answer to the question should be that Article 7(2) of regulation (EEC) no 1612/68 of the Council must be interpreted as meaning that the social advantages referred to by that provision include fares reduction cards issued by a national railway authority to large families and that this applies, even if the said advantage is only sought after the worker's death, to the benefit of his family remaining in the same Member State.'[191]

In the famous *Even* case, the ECJ gave a definition of what is meant by 'social advantages' as laid down in Regulation 1612/68:

> 'It follows from all its provisions and from the objective pursued that the advantages which this regulation extends to workers who are nationals of other member states are all those which, whether or not linked to a contract of employment, are generally granted to national workers primarily because of their objective status as workers or by virtue of the mere fact of their residence on the national territory and the extension of which to workers who are nationals of other Member States therefore seems suitable to facilitate their mobility within the Community.'

The ECJ differentiates in this case between social security benefits which are specifically mentioned in the Regulation and social grants. As a result, all differences in 'social and tax advantages' as laid down in Article 7 of Regulation 1612/68 between workers of the host Member State and migrating workers are forbidden. This is of course only valid for cross-border situations; if it is a purely national problem, it concerns social rights rather than economic rights.

3.5.3 Derived rights

Derived from the free movement of workers, the self-employed and the service providers, it has been possible for a third-country national to obtain citizenship rights through 'parasitic' rights of EU nationals who have used their free movement rights. These rights are derived rights because they are

---

[191] ECJ, Case 32/75 *Fiorinin* [1975] *ECR* 01085.

not directly given to the family members of EU workers but are considered to be part of the free movement right of the worker. It is therefore a right which is not given to those EU citizens who do not use their free movement rights. The family members can be either EU citizens or third-country nationals, as is clear from Article 2 Paragraph 2 of the Persons Directive, which does not distinguish between the two categories:

> '2. "family member" means:
> (a) the spouse;
> (b) the partner with whom the Union citizen has contracted a registered partnership, on the basis of the legislation of a Member State, if the legislation of the host Member State treats registered partnerships as equivalent to marriage and in accordance with the conditions laid down in the relevant legislation of the host Member State;
> (c) the direct descendants who are under the age of 21 or are dependants and those of the spouse or partner as defined in point (b);
> (d) the dependent direct relatives in the ascending line and those of the spouse or partner as defined in point (b);'

Only after a certain period of time does the right of the family member become an independent right. Yet, exceptions have been made to this part of the system of free movement rights. This derived right for third-country nationals, linked to free movement of workers, cannot override other binding situations, as the ECJ ruled in the *Akrich* case,[192] in which a UK national who had worked in the Republic of Ireland, wanted to have her Moroccan husband join her in the UK. He had previously been extradited. The ECJ ruled that this should not be denied, however:

> 'Conversely, where a citizen of the Union, established in a Member State and married to a national of a non-Member State without the right to remain in that Member State, moves to another Member State in order to work there as an employed person, the fact that that person's spouse has no right under Article 10 of Regulation No 1612/68 to install himself with that person in the other Member State cannot constitute less favourable treatment than that which they enjoyed before the citizen made use of the opportunities afforded by the Treaty as regards movement of persons. Accordingly, the absence of such a right is not such as to

---

[192] ECJ, Case C-109/01 *Akrich* [2003] *ECR* I-09607.

deter the citizen of the Union from exercising the rights in regard to freedom of movement conferred by Article 39 EC.

The same applies where a citizen of the Union married to a national of a non-Member State returns to the Member State of which he or she is a national in order to work there as an employed person. If the citizen's spouse has a valid right to remain in another Member State, Article 10 of Regulation No 1612/68 applies so that the citizen of the Union is not deterred from exercising his or her right to freedom of movement on returning to the Member State of which he or she is a national. If, conversely, that citizen's spouse does not already have a valid right to remain in another Member State, the absence of any right of the spouse under Article 10 aforesaid to install himself or herself with the citizen of the Union does not have a dissuasive effect in that regard.'

However, this argument has been amended by the ECJ in the *Metock* case: 'However, that conclusion must be reconsidered. The benefit of such rights cannot depend on the prior lawful residence of such a spouse in another Member State.'[193] The reasoning behind this strictly depends on the right to family life of the migrating EU citizen involved. That this is the new standpoint of the ECJ has been confirmed since in the order of the ECJ in the *Sahin* case,[194] in which the ECJ has declared a similar question an *acte éclairé*. The combination of the cases discussed above leads to the conclusion that this results in 'doctrinal uncertainty and incoherence'.[195]

It is therefore important to view the development of the position of the third-country national family member as part of the economic rights of an EU citizen. Already before the *Metock* case, the ECJ had begun to develop the line of reasoning which has led to its Metock decision. In the case of the Commission against Spain,[196] third-country spouses were refused entry to a Member State although they were married to the nationals of another Member State. The Court of Justice described the possibility of limitations to bringing spouses along:

'The right of Member State nationals and their spouses to enter and remain on the territory of another Member State is not, however, unconditional. Among the limits laid down or authorised by Community law, Article 2 of Directive 64/221

---

[193] ECJ, Case C-127/08 *Metock a.o.* [2008] *ECR* I-06241.
[194] ECJ, Case C-155/07 *Sahin* [2008] *ECR* 00000.
[195] C. Costello, 'Metock: Free Movement and "Normal Family Life" in the Union', 46 *Common Market Law Review* (2009) p. 587.

enables Member States to prohibit nationals of other Member States or their spouses who are nationals of third countries from entering their territory on grounds of public policy or public security (see, with respect to spouses, MRAX, paragraphs 61 and 62).'

In this case, the ECJ held that the only reason for refusing entry could have been that they constituted 'a genuine, present and sufficiently serious threat affecting one of the fundamental interests of society'[197] since the third-country nationals in question 'derived from their status as spouses of Member State nationals the right to enter the territory of the Member States or to obtain a visa for that purpose.'[198]

In the earlier *Carpenter* case,[199] an illegal third-country national was awarded the right of residence because her husband is an EU national who has made use of the possibilities the free movement of services had offered him:

> 'Although, in the main proceedings, Mr Carpenter's spouse has infringed the immigration laws of the United Kingdom by not leaving the country prior to the expiry of her leave to remain as a visitor, her conduct, since her arrival in the United Kingdom in September 1994, has not been the subject of any other complaint that could give cause to fear that she might in the future constitute a danger to public order or public safety. Moreover, it is clear that Mr and Mrs Carpenter's marriage, which was celebrated in the United Kingdom in 1996, is genuine and that Mrs Carpenter continues to lead a true family life there, in particular by looking after her husband's children from a previous marriage.
>
> In view of all the foregoing, the answer to the question referred to the Court is that Article 49 EC, read in the light of the fundamental right to respect for family life, is to be interpreted as precluding, in circumstances such as those in the main proceedings, a refusal, by the Member State of origin of a provider of services established in that Member State who provides services to recipients established in other Member States, of the right to reside in its territory to that provider's spouse, who is a national of a third country.'

---

[196] ECJ, Case C-503/03 *Commission* v. *Spain* [2006] *ECR* I-01097.
[197] Nos. 52 and 53 of ECJ, Case C-503/03 *Commission* v. *Spain* [2006] *ECR* I-01097.
[198] No. 42 of ECJ, Case C-503/03 *Commission* v. *Spain* [2006] *ECR* I-01097.
[199] ECJ, Case C-60/00 *Carpenter* [2002] *ECR* I-0627.

The recent cases of *Jia*[200] and *Eind*[201] added to this development to give residence to third-country national family members although these did not have prior legal residence in another Member State. In the case of Ms Jia did it concern the Chinese father of a spouse of an EU migrant self-employed citizen. The ECJ decided in this case that the *Akrich* rule that prior lawful residence in a Member State for the third-country family member is necessary cannot be interpreted strictly, or cannot even be seen as a requirement:[202]

> 'The answer to Question 1(a) to (d) must therefore be that, having regard to the judgment in Akrich, Community law does not require Member States to make the grant of a residence permit to nationals of a non-Member State, who are members of the family of a Community national who has exercised his or her right of free movement, subject to the condition that those family members have previously been residing lawfully in another Member State.'

A similar line of reasoning was followed in the *Eind* case, in which it did not concern an EU citizen who is still economically active. It is important to note that this series of ECJ decisions concerns a citizens' right which would otherwise not have been given to these citizens: the right to bring along a family member is clearly not a regular economic right of a citizen, as is shown by the protests by Member States on the implications of especially the *Metock* decision of the ECJ.[203] Due to the emphasis on the fundamental right to family life, the ECJ has shifted the decision for the right of entry of third-country nationals from the Member States as such to the Member States as part of the European system, when the third-country national is a family member of a migrating EU citizen. From this can be concluded that a new typically European Union citizenship right has thus been created: the economic right to free movement which includes the derived right to bring a family member along.

---

[200] ECJ, Case C-1/05 *Jia* [2007] *ECR* I-00001.

[201] ECJ, Case C-1/05 *Jia* [2007] *ECR* I-00001.

[202] See for this interpretation of the *Jia* case also: S. Currie, 'Accelerated Justice or a Step Too Far? Residence Rights of Non-EU family Members and the Court's Ruling in Metock', 34 *E.L. Rev.* (April 2009) p. 311.

[203] Currie, op. cit., note 202, pp. 323-326; Costello, op. cit., note 195, p. 622.

3.5.4   Student rights

A separate category of economic rights is formed by student rights. Several elements of the position of students have already been discussed above in this chapter as part of other economic rights, like the forming of the definition of 'worker' in Article 39 TEC (Art. 45 TFEU-L) and the options for students to fall under the legislation for workers when working part-time. Yet, there are also economic rights attached to the possibilities for students to study in another Member State. Part of these economic rights are linked to the right of the child of a worker or self-employed person to come with the parent to the host Member State and follow and education there without being discriminated, thus the right to education. Another part consists of independent free movement rights, mostly the right of access to student grants and the right of entry into an establishment for education. In general, both types of rights are not based on primary rights but on secondary legislation. The EC Treaty only refers to education in the form of a supporting competence in Article 149 TEC (Art. 165 TFEU-L):

> '1. The Community shall contribute to the development of quality education by encouraging cooperation between Member States and, if necessary, by supporting and supplementing their action, while fully respecting the responsibility of the Member States for the content of teaching and the organisation of education systems and their cultural and linguistic diversity.'

This competence can not be considered to be an economic right as such but can only be part of an economic right. While the student has been given free movement rights in the Persons Directive in Article 7 Paragraph 1(c) to enroll in an establishment in another Member State as long as he is not a burden on the social assistance system, the basis for this provision is not Article 149 TEC (Art. 165 TFEU-L) but the free movement rights of EU citizens. On the basis of the Persons Directive, these students are even allowed to bring along family members in the same way as workers and self-employed persons are allowed to do. Yet, Article 149 TEC (Art. 165 TFEU-L) is the basis of other relevant legislation, especially the systems of European grants under the caption of lifelong learning,[204] like the Erasmus, Socrates and Leonardo da Vinci programmes.

---

[204] Decision No. 1720/2006/EC of the European Parliament and of the Council of 15 November 2006 *OJ* L 327, 24 November 2006, pp. 45-68 establishing an action programme in the field of lifelong learning.

In addition to these European grants systems, the system of economic rights also involves the options for access to student grants in the host Member State. In the paragraph on the concept and contents of the notion of EU citizenship above, attention was already indirectly paid to the two main ways in which this can be realized: either via the migrating parent or as an independent right to a student grant or to the system of study finance.

The way via the migrating parent is laid down in the Persons Directive (and previously in Regulation 1612/68) as part of the system of non-discrimination of the migrating parent, as the ECJ decided in an early stage in the *Bernini* case:[205]

> 'The national court next wishes to know whether the child of the worker may, under Article 7(2) of Regulation No 1612/68 claim an independent right to study finance. It should be pointed out in that connection that it follows from the judgment in Lebon, cited above, that the dependent members of the family are the indirect beneficiaries of the equal treatment accorded to the migrant worker. Consequently, where the grant of financing to a child of a migrant worker constitutes a social advantage for the migrant worker, the child may itself rely on Article 7(2) in order to obtain that financing if under national law it is granted directly to the student.'

The case of Ms Meeusen[206] is another prime example of this category. In this case, the right to a Dutch national student grant was made dependent on the position of the parent:

> 'It should also be added that the Court has consistently held that the principle of equal treatment laid down in Article 7 of Regulation No 1612/68 is also intended to prevent discrimination to the detriment of descendants dependent on the worker (see Case 94/84 *ONEM* v *Deak* [1985] ECR 1873, paragraph 22). Those descendants can thus rely on Article 7(2) in order to obtain study finance under the same conditions as are applicable to children of national workers (Bernini, paragraph 28).'

The fact that the Member State is allowed to adopt its own national legislation on who has access to the system of student financing is influenced by the fact that the national legislation cannot be in breach of the principle of

---

[205] ECJ, Case C-3/90 *Bernini* [1992] *ECR* I-01071.

[206] *Meeusen* case, *supra* note 114.

non-discrimination on the basis of nationality. While the Belgian national Meeusen did not have a right to a student grant under Belgian national law, she did possess such a right under Dutch national law. Although she was resident in Belgium, the Belgian system differed from the Dutch system in that it did not have a general right to a basic grant. Thus, through the rights of the migrating parent, Ms Meeusen had a right under the Dutch system. This was also confirmed by the ECJ in the *Baumbast and R* case,[207] in which not so much the right to the grant itself was at stake but rather the right to pursue an education in the host Member State, and consequently also have access to the same options for financing as the nationals of the host Member State.

Another example of the influence of European Union law on the national system of student grants is the case of Ms Gürol,[208] in which Germany had set its limits based on the Association Agreement with Turkey. Under this system, the family members of Turkish migrant workers have only derived rights and can only exercise these when they have their place of residence with the parents. However, Ms Gürol wanted to study and live in another city than the one her parents lived in and thus use the German option for a secondary residence:

'The condition of residing with parents in accordance with the first sentence of Article 9 is met in the case of a Turkish child who, after residing legally with his parents in the host Member State, establishes his main residence in the place in the same Member State in which he follows his university studies, while declaring his parents' home to be his secondary residence only.'

Moreover, the right to financing for an exchange programme should be given in a similar manner:

'The second sentence of Article 9 of Decision No 1/80 has direct effect in the Member States. That provision guarantees Turkish children a non-discriminatory right of access to education grants, such as that provided for under the legislation at issue in the main proceedings, that right being theirs even when they pursue higher education studies in Turkey.'

While this derived economic right to a student grant is in fact the right of the migrating EU national like the right to bring your family member along when

---

[207] ECJ, Case C-413/99 *Baumbast and R* [2002] *ECR* I-07091.
[208] ECJ, Case C-374/03 *Gürol* [2005] *ECR* I-06199.

you migrate, this economic right has also developed as an independent right of an EU national. Originally, this right was only available to EU nationals who used the right to free movement of workers in the past. Since the introduction of the notion of EU citizenship in the EU system, this became an independent economic right, formalized in the Persons Directive. The first instance in which this was established by the ECJ was the *Grzelczyk* case,[209] which was already discussed above because the status of the notion of EU citizenship was confirmed by the ECJ in this case at a very early stage. Yet, the facts concerned the right to study financing after having been a worker in the host Member State:

'The fact that a Union citizen pursues university studies in a Member State other than the State of which he is a national cannot, of itself, deprive him of the possibility of relying on the prohibition of all discrimination on grounds of nationality laid down in Article 6 of the Treaty.

(…)

It follows from the foregoing that Articles 6 and 8 of the Treaty preclude entitlement to a non-contributory social benefit, such as the minimex, from being made conditional, in the case of nationals of Member States other than the host State where they are legally resident, on their falling within the scope of Regulation No 1612/68 when no such condition applies to nationals of the host Member State.'

Whereas in the *Morgan* case,[210] the application of the EU citizenship rights made the ECJ be even clearer in its conclusion:

'Articles 17 EC and 18 EC preclude, in circumstances such as those in the cases before the referring court, a condition in accordance with which, in order to obtain an education or training grant for studies in a Member State other than that of which the students applying for such assistance are nationals, those studies must be a continuation of education or training pursued for at least one year in the Member State of origin of those students.'

Before this case, the ECJ had already established a direct link between EU citizenship and the independent right of the child of a migrant worker to a student grant in the *Bidar* case,[211] although the conditions under which this

---

[209] *Grzelczyk* case, *supra* note 19.
[210] ECJ, Joined Cases C-11/06 and C-12/06 *Morgan* [2007] *ECR* I-00000.
[211] *Bidar* case, *supra* note 113.

right is established have been amended by the ECJ in the *Förster* case. Where the ECJ made the decision of the necessary degree of integration dependent upon an individual assessment in the *Bidar* case, it decided in the *Förster* case that:

> 'In the light of the foregoing, the response to the second to fourth questions must be that a student who is a national of a Member State and travels to another Member State to study there can rely on the first paragraph of Article 12 EC in order to obtain a maintenance grant where he or she has resided for a certain duration in the host Member State. The first paragraph of Article 12 EC does not preclude the application to nationals of other Member States of a requirement of five years' prior residence.'

This shows that the Member States can still lay conditions on the application of this independent economic right of EU citizens.

3.6   CONCLUSIONS

The economic rights of citizens in the EU, and therefore the free movement rights, show that the European Union has gone very far in applying rights. The basis of the right of free movement is equal treatment, as Article 39 TEC (Art. 45 TFEU-L) shows. Equal treatment between migrating workers and the workers from the host Member State means that there cannot be any form of discrimination. The definitions applied to workers, establishment and services show that it is relatively easy to fall in one of these categories, even if there is no full time economic activity involved. If a citizen falls in any of these categories, the consequences go beyond equal treatment and non-discrimination. European law does more than prohibit discrimination on the basis of nationality, it promotes the exercise of the right of free movement. To bring it to the extreme: the ideal could be that every EU citizen would use the free movement rights. Member States should not make it less attractive for someone to work in another Member State. Moreover, a citizen must be treated equally and have the same rights as a worker (for instance) of the host Member State and at the same time retain rights which he had at home which workers from the host Member State cannot exercise. Examples of this are the rights to the surname system as has been discussed in the preceding chapter, and the right to pay specific taxes in another Member State. In addition, the exercise of the right to free movement gives an EU citizen rights which he would not have possessed had he not used the free movement right. The concerns mostly the right to either bring your third-country national family member along or to prevent this spouse from being extradited. Had the EU citizen not used the free movement right, it would have been a matter of national law instead of European law. The case-law of the ECJ shows that, under national law, the similar right for the family member to stay would not have existed.

Thus, the exercise of free movement rights triggers other rights to come into existence. Member States are in principle free to make any decisions about the economic rights but these decisions may have EU consequences.

Chapter 4

SOCIAL RIGHTS FOR EU CITIZENS

Chapter 4

SOCIAL RIGHTS FOR EU CITIZENS

Within the system of European Union law, the concept of social rights in the development of citizenship rights, as set up by Marshall,[212] is spread over different aspects of the legal system:

> 'By the social element I mean the whole range from the right to a modicum of economic welfare and security to the right to share to the full in the social heritage and to live the life of a civilised being according to the standards prevailing in the society. The institutions most closely connected with it are the educational system and the social services.'[213]

The diverse aspects in this definition by Marshall fall in different parts of European Union law. The category of social rights applies to more 'traditional' social rights such as equal treatment, access to social benefits, and access to social security, as well as to the officially non-EU areas like education[214] and the national social security systems.[215] Yet, the case-law of the ECJ shows that this cannot be applied as strict as it seems and that subjects

---

[212] See Chapter 1 of this book.

[213] Marshall, op. cit., note 121, pp. 10-11.

[214] Art. 149 Para. 1 EC: 'The Community shall contribute to the development of quality education by encouraging cooperation between Member States and, if necessary, by supporting and supplementing their action, while fully respecting the responsibility of the Member States for the content of teaching and the organisation of education systems and their cultural and linguistic diversity.'

[215] See for instance: ECJ, Case 11/70, *Internationale Handelsgesellschaft* [1970] *ECR* I-01125: 'First, it should be recalled that it is clear, both from the case-law of the Court and from Art. 152(5) EC, that Community law does not detract from the power of the Member States to organise their social security systems and to adopt, in particular, provisions intended to govern the organisation and delivery of health services and medical care.'

F. Goudappel, The Effects of EU Citizenship
© 2010, T·M·C·ASSER PRESS, *The Hague, The Netherlands and the Author*

like national education and social security systems may have a European Union edge to them:

> 'First, it should be recalled that it is clear, both from the case-law of the Court and from Article 152(5) EC, that Community law does not detract from the power of the Member States to organise their social security systems and to adopt, in particular, provisions intended to govern the organisation and delivery of health services and medical care. In exercising that power, however, the Member States must comply with Community law, in particular the provisions of the Treaty on the freedoms of movement, including freedom of establishment. Those provisions prohibit the Member States from introducing or maintaining unjustified restrictions on the exercise of those freedoms in the healthcare sector.'[216]

Many elements of the citizens' social rights form part of the welfare state system, which is thus traditionally in the hands of the Member States (like social benefits, social security and education). The European Union rights, however, have either influenced the systems at the national level or in some cases even set the standard. These standards have, on the other hand, also been influenced by the European Social Charter, which was closed under the Council of Europe. In general the European Union has its own social policy which includes exportable and non-exportable rights, as well as non-cross-border social rights.

In addition, the Marshall definition comprises elements of fundamental rights. Although the elements of Marshall's definition all form part of European Union law in some form, they have not developed as one coherent policy area but rather one by one at different speeds at different moments. Equal treatment of men and women in the working environment, for instance, was part of the original EEC Treaty in 1957, while the European influence on the national education systems of the Member States developed in case-law over recent years. It is therefore not part of a linear development from economic rights via social rights to political rights. Moreover, some of the rights are only available to EU nationals while others have a more general nature. Some are typical for the European Union system as they are cross-border while others go beyond this and have directly led to obligations in the legal orders of the Member States whether cross-border or not.

Considering all this, the following elements need to be discussed in more detail in order to obtain an overview of the social rights citizens possess

---

[216] ECJ, Case 11/70, *Internationale Handelsgesellschaft* [1970] *ECR* I-01125.

within the European Union system. First, the more traditional European cross-border social rights and the European social policy will be discussed, followed by social rights which do not necessarily have a cross-border element. In addition, attention will be paid to the social fundamental rights applied in European Union law.

4.1   CROSS-BORDER SOCIAL RIGHTS

Cross-border or cross-border social rights in European Union law are a typical element of European law by nature and are in fact an integral part of the economic free movement rights.

Art. 39 Paragraph 2 TEC (Art. 45 TFEU-L) states:

> 'Such freedom of movement shall entail the abolition of any discrimination based on nationality between workers of the Member States as regards employment, remuneration and other conditions of work and employment.'

These rights have not developed at a different speed than the free movement right itself but are an indivisible part of the free movement right. They are only available to EU citizens and only to those who use their free movement rights. The cross-border social rights are mostly defined as 'social advantages' in EU law, in comparison to 'social benefits' which are not exportable.[217] The definition of these stems from the *Even* case:[218]

> 'Which, whether or not linked to a contract of employment, are generally granted to national workers primarily because of their objective status as workers or by virtue of the mere fact of their residence on the national territory and the extension of which to workers who are nationals of the other Member States therefore seems suitable to facilitate their mobility within the Community.'

The underlying rule is that this category of rights falls under European Union law at the moment there is discrimination on the basis of nationality.[219] In all

---

[217] Fairhurst, op. cit., note 146, p. 504.

[218] ECJ, Case 207/78 *Criminal Proceedings against Gilbert Even* [1979] *ECR* 02019.

[219] Art. 7 Para. 2 of Regulation 1612/68 of the Council of 15 October 1968 *OJ* L 257, 19 October 1968, pp. 2-12 on freedom of movement for workers within the Community.

other situations, it concerns a national issue not touched by EU law. However, the social side of European integration is often considered to be an
important element in order for the democratic welfare system:

> 'The exclusion of the social sphere from the integration project provides the recipe
> for potential failure which could be of constitutional significance for those who
> assume that the citizens of constitutional democracies are entitled to vote in favour
> of welfare policies.'[220]

The cases of *Viking* and *Laval* have already been discussed above as part of
the fundamental right protection under the citizens' economic rights. They
are excellent examples of the way in which European law influences both
the economic rights of citizens and the social aspects of these economic rights.
Thus, the social cross-border rights are considered a secondary form of economic rights. This includes the right to bring along pension and other social
security rights across the border.

An example of this is the *Van Lent* case,[221] in which the right to equal pay
in a cross-border situation was considered to be breached by not allowing
him to drive a Luxembourg registered leased car in Belgium: 'Such a measure, which has the effect of preventing a worker from benefiting from certain advantages, in particular, the provision of a vehicle, may deter him from
leaving his country of origin in order to exercise his right to free movement.'

Other elements of the exportability of social rights concern an answer to
the questions which Member States has to pay the old-age pension of a former
migrating worker and how the pension has to be calculated. For this, Regulation 1408/71[222] lays down basic rules:

> 'Provisions concerning reduction, suspension or withdrawal of benefit provided
> for in the legislation of a Member State in the case of overlapping with other
> social security benefits or other income may be invoked, even if the right to such
> benefits was acquired under the legislation of another Member State or such in-

---

[220] C. Joerges and F. Rödl, 'Informal Politics, Formalised Law and the "Social Deficit" of
European Integration: Reflections after the Judgments of the ECJ in *Viking* and *Laval*',
15 *European Law Journal* (January 2009) p. 3.

[221] ECJ, Case C-232/01 *Van Lent* [2003] *ECR* I-11525.

[222] Regulation (EEC) No. 1408/71 of the Council of 14 June 1971 *OJ* L 149, 5 July 1971,
pp. 2-50 on the application of social security schemes to employed persons and their families
moving within the Community, and amending acts.

come arises in the territory of another Member State. However, this provision does not apply when the person concerned receives benefits of the same kind in respect of invalidity, old age, death (pensions) or occupational disease that are awarded by the institutions of two or more Member States, in conformity with the relevant Community provisions.'

Similar questions concern the right to other benefits. Yet, the Member State of residence needs to pay and take into account all rights acquired in other Member States., as the *Noteboom* case shows.[223]

The most recent discussion concerned the question whether a citizen needs to be a resident in order to exercise certain pension rights. In the *Tas-Hagen* case,[224] in which the Dutch government had made residence a main requirement for a pension benefit under the Law on Benefits for Civilian War Victims 1940-1945. The ECJ decided that:

'The objective of limiting the obligation of solidarity with civilian war victims to those who had links with the population of the Member State concerned during and after the war, by means of a residence condition regarded as an expression of the extent to which those persons are connected to that society, may constitute an objective consideration of public interest capable of justifying a restriction on the freedoms conferred by Article 18(1) EC on every citizen of the Union.

However, the setting of a residence criterion based solely on the date on which the application for the benefit is submitted is not a satisfactory indicator of the degree of attachment of the applicant to the society which is thereby demonstrating its solidarity with him, and therefore fails to comply with the principle of proportionality.'

This line of reasoning has been described as 'to narrow down the limitation of the freedoms and to broaden the freedoms themselves.'[225] It can, however, not be denied that this case represents a steady development in ECJ case-law, which was recently re-affirmed in the case of Mrs Zablocka-Weyher-müller,[226] in which the ECJ applied the same reasoning, referring to the *Tas-Hagen* case, on the surviving spouse of a victim of war, even though the only link for the widow was the fact that she resided in Germany.

---

[223] ECJ, Case C-101/04 *Noteboom* [2005] *ECR* I-00771.

[224] ECJ, Case C-192/05 *Tas-Hagen & Tas* [2006] *ECR* I-10451.

[225] T. Yaneva, 'Borderlines of Union Citizenship', 34 *Legal Issues of Economic Integration* (2007) p. 418.

[226] ECJ, Case C-221/07 *Zablocka-Weyhermüller* [2008] *ECR* 00000.

4.2   NON-CROSS-BORDER SOCIAL RIGHTS

Contrary to the social rights discussed above, non-cross-border European social rights are part of European Union law although they do not fall in the more traditional perception of European integration. The non-cross-border social rights are therefore more interesting from a citizen's point of view. These rights are a direct influence on citizens' rights, whether the citizens involved are EU nationals or not. The influence is a direct influence in the national legal order, and therefore a very positive element of citizens' rights as far as European influence on the position of the citizen is concerned. Without the EU, many of these rights would not have existed in several Member States, or at least would not have developed as much as they have now.

Interestingly, the right to equal pay for men and women has been part of European law from the beginning, although it is a non-cross-border right and influences the internal system of the Member States. Although its introduction in the original Treaty of Rome in 1957 was motivated by economic reasons because France already had this principle laid down in its national legislation and was afraid for a negative competition position compared to the other Member States,[227] this element has been very influential. The landmark case in this was the *Defrenne* case,[228] in which a Belgian air hostess opposed that her contract would end much earlier than that of her male collegues. The ECJ ruled that the provision in the then EEC Treaty had direct effect in the Member States and could be applied by national courts.

On top of the right to equal pay, the Treaty of Maastricht introduced Article 13 TEC (Art. 19 TFEU-L), in which equal treatment without a cross-border element has been given a legal basis:

'1. Without prejudice to the other provisions of this Treaty and within the limits of the powers conferred by it upon the Community, the Council, acting unanimously on a proposal from the Commission and after consulting the European Parliament, may take appropriate action to combat discrimination based on sex, racial or ethnic origin, religion or belief, disability, age or sexual orientation.'

While this represents a rather broad non-discrimination principle, the social rights aspect in this book concentrates on the position of workers or at least

---

[227] D. Rodrik, *Has Globalization Gone Too Far?* (Washington 1997) p. 38.
[228] ECJ, Case 43/75 *Defrenne* [1976] *ECR* 00455.

work-related elements. This does not mean that for instance equal treatment rights based on sexual orientation or ethnic origin are not important as general citizenship rights but rather that the focus on the development of citizenship rights as Marshall described lies with the position of workers and like categories of citizens. For this paragraph, some of the landmark legislation and cases in this policy area are therefore selected which show that these social rights have had a large influence in the legal systems of the Member States without containing a cross-border element.

The first one contains legislation and case-law on the equal treatment for the establishment of a pension age, following the *Defrenne* case. The basis can be found in Directive 76/207/EEC[229] and Directive 79/7/EEC.[230] This has led to very different cases, like for instance the *Marshall* case[231] and the *Vergani* case.[232] In the *Marshall* case, Ms Marshall was discriminated against by her employer, the State, concerning the pension age. The ECJ ruled that under such circumstances, Ms Marshall had the right to be compensated and could rely on the direct application of the Directive:

'A person who has been injured as a result of discriminatory dismissal may rely on the provisions of Article 6 of the Directive as against an authority of the State acting in its capacity as an employer in order to set aside a national provision which imposes limits on the amount of compensation recoverable by way of reparation.'

The *Vergani* case, on the other hand, shows that equal treatment also means that men should not be discriminated against women being allowed to retire earlier:

'Council Directive 76/207/EEC of 9 February 1976 on the implementation of the principle of equal treatment for men and women as regards access to employ-

---

[229] Council Directive 76/207/EEC of 9 February 1976 *OJ* L 39, 14 February 1976, pp. 40-42 on the implementation of the principle of equal treatment for men and women as regards access to employment, vocational training and promotion, and working conditions.

[230] Council Directive 79/7/EEC of 19 December 1978 *OJ* L 6, 10 January 1979, pp. 24-25 on the progressive implementation of the principle of equal treatment for men and women in matters of social security.

[231] ECJ, Case C-271/91 *Marshall* [1993] *ECR* I-04367.

[232] ECJ, Case C-207/04 *Vergani* [2005] *ECR* I-07453.

ment, vocational training and promotion, and working conditions must be interpreted as precluding a provision such as that at issue in the main proceedings, which grants to workers who have passed the age of 50 years in the case of women and 55 years in the case of men, as a voluntary redundancy incentive, an advantage consisting in taxation at a rate reduced by half, of sums paid on cessation of the employment relationship.'

This broad range of options under the Directives is also applied on other equal treatment subjects, most notably the definition of working time, as laid down in Directive 93/104/EC.[233] While the maximum European working week contains 48 hours, this Directive harmonizes all minimum requirements for working time in the legislative systems of the Member States. The application of these requirements on on-call duty has led to several cases, like the *Dellas* case:

'According to that case-law, although periods of professional inactivity are inherent in on-call duty performed by workers where they are required to be physically present on the employer's premises, given that, unlike during normal working hours, the need for urgent interventions during such duty cannot be planned in advance and the activity actually performed depends on the circumstances, the decisive factor in considering that the characteristic features of the concept of "working time" within the meaning of Directive 93/104 are present in the case of such on-call duty performed by a worker at his actual workplace is that he is required to be physically present at the place determined by the employer and to be available to the employer in order to be able to provide the appropriate services immediately in case of need. Those obligations must therefore be regarded as coming within the ambit of the performance of that worker's duties.'

This means that hours spent on on-call duty are considered to be working hours. As a result, Member States have had to amend legislation and contracts for hospital workers, fire fighters[234] and others. Other European legislation and case-law which have influenced the social rights in the national legal systems are first the rules of redundancy in case of collective redundan-

---

[233] Council Directive 93/104/EC of 23 November 1993 *OJ* L 307, 13 December 1993, pp. 18-24 concerning certain aspects of the organization of working time.

[234] See for instance 'Rotterdamse Brandweer Krijgt Kortere Werkweek', *de Volkskrant*, 2006, <www.volkskrant.nl/economie/article380633.ece/Rotterdamse_brandweer_krijgt_kortere_werkweek> (last visited on 21 August 2009).

cies[235] as the *Junk* case[236] shows. In this case, it was established that the moment the employers announces his intention to terminate the contract of employment is the moment of redundancy. From that moment, the right to social benefits begins. Another situation concerned the decision that maternity leave cannot be counted as holiday leave even when there is a collective agreement which contains an general annual leave which happened to coincide with the maternity leave, as the *Merino Gomez* case[237] shows. And finally, apart from the examples above, the European Union stimulates affirmative action for women in the public service, as the ECJ decided in the *Marschall* case,[238] in which Mr Marschall complained about the fact that he female competitors for a government position had better chances because of affirmative action.

4.3   SOCIAL FUNDAMENTAL RIGHTS

As stated above, the application by the ECJ of the equal treatment rights as social fundamental rights can be described in some cases as 'to narrow down the limitation of the freedoms and to broaden the freedoms themselves.'[239] Social fundamental rights can be either fundamental rights laid down in the EU Charter on Fundamental Rights, like the right to collective bargaining and action in Article 28 or the right to fair and just working conditions in Article 31, or the non-work related social rights falling under the heading of Article 13 TEC (Art. 19 TFEU-L). The latter category has given rise to secondary legislation covering all aspects of Article 13 TEC (Art. 19 TFEU-L), like a directive on equal treatment irrespective of ethnic origin.[240]

Several important cases have followed from this secondary legislation, framing the social fundamental rights within the European Union. In the

---

[235] Council Directive 98/59/EC of 20 July 1998 *OJ* L 225, 12 August 1998, pp. 16-21 on the approximation of the laws of the Member States relating to collective redundancies.

[236] ECJ, Case C-188/03 *Junk* [2005] *ECR* I-00885.

[237] ECJ, Case C-342/01 *Merino Gomez* [2004] *ECR* I-02605.

[238] ECJ, Case C-409/95 *Marschall* [1997] *ECR* I-06363.

[239] Yaneva, op. cit., note 225, p. 418.

[240] Council Directive 2000/43/EC of 29 June 2000 *OJ* L 180, 19 July 2000, pp. 22-26 implementing the principle of equal treatment between persons irrespective of racial or ethnic origin.

famous *Dory* case,[241] Mr Dory claimed unequal treatment because the compulsory military service in Germany only applied to men. He feared unequality in access to the labour market because women did not have to fulfill military service in between. Although the ECJ in principle agreed with Mr Dory, it also stated that national defense forms an exception:

> 'Nevertheless, the delay in the careers of persons called up for military service is an inevitable consequence of the choice made by the Member State regarding military organisation and does not mean that that choice comes within the scope of Community law. The existence of adverse consequences for access to employment cannot, without encroaching on the competences of the Member States, have the effect of compelling the Member State in question either to extend the obligation of military service to women, thus imposing on them the same disadvantages with regard to access to employment, or to abolish compulsory military service.'

Equal treatment has its limits, as the ECJ decided in this case. Other cases on social fundamental rights have, on the other hand, expanded such limits. In the *Richards* case,[242] for instance, the right to equal treatment was expanded to a transsexual who has undergone male-to-female gender reassignment surgery. Because Ms Richards had become a woman, the retirement age for women in the UK had to be applied to her. Because of cases like these, it is possible to conclude that European social fundamental rights are expanding, mostly through case-law of the European Union. Internal situations in the Member States have a European dimension.

4.4   SOCIAL RIGHTS AS PART OF CITIZENS' RIGHTS

An overall assessment of the social rights in European Union law is that they are rather diverse. Cross-border rights may or may not be exportable. Non-cross-border rights have an impact on the legal systems of the Member States and have partially grown into full-fledged European fundamental rights. A combination of secondary legislation and the case-law of the ECJ have given form and substance to a European social policy. However, many of these

---

[241] ECJ, Case C-186/01 *Dory* [2003] *ECR* I-02479.
[242] ECJ, Case C-423/04 *Richards* [2006] *ECR* I-03585.

rights can only with difficulty be distinguished from the economic rights and the political rights. Only the non-cross-border rights have an independent status. Moreover, they have had a major impact on the development and details of the social rights in the Member States.

Chapter 5

POLITICAL RIGHTS FOR EU CITIZENS

Chapter 5

POLITICAL RIGHTS FOR EU CITIZENS

'Democracy is government accountable to citizens'[243] is a basic statement on the political rights of citizens. One of the key elements in the notion of citizenship contains the political rights of a citizen. Such political rights may take different forms. One the one hand, there are the different forms of the right of suffrage, including the right to vote and the right to be elected. It needs to be noted that part of these rights may be granted to non-nationals, especially in the European Union context. The right to vote forms also an inherent part of democratic, political rights which means that the options for EU citizens to influence the democratic system need to be explored for an overview of their political rights. This basic human right simultaneously brings the question how human rights in general and democratic rights in particular can be protected, most notably in court.

One approach in view of the political rights in a European Union context is checking whether the democratic legitimacy of the overall constellation of democratic institutions and procedures fits the standards. This can be done by means of an inventarisation of the 'procedural, substantive and adjudicative legitimacy.'[244] In this theoretical approach, 'procedural legitimacy' means 'the right of all citizens to participate in the deliberation and decision-making stages of the law-making process.'[245] 'Substantive legitimacy' and 'adjudicative legitimacy' refer to the substantive values in the legislative process and the role of the courts in upholding the democratic values respectively.

---

[243] As can be found on the website 'Launching an Observatory on Citizenship in Europe', <http://eudo-citizenship.eu/> (last visited on 28 October 2009).

[244] A. José Menéndez, 'The European Democratic Challenge: The Forging of a Supranational *Volonté Générale*', 15 *European Law Journal* (May 2009) p. 283.

[245] Menéndez, op. cit., note 244, p. 283.

F. Goudappel, The Effects of EU Citizenship
© 2010, T·M·C·ASSER PRESS, *The Hague, The Netherlands and the Author*

For an in-depth analysis of the political rights of the citizen in the European Union, the procedural legitimacy is what represents the citizen best. However, it means more than the right to vote[246] for The European Parliament does not paint the whole picture. What needs to be added is firstly the right to vote for local elections, which is a right given to EU citizens specifically in the EC Treaty. However, the procedures to participate in the European legislative process include the role of national parliaments and the role of the national ministers in the Council. For this, an insight into the transparency of the procedures and the decisions taken is necessary as well.

This means a study of both the European and the national level for the procedural elements in particular. Who has which rights? The Member States can create their own procedures, like they do for the economic and social rights, but there are European consequences attached to these national decisions on procedures.

5.1   REPRESENTATION THROUGH THE EUROPEAN PARLIAMENT AND NATIONAL PARLIAMENTS

The basic element of democratic representation at the European level lies in the system of representation of the citizens through The European Parliament. For this, both the scope of the right to vote and the powers of the European Parliament are important. In the Treaty of Lisbon, this form of representation is laid down in Article 10 TEU (new):

'1. The functioning of the Union shall be founded on representative democracy.
2. Citizens are directly represented at Union level in the European Parliament. Member States are represented in the European Council by their Heads of State or Government and in the Council by their governments, themselves democratically accountable either to their national Parliaments, or to their citizens.
3. Every citizen shall have the right to participate in the democratic life of the Union. Decisions shall be taken as openly and as closely as possible to the citizen.
4. Political parties at European level contribute to forming European political awareness and to expressing the will of citizens of the Union.'

---

[246] In which the right to be elected may be included when being referred to in a general sense.

Thus, there is a double system of representation, which already exists under the old Treaties but which has not been formulated as directly as it has been done in the Treaty of Lisbon. The double representation means both representation through direct elections for European Parliament and indirectly through the European Council and the Council.

For the right to vote, the basis is laid down in Article 189 of the EC Treaty (repealed as such in the Treaty of Lisbon). Each Member State has been assigned a certain number of seats in the European Parliament, ranging from five seats for Malta to 99 seats for Germany.[247] The differences in this system of seats have been taken as an important argument by the German *Bundesverfassungsgericht* in its decision concerning the Treaty of Lisbon,[248] in which the list of numbers of seats is replaced by Article 14 Paragraph 2 TEU-L:

'The European Parliament shall be composed of representatives of the Union's citizens. They shall not exceed seven hundred and fifty in number, plus the President. Representation of citizens shall be degressively proportional, with a minimum threshold of six members per Member State. No Member State shall be allocated more than ninety-six seats.'

Apart from the fact that this means that amendments on the number of seats per Member State can be negotiated by all without the necessity of a Treaty amendment but be laid down in a Decision, the Bundesverfassungsgericht has noted a substantive difference in the number of citizens represented by the respective Members of the European Parliament:

'The Federal Republic of Germany is allotted 96 seats (Article 2 of the draft Decision). According to the Draft decision, a Member of the elected in France would represent approximately 857,000 citizens of the Union and thus as many as a Member elected in Germany, who represents approximately 857,000 as well. In contrast, a Member of the European Parliament elected in Luxembourg would, however, only represent approximately 83,000 Luxembourg citizens of the Union, i.e. a tenth of them, in the case of Malta, it would be approximately 67,000, or only roughly a twelfth of them; as regards a medium-sized Member State such as

---

247 Art. 190 Para. 2 TEC *OJ* C 306 of 17 December 2007.
248 Judgment of the Bundesverfassungsgericht of 30 June 2009: BVerfG, 2 BvE 2/08 vom 30.6.2009, Absatz-Nr. (1-421), <www.bverfg.de/entscheidungen/es20090630_2bve000208en. html> (last visited on 29 August 2009).

Sweden, every elected Member of the European Parliament would represent approximately 455,000 citizens of the Union from his or her country in the European Parliament (as regards the population figures on which these calculations are based see Eurostat, Europe in figures, *Eurostat yearbook 2008*, 2008, p. 25).'[249]

While the *Bundesverfassungsgericht* consequently remarks that 'In federal states, such marked imbalances are, as a general rule, only tolerated for the second chamber existing beside Parliament', and that it the system is meant to represent the distribution of political power in the Member States because the Members of European Parliament are not representatives of their Member States as such but more representatives of the political spectrum in the Member States. After all the elected members form European fractions after election: 'Political parties at European level contribute to forming European political awareness and to expressing the will of citizens of the Union.'[250] This emphasizes the political ideas across the Member States rather than a national representation.

However, the Member States themselves decide at the national level who has the right to vote for these representatives in the European Parliament. This usually follows the national system of election with the UK for instance opting for a district system and a Member State like the Netherlands for a direct system. These two Member States have also been involved in court cases concerning the question who has the right to vote. In principle, the own citizens and the citizens of other Member States in their host Member State have the right to vote for the European Parliament. For both situations, the citizens involved resided in Gibraltar and Aruba respectively, overseas territories on the basis of Article 299 Paragraph 2 TEC (Art. 355 TFEU-L). The central question in both cases is how far the independence of the Member States reaches to decide who of their nationals have the right to vote in European elections.

In the case of *Eman and Sevinger*,[251] Dutch citizens on Aruba and the Netherlands Antilles complained that they did not have the right to vote for the European Parliament although they are Dutch and reside in the Kingdom of the Netherlands. In the first place, they claimed that European Union law is (voluntarily) implemented in Aruba and the Netherlands Antilles and thus

---

[249] Para. 285 of the Lisbon Decision of the *Bundesverfassungsgericht*.
[250] Art. 10 Para. 4 TEU-L, see now also Art. 191 TEC.
[251] ECJ, Case C-300/04 *Eman & Sevinger* [2006] *ECR* I-08055.

has an effect on local legislation. However, at that time, the Netherlands Antilles and Aruba did not have any means of influencing the decision-making process resulting in the relevant European Union law. This could change, according to Eman and Sevinger, by having the right to vote for European Parliament. Secondly, Eman and Sevinger pointed out that they are Dutch nationals and should therefore be able to vote for European Parliament. The Advocate-General (A-G) had concluded that the Dutch Kieswet (i.e., the law on elections) violated the right to equal treatment by discriminating between Dutch nationals because it combines the right to vote for European Parliament with the right to vote for the Dutch national parliament (in this case the Second Chamber of Parliament, the *Tweede Kamer*). It therefore meant that there are three categories of Dutch nationals: the Dutch on the territory in Europe, the Dutch living in third countries, and the Dutch on the Netherlands Antilles and Aruba. Only the first two categories have the right to vote for European Parliament. The conclusion by the A-G in this case[252] points at the following co-occurrence of problems of European law: Article 12 TEC (Art. 20 TFEU-L) forbids any discrimination on the basis of nationality, while equal treatment either is part of this non-discrimination on the basis of nationality or part of basic right protection (also laid down in Art. 13 TEC (Art. 21 TFEU-L) as the more traditional prohibition of discrimination. In addition, Article 19 TEC gives every EU citizen (i.e., everyone with the nationality of one of the Member States) the right to vote for European Parliament.

However, the ECJ argued that there is inequality between the Dutch who live in third countries and the Dutch on Aruba and the Netherlands Antilles. The Netherlands does not have any system of parted nationality for former colonies as France and the UK have. This means that the Netherlands only has one type of nationality and needs to act according to the European system in this respect. This reasoning of the ECJ is interesting because the EC Treaty only refers to discrimination of nationals of other Member States, not between nationals of one and the same Member State.

For the UK, the question was raised by Ms Matthews whether she, as a UK citizen residing in Gibraltar, could exercise the right to vote. The situation is slightly different from the Dutch one because Gibraltar is an overseas

---

[252] Conclusion by A-G A. Tizzano of 6 April 2006, in ECJ, Case C-145/04 *Spain v. United Kingdom* [2006] *ECR* I-07917 and ECJ, Case C-300/04 *Eman & Sevinger* [2006] *ECR* I-08055.

territory in Europe. Ms Matthews took this problem to the ECHR in Strasbourg, which decided that:

> 'However, in the present case the applicant, as a resident of Gibraltar, was com-
> pletely denied any opportunity to express her opinion in the choice of the mem-
> bers of the European Parliament. The position is not analogous to that of persons
> who are unable to take part in elections because they live outside the jurisdiction,
> as such individuals have weakened the link between themselves and the jurisdic-
> tion. In the present case, as the Court has found (see paragraph 34 above), the
> legislation which emanates from the European Community forms part of the leg-
> islation in Gibraltar, and the applicant is directly affected by it.
> In the circumstances of the present case, the very essence of the applicant's right
> to vote, as guaranteed by Article 3 of Protocol No. 1, was denied.
> It follows that there has been a violation of that provision.'

As a follow-up, the UK amended its legislation but this amendment was not accepted by Spain, which complained with the ECJ about this.[253] Spain claimed in this case that the UK gave too many people in Gibraltar the right to vote because the system included Commonwealth citizens. However, the ECJ decided that the UK only fulfilled the promise they made in reference to the *Matthews* case and transposed their national electoral system for European Parliament to Gibraltar.

The above cases show that European law has its own requirements and limitations for the freedom of the Member States to decide to whom they give the right to vote for the European Parliament. In addition, the position of the European Parliament is defined by its role in the European decision-making process. While the European Parliament only has the competence to decide with the Council under the co-decision procedure in Article 251 TEC at present, this procedure is to be applied for most legislative proposals but not for all. Under the Treaty of Lisbon, however, this procedure, laid down in Articles 289 and 294 TFEU-L as the 'ordinary legislative procedure', will be applied in more or less all procedures, leading to the statement that the European Parliament is in this way the 'winner' in the legislative process under Lisbon.[254] Yet, nothing changes for the right of initiative: under the Treaty of Lisbon, this will exclusively remain in the hands of the Commission.

---

[253] ECJ, Case C-145/04 *Spain* v. *United Kingdom* [2006] *ECR* I-07917.

[254] P. Craig, 'The Role of the European Parliament under the Lisbon Treaty', in S. Griller and J. Ziller (eds.), *The Lisbon Treaty, EU Constitutionalism without a Constitutional Treaty?* (Vienna/New York 2009) p. 110.

All this is important in combination with the competences which the European Parliament has been given in the Treaties, and the so-called democratic deficit. In the Treaty of Lisbon, these competences are summarized in Article 14 Paragraph 1 TEU-L:

'The European Parliament shall, jointly with the Council, exercise legislative and budgetary functions. It shall exercise functions of political control and consultation as laid down in the Treaties. It shall elect the President of the Commission.'

While the European Parliament lacks the right of initiative for legislation, these competences have to be considered together with the position of the national parliaments. After all, these national parliaments have retained the competence to exercise control on the national input at the European level. For this, a system of interparliamentary cooperation has recently been created,[255] also with a view of the coming into force of the Treaty of Lisbon, which prescribes such a system in Article 12 sub f TEU-L.

For the national parliaments, the role in the European processes is therefore twofold: on the one hand, they have to use their national control mechanisms to check the actions of their cabinet ministers in the European Council and the Council, and on the other hand they have the option to be pro-active in the legislative process, which will become particularly strong under the Treaty of Lisbon.

Art. 12 TEU (new) states:

'National Parliaments contribute actively to the good functioning of the Union:
(a) through being informed by the institutions of the Union and having draft legislative acts of the Union forwarded to them in accordance with the Protocol on the role of national Parliaments in the European Union;
(b) by seeing to it that the principle of subsidiarity is respected in accordance with the procedures provided for in the Protocol on the application of the principles of subsidiarity and proportionality;
(c) by taking part, within the framework of the area of freedom, security and justice, in the evaluation mechanisms for the implementation of the Union poli-

---

[255] European Parliament Relations with National Parliaments, <www.europarl.europa.eu/webnp/cms/lang/en/pid/1;jsessionid=3D23A92CBC2E5DA62D013BB1A6E6F5D5> (last visited on 28 October 2009]; and IPEX, Interparliamentary EU Information Exchange, <www.ipex.eu/ipex/cms/pid/> (last visited on 28 October 2009).

cies in that area, in accordance with Article 70 of the Treaty on the Functioning of the European Union, and through being involved in the political monitoring of Europol and the evaluation of Eurojust's activities in accordance with Articles 88 and 85 of that Treaty;

(d) by taking part in the revision procedures of the Treaties, in accordance with Article 48 of this Treaty;

(e) by being notified of applications for accession to the Union, in accordance with Article 49 of this Treaty;

(f) by taking part in the inter-parliamentary cooperation between national Parliaments and with the European Parliament, in accordance with the Protocol on the role of national Parliaments in the European Union.'

Together, the national parliaments and the European Parliament cover what is considered a citizen's right to vote and to influence the decision-making procedures. In order to strengthen this, the Treaty of Lisbon, like the European Constitution, contains a specific protocol on the role of national parliaments[256] along with a protocol on the application of the principles of subsidiarity[257] and proportionality, in which the national parliaments play a large role as well. In these protocols the national parliaments are given the competence not only to participate in the European decision-making process but also to have a distinct say in it.

5.2   Right to Vote in Local Elections

In addition to the right to vote for European Parliament, EU citizens have been given the right to vote in local elections as well.

Article 19 Paragraph 1 TEC (Art. 22 Para. 1 TFEU-L) states:

'Every citizen of the Union residing in a Member State of which he is not a national shall have the right to vote and to stand as a candidate at municipal elections in the Member State in which he resides, under the same conditions as nationals of that State. This right shall be exercised subject to detailed arrangements adopted by the Council, acting unanimously on a proposal from the Commission and after consulting the European Parliament; these arrangements may provide for derogations where warranted by problems specific to a Member State.'

---

[256] Protocol No. 1 on the role of national parliaments in the European Union.
[257] Protocol No. 2 on the application of the principles of subsidiarity and proportionality.

A similar right has been laid down in Article 40 of the EU Charter on Fundamental Rights, which indicates that the Member States consider this a fundamental right of their citizens. While this means that this right to vote only exists for those residing in another Member State to participate in the political life of their new place of residence, it also indicates the wish for integration in society like for instance the right to bring a family member along when migrating does as well. As such, the right to vote in local elections is a special European citizenship right, which does not exist outside the European Union system.

5.3   TRANSPARENCY

One of the ways in which democratic control can be exercised in the European Union system is by means of transparency. As the Commission itself indicates: 'The Union must be open to public scrutiny and accountable for its work. This requires a high level of openness and transparency.'[258] The idea of transparency or openness in the European context developed from national systems which had a need to evaluate government and governmental actions over the last thirty years, especially in the UK and Sweden.[259] In the 1990s, a similar system was adopted for achievements and cost-effectiveness by the EU, based on experiences in the Member States.[260] The need for evaluation is thus seen as part of the claim for sovereignty, accountability, legitimacy and effective implementation.[261] However, the terms 'transparency' and 'openness' can be used interchangeably.[262] In European terms, an important part of transparency is formed by the need for 'traceability' of Community legislation.[263] This is of course not just an European issue, the

---

[258] Strategic objectives 2005-2009; Europe 2010: A Partnership for European Renewal; Prosperity, Solidarity and Security. Communication from the President in agreement with Vice-President Wallström, COM(2005)12, p. 5.

[259] H. Summa (rapporteur) and H. Schmitt von Sydow (pilot), 'Report of the Working Group Evaluation and Transparency' (Group 2b), p. 4.

[260] Summa and Schmitt von Sydow, op. cit., note 259, p. 6.

[261] Summa and Schmitt von Sydow, op. cit., note 259, p. 4.

[262] P. Nikiforos Diamandouros, FOI: A European Perspective Speech by the European Ombudsman, Professor P. Nikiforos Diamandouros, at the 4th International Conference of Information Commissioners, Manchester, 23 March 2006, to be found on <www.ombudsman. europa.eu/speeches/en/2006-05-23.htm> [last visited on 2 December 2008].

[263] Summa and Schmitt von Sydow, op. cit., note 259, p. 16.

European transparency demands can increasingly be seen at the national level in the Member States and even in national case-law.[264] Moreover, in the EU Charter of Fundamental Rights, the elements are laid down in Article 41 (right to good administration), Article 42 (right of access to documents) and Article 43 (European Ombudsman). Not only will this Charter be part of the system of the Treaty of Lisbon through the Declaration to the Treaty, several of these rights are laid down in the Treaty itself. In this way, the principle of transparency will become an even stronger right in the European system.

The importance of transparency at the European Union level is large. Not only is it considered to be one of the basic rights on which the European Union was founded,[265] it is also deemed important for an understanding by the public in general of what is happening at the European level. Some state that the Irish rejection of the Treaty of Lisbon in 2008 was partially based on a lack of transparency.[266]

The approach of transparency of European Union decisions and actions manifests itself twofold: in the stages leading to legislation by means of consultation and in access to documents afterwards. In order to give these approaches form and substance, legislation has been adopted and internal EU documents have been created. In order to obtain a full overview of the width of transparency in the EU, four manifestations will be discussed in detail. First, the process and procedures of consultation rounds by – most notably – the Commission will be described, along with an evaluation of the transparency of the process. Access to documents used by any of the institutions will then be discussed, both from a legislative point of view and from case-law. A third method of transparency goes via the European Ombudsman, whose main task it is the following:

'the Ombudsman shall help to uncover maladministration in the activities of the Community institutions and bodies, with the exception of the Court of Justice and the Court of First Instance acting in their judicial role (...).'[267]

---

[264] S. Prechal, 'De emancipatie of "het algemene transparantiebeginsel"', 9 *SEW* (September 2008) p. 316.

[265] Art. 42 of the European Union Charter on Basic Rights.

[266] S. Peers, 'Statewatch Analysis. Proposals for Greater Openness, Transparency and Democracy in the EU', October 2008, p. 1, <www.statewatch.org/analyses/proposals-for-greater-openness-peers-08.pdf> (last visited on 27 October 2008).

[267] Art. 2 Para. 1 of the Decision of the European Parliament on the regulations and general conditions governing the performance of the Ombudsman's duties, Adopted by Parlia-

Finally, the voting in the Council has to be taken into consideration, especially the public voting in the co-decision procedure.

From a practical point of view, transparency of the decision-making process has been ensured by the institutions in different ways. The Pre-lex system on the Europa website,[268] for instance, gives all background information for each step in the decision-making process for pending legislation.

5.4   ACCESS TO DOCUMENTS

Access to documents is a traditional part of transparency in view of democratic control of decisions taken by institutions. In the European system, the first steps towards this were taken in 1992 in an Annex to the Treaty of Maastricht:

The Conference considers that transparency of the decision- making process strengthens the democratic nature of the institutions and the public's confidence in the administration. The Conference accordingly recommends that the Commission submit to the Council no later than 1993 a report on measures designed to improve public access to the information available to the institutions.[269]

The most notable results of the process of providing access to documents were subsequent decisions in which this was ensured for the respective institutions.[270] In 2001, these separate decisions were replaced by one comprehensive regulation on the issue.[271] In the Treaty of Amsterdam, the right to access to documents for the EU citizens was laid down in Article 255 EC, on

---

ment on 9 March 1994 (*OJ* L 113, 4 May 1994, p. 15) and amended by its decisions of 14 March 2002 (*OJ* L 92, 9 April 2002, p. 13) and 18 June 2008 (*OJ* L 189, 17 July 2008, p. 25).

[268] <http://ec.europa.eu/prelex/apcnet.cfm?CL=en>.

[269] Declaration 17 to the Treaty of Maastricht.

[270] Council Decision 93/731/EC on public access to Council documents, *OJ* L 340 31 December 1993; Decision 94/90/ECSC, EC, Euratom on public access to Commission documents, *OJ* L 46, 18 February 1994; 97/632/EC, ECSC, Euratom Decision of the European Parliament of 10 July 1997 on public access to document of the European Parliament, *OJ* L 263 25 September 1997.

[271] Regulation (EC) 1049/2001 of the European Parliament and of the Council of 30 May 2001 *OJ* L 145, 31 May 2001, pp. 43-48 regarding public access to European Parliament, Council and Commission documents.

the basis of which specific legislation was adopted in order to ensure this access to document.[272] Access to documents will re-obtain a direct legal basis in the Treaty of Lisbon in Article 16A TFUE. The system is being reviewed on a regular basis, the latest review process started in 2007.[273]

Thus, new influences can be detected. As case-law of the ECJ shows,[274] Member States may be forced to give access to documents following from European law even when their national legislation does not provide for this option.[275] This process goes even further because the European Union also experiences top-down influence on this issue from international obligations, which may then influence the national level. As the implementation of the Arhus Convention shows,[276] environmental issues are a matter for everybody, which means that access to information needs to be ensured at all levels. In several of the European anti-terrorism cases, on the other hand, the Court of Justice has decided that this European principle even applies to European obligations which follow directly from international obligations.[277]

5.5   EUROPEAN OMBUDSMAN

The institution of the European Ombudsman was meant to help limit the democratic deficit through The European Parliament as a 'complementary instrument of political accountability over other Community institutions and bodies'.[278] This institution was proposed by Spain and Denmark on the basis

---

[272] Regulation (EC) No. 1049/2001 of the European Parliament and of the Council of 30 May 2001 regarding public access to Eruopean Parliament, Council and Commission documents.

[273] Public Access to Documents held by the institutions of the European Community; A Review, Commission Green Paper, 18 April 2007, COM(2007)185 final.

[274] A prime example is ECJ, Case C-64/05 *Sweden* v. *Commission* [2007] *ECR* I-11389.

[275] S. Prechal and M.E. de Leeuw, 'Transparency: A General Principle of EU Law?', in U. Bernitz a.o. (eds.), *General Principles of EC Lawa in a Process of Development* (The Hague 2008) pp. 212-214.

[276] See Public Access to Documents held by the institutions of the European Community; A Review, Commission Green Paper, 18 April 2007, COM(2007)185 final, for a review of this influence. See also Prechal and De Leeuw, op. cit., note 275, pp. 214-215.

[277] For instance ECJ, Joined Cases C-402/05 P and C-415/05 P *Kadi and Barakaat* [2008] *ECR* I-06351.

[278] W. Song and V. Della Sala, 'Eursceptics and Europhiles in Accord: The Creation of the European Ombudsman as an Institutional Isomorphism', 36(4) *Policy and Politics* (2008) p. 482.

of their own national experiences with national ombudsmen.[279] Eight of the twelve Member States at the time had Ombudsman-type institutions in their national system. The remaining Member States, therefore had a top-down influence from the European level because of this new institution.[280] It needs to be noted here that, because the concept of the European Ombudsman was adopted in the text of the EC Treaty in Article 195 EC, all (new) Member States had to accept this notion, even if they did not know it in their national constitutional structure since the procedure for amending the EC Treaty has always required unanimity of the Member States. For Member States which acceded later, the institution of the European Ombudsman was part of the whole package and might therefore have entered their legal system without prior express consent.

Yet, before the ombudsman-concept became part of the European system, the development of this concept was subject to transnational influence, developing from a Nordic invention in the early twentieth century to a more general Western European concept in the second half of the twentieth century.[281] Of the two models for an ombudsman which have developed in this period (control or redress),[282] the European Ombudsman has proven to be more of a redress type of ombudsman.[283] It is therefore part of both the national systems and the European system as a political right of the citizens.

5.6 VOTING IN THE COUNCIL

Voting in the Council is important in two ways for the political rights of the citizens. It is both the Council representing the Member States at the European level and control at Member State level by national parliaments as part of the process of transparency. As the Council is composed by national ministers as Article 203 TEC states, as replaced by Article 16 TEU-L, it indirectly represents the citizens of the Member States.

---

[279] Song and Della Sala, op. cit., note 278, p. 493.
[280] Song and Della Sala, op. cit., note 278, p. 493.
[281] Song and Della Sala, op. cit., note 278, p. 490.
[282] K. Heede, *European Ombudsman: Redress and Control at Union Level* (The Hague 2000) p. 112.
[283] Heede, op. cit., note 282, pp. 27-271.

For the transparency of the political decisions of the Council, several practical measures have been taken at the European level in order to promote openness in the decision-making process. One of the measures resulting from this can be found in Article 1 TEU, in which was stated:

> 'This Treaty marks a new stage in the process of creating an ever closer union among the peoples of Europe, in which decisions are taken as openly as possible and as closely as possible to the citizen.'

This can be seen as a method to implement also the constitutional traditions common to the Member States as Article 6 Paragraph 2 TEU (Art. 6 TEU-L) states. The most important decision in this strife for openness was taken in 2006, when the Council adopted new Rules of Procedure.[284] Part of these new Rules is the public voting of the Council in co-decision procedures under Article 251 TEC. As it is stated in the preamble to the Council decision, the reason behind the public voting is openness and transparency because a Member State can be outvoted in this procedure. Because the Council is composed of members of the governments of the Member States, the actions of these members can only be checked by the national parliaments according to national rules. As a consequence, the voting in the Council needs to be public so that a control system can be maintained. It goes without saying that such a public vote is not necessary in cases in which unanimity is prescribed[285] because it is clear that each member has voted in favour in case of adoption of the legislation.

It is important to note that this way of voting in the Council goes further than is usual at Member State level. However, it is at the same time a method to open possibilities for the national parliaments for transparency.

5.7   BASIC RIGHTS PROTECTION AS A POLITICAL RIGHT

While basic rights or fundamental rights form part of all the rights under the Marshall division of citizenship rights into economic, social and political

---

[284] Council decision of 15 September 2006 *OJ* L 285, 16 October 2006, pp. 47-71 adopting the Council's Rules of Procedure (2006/683/EC, Euratom).

[285] Examples: voting in the second and most of the third pillar; voting in a advisory procedure when it is different from the draft legislation of the Commission under Art. 250 EC.

rights, the right of access to justice is also a part of the political rights because it adds to the transparency of the decisions made. Although the status of fundamental rights has been discussed above as part of the economic rights and as part of the general theoretical citizenship rights, the evaluation of their position may be different as a political right.

Access to justice was most prominently at the forefront in several cases concerning the Security Council blacklists as decided by the ECJ in the fight against terrorism. As described above, the case of *Gestoras Pro Amnistia*[286] is a good example of a case in which the ECJ discussed access to justice for third parties affected by third-pillar measures. Interestingly, the Court of Justice suggests that it is against a narrow interpretation of its powers under Article 35 TEU.[287] but practical application of its broad interpretation leaves many questions unanswered. Firstly, there is the question how a case concerning the Security Council blacklists and its implementation measures in the third pillar would come before a national court. Secondly, the suggestion that Member States could bring a case to the Court of Justice against the lawfulness of a third-pillar common position does not seem to take into account that Article 34 TEU prescribes unanimity for such common positions, which would lead to a Member State bringing a case against its own voting in favour of it in the past. Yet, the underlying idea that national courts have jurisdiction when the Court of Justice does not is in harmony with both the system of the Treaties (Art. 5 TEC) and the steady case-law of the Court of Justice on this matter. In this way, access to justice especially in the third pillar shows a limitation of the political rights of the citizens, and even wider than this: for all without distinction concerning nationality, thus including third-country nationals.

5.8 IS THERE A EUROPEAN DEMOCRATIC DEFICIT?

In conclusion, the political rights of the citizens under European Union law can be summarized in an evaluation of a possible European democratic deficit. The double system of the right to vote and the political control by both the European Parliament and the national parliaments seems to fill all the

---

[286] ECJ, Case C-354-04 P *Gestoras Pro Amnistia a.o.* v. *the Council of the European Union* [2007] *ECR* I-01579.
[287] Para. 53 of the judgment.

holes in a democratic deficit. Especially under the Treaty of Lisbon, the role of national parliaments will be strengthened and complement the role of the European Parliament. Moreover, with the help of the control on the Council, the citizens in the European system have an almost complete influence on the decision-making process, with the very notable exception of the right of initiative. As citizenship rights, these political rights fill the requirements and even contain an additional European citizenship right of the right to vote in local elections. The progress recently made in transparency of the decision-making process in different ways augments this closing of the democratic deficit although this closing is clearly not reached as a goal yet.

Chapter 6

THIRD-COUNTRY NATIONALS AND EU CITIZENSHIP RIGHTS

Chapter 6

THIRD-COUNTRY NATIONALS AND EU CITIZENSHIP RIGHTS

6.1   EU CITIZENSHIP AND VISA, ASYLUM AND IMMIGRATION

In European Union terms, the problem of awarding citizenship and citizenship rights is the problem of immigration by third-country nationals. When legal in an EU Member State, do third-country nationals become EU citizens with all the rights and duties attached to it, or do they only obtain a limited number of rights? The right to give access and residence for third-country nationals is traditionally a national competence of the Member States.[288] These third-country nationals do not have the option to obtain full EU citizenship rights but only a limited number of these rights, leading to partial citizenship or quasi-citizenship.

For any issue concerning immigration of third-country workers, the Member States have even maintained unanimity voting because Germany wanted to protect its labour market.[289] It is for these reasons that the EC Treaty only contains the option of minimum standards in the present text of Article 61 TEC (which will disappear once the Treaty of Lisbon comes into force) although the Commission has the aim of creating a common immigration policy in the future, which is reflected in the Hague Programme[290] and the draft

---

[288]   S. Peers, 'Free Movement, Immigration Control and Constitutional Conflict', 5 *European Constitutional Law Review* (2009) p. 173.

[289]   P. Bendell, 'Immigration Policy in the European Union: Still Bringing up the Walls for Fortress Europe?', <www.migrationletters.com/200501/20050103_EU_Bendel.pdf> (last visited on 12 October 2009).

[290]   The Hague Programme: strengthening freedom, security and justice in the European Union, European Council of 5 November 2004.

F. Goudappel, The Effects of EU Citizenship
© 2010, T·M·C·ASSER PRESS, *The Hague, The Netherlands and the Author*

Stockholm Programme.[291] As a result, the citizens' rights of third-country nationals are only limitedly regulated at the European level (like the right of residence and the right to move and reside freely), with the emphasis remaining on the national level.

In the EC Treaty, Title IV is the basis for the position of third-country nationals. It follows from Article 61 TEC that third-country nationals do not have citizen rights in their own capacity on the basis of the structure of the internal market; free movement only exists for the nationals of the Member States. Yet, Article 61 TEC together with one of its results, the Directive concerning the status of third-country nationals who are long-term residents[292] has given free movement of third-country nationals after five years of legal stay immediately prior to the submission of the relevant application.[293] However, the rights to be obtained stop with free movement, although this already is a leap forward for third-country nationals in the European Union.[294] Only the right of residence and free movement between the Member States can therefore be obtained by third-country nationals, not full-fledged EU citizenship. Full EU-citizenship is only awarded to nationals of the Member States. An important element of the position of third-country nationals is formed by the Schengen Agreement because not all Member States fully participate in all elements of visa, asylum and immigration: the UK and Ireland have an opt-in option and therefore do not participate in every element, while Cyprus, Bulgaria and Romania have not met the criteria for membership yet. In addition, some non-EU Member States are party to the Schengen Agreement.

Under the Treaty of Lisbon, the legal basis for the European legislation concerning third-country nationals will undergo large amendments. The system of the present Title IV TEC, containing the requirement that legislation has to be adopted within five years after the Treaty of Amsterdam came into force and containing the legal basis for minimum standards in most cases,

---

[291] Communication from the Commission to the European Parliament and the Council; an area of freedom, security and justice serving the citizen, 10 June 2009.

[292] Council Directive 2003/109 of 25 November 2003 (*OJ* L 16/44 of 23 January 2004).

[293] J.W. de Zwaan, 'EU Asylum and Immigration Law and Policy: State of Affairs in 2005', in J.W. de Zwaan and F.A.N.J. Goudappel (eds.), *Freedom, Security and Justice in the European Union; Implementation of the Hague Programme* (The Hague 2006) pp. 130-131.

[294] P. Boeles, 'What Rights Have Migrating Third-country Nationals?', in J.W. de Zwaan and F.A.N.J. Goudappel (eds.), *Freedom, Security and Justice in the European Union; Implementation of the Hague Programme* (The Hague 2006) pp. 151-152.

will be replaced by a system which has a more general nature working towards policies and common policies.[295]

Article 67 Paragraph 2 TFEU-L states:

'It shall ensure the absence of internal border controls for persons and shall frame a common policy on asylum, immigration and external border control, based on solidarity between Member States, which is fair towards third-country nationals. For the purpose of this Title, stateless persons shall be treated as third-country nationals.'

Both under the old and the new system, there are different categories of third-country nationals depending on the citizenship rights to be obtained and the way in which they can be obtained. The most general category is the one listed as visa and immigration, which means both short-term and long-term stay. Asylum seekers are a separate category, with separate European legislation. In addition, special attention needs to be paid to family members of either EU citizens or legally resident third-country nationals, as well as to third-country nationals who are long-term residents who might belong to several of the categories above.

6.2   VISAS

Visas are given to third-country nationals who want a short-term stay of a maximum of three months in the European Union, which can be for leisure, tourism or business:

'For the purposes of this Regulation, 'visa' shall mean an authorisation issued by a Member State or a decision taken by such State which is required with a view to:
– entry for an intended stay in that Member State or in several Member States of no more than three months in total,
– entry for transit through the territory of that Member State or several Member States, except for transit at an airport.'[296]

---

[295] J.H. Reestman and F.A.N.J. Goudappel, 'The Verdrag of Lissabon en de ruimte of vrijheid, veiligheid en recht', *SEW* (November 2008) pp. 441-445.

[296] Council Regulation (EC) No. 539/2001 of 15 March 2001 *OJ* L 81, 21 March 2001, pp. 1-7 listing the third countries whose nationals must be in possession of visas when crossing the external borders and those whose nationals are exempt from that requirement, Art. 2.

In fact, for the Schengen countries, this subject has become an overall European subject with the introduction of the common visa model for the Schengen area. The criteria for obtaining a Schengen visa have been given uniform standards, which means that this is the most 'Europeanized' part of European immigration law. In terms of citizenship rights, third-country nationals may obtain a very limited right to free movement: the right to move freely within the territory of the associated Schengen states for a limited time.

An important aspect of the Schengen visa system is who may obtain a visa and who cannot. For this, a distinction needs to be made between the so-called 'visa positive' and 'visa negative' lists.[297] This is given form and substance in the Schengen Information System (SIS) and Visa Information System (VIS). As it is officially described in a Commission press release in 2007, it contains the following information:

> 'The Visa Information System will store data on up to 70 million people concerning visas for visits to or transit through the Schengen Area. This data will include the applicant's photograph and their ten fingerprints. The VIS will become the largest ten fingerprint system in the world. High levels of security are being built into the system to ensure it remains robust and available at all times and that data is only accessed by authorised persons for authorised purposes. Once it is fully operational, the VIS will be connected to all visa-issuing consulates of the Schengen States and to all their external border crossing points.'[298]

This means that once a third-country national has legally entered one of the Schengen states with a Schengen visa, he has the right to move freely within the territories of the Schengen states without the right to reside there. No other citizenship rights can be obtained for the persons falling in these categories.

---

[297] Council Regulation (EC) No. 539/2001 of 15 March 2001 listing the third countries whose nationals must be in possession of visas when crossing the external borders and those whose nationals are exempt from that requirement; see also Regulation (EC) No. 810/2009 of the European Parliament and of the Council of 13 July 2009 establishing a Community Code on Visas *OJ* L 243, 15 September 2009, pp. 1-58.

[298] Visa Information System (VIS): The JHA-Council reaches a political agreement on the VIS Regulation and VIS Decision, <http://europa.eu/rapid/pressReleasesAction.do?reference=IP/07/802&format=HTML&aged=0&language=EN&guiLanguage=en> (last visited on 12 October 2009).

Taken this all together, there are different categories of third-country nationals who want to obtain a visa to enter the European Union for a maximum of three months. The largest category is of those who need a Schengen visa and whose personal information will be stored in the Visa Information System. For them, there may be questions concerning data protection. As a result of the VIS registration, it is possible, for instance, to access information on individuals who have applied for a Schengen visa in another Schengen state. It also means that once you have been refused a Schengen visa, other Schengen states will be aware of this. For third-country nationals of states which are on the visa positive list, the visa waiver programme leads to a system which is not checked the way a citizen of a 'visa negative' state is, which gives more options for non-refusal. The only element of citizenship rights, however, which can be obtained this way for third-country nationals, is the right to move freely among the territories of the Schengen states. It needs to be noted that it is still the individual Schengen states which decide on admittance and issuing of the visa, but with consequences for admittance to the other Schengen states. For third-country nationals travelling to non-Schengen EU Member States, most notably to the UK and Ireland, the above is not valid. They may only obtain a visa for that particular state without the right to free movement to other Member States.

Under the Treaty of Lisbon, the reference to visas will be omitted and will be replaced by the more general reference to border checks.[299] Because a common policy on visas and other short-stay residence permits has been achieved under the old system, the Treaty of Lisbon focuses on the practical application of this common policy.

6.3 IMMIGRATION

The legislation for immigration, i.e. long-term stay for third-country nationals, is in another phase of development, a common policy has not been achieved (yet). Although the position of some third-country nationals has been described above for the derived right of third-country family members of migrating EU citizens, this does not cover all categories of third-country nationals having the possibility to immigrate into the European Union. First,

---

[299] Art. 77 TFEU-L.

there is the group of third-country nationals who wants to work in the European Union, for whom the options are limited. Secondly, asylum seekers form a separate category because the general legislation for immigration does not apply to them. Thirdly, the family members mentioned above can obtain independent citizenship rights in time as long-term residents.

The basis for the EU third-country immigration policy is at present laid down in Article 63 TEC, which will be replaced by the more progressive Article 79 TEU-L, which has a goal instead of a minimum requirement:

'1. The Union shall develop a common immigration policy aimed at ensuring, at all stages, the efficient management of migration flows, fair treatment of third-country nationals residing legally in Member States, and the prevention of, and enhanced measures to combat, illegal immigration and trafficking in human beings.

2. For the purposes of paragraph 1, the European Parliament and the Council, acting in accordance with the ordinary legislative procedure, shall adopt measures in the following areas:

(a) the conditions of entry and residence, and standards on the issue by Member States of long-term visas and residence permits, including those for the purpose of family reunification;

(b) the definition of the rights of third-country nationals residing legally in a Member State, including the conditions governing freedom of movement and of residence in other Member States;

(c) illegal immigration and unauthorised residence, including removal and repatriation of persons residing without authorisation;

(d) combating trafficking in persons, in particular women and children.'

The final goal of a common immigration policy stems from the Hague Programme, in which the steps have been laid down for reaching this goal. The Member States are responsible for deciding whom to give a permit to, but this decision may have European consequences. The immigrants do not obtain the right to free movement but only the right of residence, thus the opposite of the short-term stay. In the proposal for the follow-up of the Hague Programme, the Stockholm Programme,[300] the European Council states:

---

[300] The Stockholm Programme – An open and secure Europe serving the citizen, Council of the European Union, Presidency, Draft, 16 October 2009, 14449/09.

'The European Council believes that the objective of granting third-country nationals legally resident in the Member States of the EU a uniform level of rights comparable with that of Union citizens should remain the objective of a common immigration policy and should be implemented as soon as possible, and no later than 2014.'

The aim is therefore to give more than partial citizenship rights to third-country nationals in the future. Yet, until now, measures have been taken to manage two elements of immigration: economic immigration and illegal immigration. While illegal immigration cannot lead to any citizenship right except fundamental right protection, the Member States decide on the right of entry and residence. However, once denied entry and residence, The Schengen Information System and European cooperation lead to removal.[301] For economic immigration, only partial measures have been taken so far. The Member States decide on individual applications but with European limits. Thus, specific categories of third-country nationals can obtain a work permit on the basis of Directives, which have to be implemented in the legal systems of the Member States and therefore break the independence of the Member States to make their own decisions. Until now, one such Directive has been adopted, for scientists.[302]

6.4   Asylum Seekers

Although asylum seekers are in basis third-country nationals as well,[303] different European legislation applies to their situation, partially because of the

---

[301] For instance: Council Directive 2001/40/EC of 28 May 2001 *OJ* L 149, 2 June 2001, pp. 34-36 on the mutual recognition of decisions on the expulsion of third-country nationals; or 2004/573/EC, Council Decision of 29 April 2004 *OJ* L 261, 6 August 2004, pp. 28-35 on the organisation of joint flights for removals from the territory of two or more Member States, of third-country nationals who are subjects of individual removal orders.

[302] Council Directive 2005/71/EC *OJ* L 289, 3 November 2005, pp. 15-22 on a specific procedure for admitting third-country nationals for the purposes of scientific research.

[303] Protocol on asylum for nationals of Member States, Protocol No. 22 to the Treaty of Maastricht, and Protocol No. 24 to the Treaty of Lisbon, lay down that EU citizens cannot be granted asylum in another Member State: 'Given the level of protection of fundamental rights and freedoms by the Member States of the European Union, Member States shall be regarded as constituting safe countries of origin in respect of each other for all legal and practical purposes in relation to asylum matters.'

international obligations of the Member States under several international treaties which is recognized in both the old and the new Treaties.

Article 78 Paragraph 1 TFEU-L states:[304]

> 'The Union shall develop a common policy on asylum, subsidiary protection and temporary protection with a view to offering appropriate status to any third-country national requiring international protection and ensuring compliance with the principle of non-refoulement. This policy must be in accordance with the Geneva Convention of 28 July 1951 and the Protocol of 31 January 1967 relating to the status of refugees, and other relevant treaties.'

The Member States have the right to decide on entry and residence by granting the status of refugee to asylum seekers but this right is limited by both international and European obligations. On top of the obligations following from, for instance, the Geneva Convention, for which subsidiary protection has been decided upon by the Member States, the details of which have been laid down in the so-called Qualification Directive.[305] This Directive contains provisions for the situation in which a Member State has to give the citizenship rights to residence permits, and access to social welfare, health care and the labour market. The ECJ has recently given its first judgment on the application of these obligations in the *Elgafaji* case,[306] in which it concluded that:

> 'Article 15(c) of Council Directive 2004/83/EC of 29 April 2004 on minimum standards for the qualification and status of third-country nationals or stateless persons as refugees or as persons who otherwise need international protection and the content of the protection granted, in conjunction with Article 2(e) thereof, must be interpreted as meaning that:
> – the existence of a serious and individual threat to the life or person of an applicant for subsidiary protection is not subject to the condition that that applicant adduce evidence that he is specifically targeted by reason of factors particular to his personal circumstances;
> – the existence of such a threat can exceptionally be considered to be established where the degree of indiscriminate violence characterising the armed conflict

---

[304] Now Art. 63 points 1 and 2 TEC.

[305] Council Directive 2004/83/EC of 29 April 2004 *OJ* L 304, 30 September 2004, pp. 12-23 on minimum standards for the qualification and status of third-country nationals or stateless persons as refugees or as persons who otherwise need international protection and the content of the protection granted.

[306] ECJ, Case C-465/07 *Elgafaji* [2009] *ECR* 00000.

taking place – assessed by the competent national authorities before which an application for subsidiary protection is made, or by the courts of a Member State to which a decision refusing such an application is referred – reaches such a high level that substantial grounds are shown for believing that a civilian, returned to the relevant country or, as the case may be, to the relevant region, would, solely on account of his presence on the territory of that country or region, face a real risk of being subject to that threat.'

The Commission has recently proposed to amend this Qualification Directive, among other reasons in order to

'eliminate the differences in the level of rights granted to refugees and beneficiaries of subsidiary protection which can no longer be considered as justified. The amendments concern the duration of residence permits, access to social welfare, health care and the labour market.'[307]

The access to citizenship rights should be enlarged in this way in the future. The right of entry and of residence for asylum seekers is also partially ruled by the Dublin II Regulation at present,[308] which 'lays down the criteria and mechanisms for determining the Member State responsible for examining an application for asylum lodged in one of the Member States by a third-country national' as Article 1 of the Regulation states. This influences the options for access for asylum seekers and therefore also the options for obtaining partial citizenship rights.

In the future, not only the 'asylum package' of which the Qualifications Directive forms part will be important but also the goal of the Common European Asylum System, which was already announced in the Hague Programme, but which was given its first form by the Commission in 2008.[309]

---

[307] A single and fairer asylum procedure for a uniform status in the EU: putting in place the final building blocks for international protection, <http://europa.eu/rapid/pressReleases Action.do?reference=IP/09/1552&format=HTML&aged=0&language=EN&guiLanguage =en> (last visited on 24 October 2009).

[308] Council Regulation (EC) No. 343/2003 of 18 February 2003 *OJ* L 50, 25 February 2003, pp. 1-10 establishing the criteria and mechanisms for determining the Member State responsible for examining an asylum application lodged in one of the Member States by a third-country national.

[309] Communication from the Commission to the European Parliament, the Council, the European Economic and Social Committee and the Committee of Regions, 'Policy Plan on Asylum, An Integrated Approach to Protection across the EU', 17 June 2008, COM(2008)360 final.

This aim is repeated in the Treaty of Lisbon in Article 78 Paragraph 2 TFEU-L:

'For the purposes of paragraph 1, the European Parliament and the Council, acting in accordance with the ordinary legislative procedure, shall adopt measures for a common European asylum system comprising:
(a) a uniform status of asylum for nationals of third countries, valid throughout the Union;
(b) a uniform status of subsidiary protection for nationals of third countries who, without obtaining European asylum, are in need of international protection;
(c) a common system of temporary protection for displaced persons in the event of a massive inflow;
(d) common procedures for the granting and withdrawing of uniform asylum or subsidiary protection status;
(e) criteria and mechanisms for determining which Member State is responsible for considering an application for asylum or subsidiary protection;
(f) standards concerning the conditions for the reception of applicants for asylum or subsidiary protection;
(g) partnership and cooperation with third countries for the purpose of managing inflows of people applying for asylum or subsidiary or temporary protection.'

This list, which continues from the minimum standards in the Treaty of Amsterdam, shows that different measures have to be taken in order to reach this Common European Asylum System:

'Vice-President Jacques Barrot, Commissioner responsible for Freedom, Security and Justice, stated: "Today, the Commission puts in place the final building blocks of the Common European Asylum System. Significant progress has been accomplished in recent years as a result of the implementation of common standards, but considerable disparities remain between Member States. Our proposals represent a major step forward towards achieving higher standards of protection, a more equal level playing field as well as higher efficiency and coherence for the system".'[310]

---

[310] A single and fairer asylum procedure for a uniform status in the EU: putting in place the final building blocks for international protection, <http://europa.eu/rapid/pressReleasesAction.do?reference=IP/09/1552&format=HTML&aged=0&language=EN&guiLanguage=en> (last visited on 24 October 2009).

Once achieved, the contents of the decisions on entry and residence will be laid down at the European level instead of the national level, which means that the responsibility of the protection of citizenship rights will also shift to the European level.

6.5   FAMILY MEMBERS

As discussed in the third chapter of this book, family members of migrating European citizens have the possibility to migrate together with this European citizen. The Persons Directive does not distinguish between family members who are EU nationals and those who are third-country nationals. All have been given the right to move along with the EU national. Yet, if this bond between the EU national and the family member is broken in some way, there may be limits on the options for the third country family member to stay in the host Member State. While the Treaties are silent on the subject, secondary legislation discusses the contents and scope of this derived right.

> 'The right of all Union citizens to move and reside freely within the territory of the Member States should, if it is to be exercised under objective conditions of freedom and dignity, be also granted to their family members, irrespective of nationality. For the purposes of this Directive, the definition of "family member" should also include the registered partner if the legislation of the host Member State treats registered partnership as equivalent to marriage.'[311]

It is therefore possible for these family members to shift from dependent citizenship rights to autonomous citizenship rights without for instance the right to vote because they are not nationals of one of the Member States.

Thus, where a citizen of the Union, established in a Member State and married to a national of a non-Member State without the right to remain in that Member State, moves to another Member State in order to work there as an employed person, the fact that that person's spouse has no right under Article 10 of Regulation No. 1612/68 to install himself with that person in the other Member State cannot constitute less favourable treatment than that which they enjoyed before the citizen made use of the opportunities afforded by the Treaty as regards movement of persons. Accordingly, the absence of

---

[311]   Recital 5 to Directive 2004/38/EC.

such a right is not such as to deter the citizen of the Union from exercising the rights in regard to freedom of movement conferred by Article 39 EC.

The same applies where a citizen of the Union married to a national of a non-Member State returns to the Member State of which he or she is a national in order to work there as an employed person. If the citizen's spouse has a valid right to remain in another Member State, Article 10 of Regulation No. 1612/68 applies so that the citizen of the Union is not deterred from exercising his or her right to freedom of movement on returning to the Member State of which he or she is a national. If, conversely, that citizen's spouse does not already have a valid right to remain in another Member State, the absence of any right of the spouse under Article 10 aforesaid to install himself or herself with the citizen of the Union does not have a dissuasive effect in that regard.

In the case of the Commission against Spain,[312] third-country spouses were refused entry to a Member State although they were married to the nationals of another Member State. The Court of Justice described the possibility of limitations to bringing spouses along:

The right of Member State nationals and their spouses to enter and remain on the territory of another Member State is not, however, unconditional. Among the limits laid down or authorised by Community law, Article 2 of Directive 64/221 enables Member States to preclude nationals of other Member States or their spouses who are nationals of third countries from entering their territory on grounds of public policy or public security (see, with respect to spouses, MRAX, Paras. 61 and 62).

Moreover, in the *Singh* case,[313] the Court of Justice specifically ruled against abuse of the possibilities to obtain citizenship rights by third-country nationals as described above:

'As regards the risk of fraud referred to by the United Kingdom, it is sufficient to note that, as the Court has consistently held (see in particular the judgments in Case 115/78 Knoors v Secretary of State for Economic Affairs [1979] *ECR* 399, paragraph 25, and Case C-61/89 Bouchoucha [1990] *ECR* I-3551, paragraph 14), the facilities created by the Treaty cannot have the effect of allowing the persons who benefit from them to evade the application of national legislation and of precluding Member States from taking the measures necessary to prevent such abuse.

---

[312] ECJ, Case C-503/03 *Commission* v. *Spain* [2006] *ECR* I-01097.
[313] ECJ, Case C-370/90 *Singh* [1992] *ECR* I-04265.

The answer to the question referred for a preliminary ruling must therefore be that Article 52 of the Treaty and Directive 73/148, properly construed, require a Member State to grant leave to enter and reside in its territory to the spouse, of whatever nationality, of a national of that State who has gone, with that spouse, to another Member State in order to work there as an employed person as envisaged by Article 48 of the Treaty and returns to establish himself or herself as envisaged by Article 52 of the Treaty in the territory of the State of which he or she is a national. The spouse must enjoy at least the same rights as would be granted to him or her under Community law if his or her spouse entered and resided in the territory of another Member State.'

In recapitulation, it needs to be noted that the award of citizenship and citizenship rights in the European Union is based upon nationality, while giving citizenship rights to nationals of the other Member States.[314] This excludes third-country nationals, who can only obtain limited citizenship rights, either by means of residence in a Member State awarded by that specific Member State or through a link with a national of a Member State who has used the possibilities of free movement.

More rights for the third-country family members are laid down in the so-called family reunification directive.[315] This directive aims at harmonizing the rules for family reunification but has met significant resistance from the Member States. The non-Schengen states Denmark, the UK and Ireland do not participate in it, for instance. For protection of the fundamental rights for minor citizens, the European Parliament has tried a case for annulment against the Council.[316] Although the ECJ decided that of course fundamental rights protection is applicable, the right to family life is not violated in this Directive.

6.6 Rights of Long-term Residents

For both family reunification and third-country workers, the citizenship right above only contain the right of entry and residence, apart from the general

---

[314] N. Reich, 'Union Citizenship – Metaphor or Source of Rights?', 7 *European Law Journal* (March 2001) pp. 4-23.

[315] Council Directive 2003/86/EC of 22 September 2003 *OJ* L 251, 3 October 2003, pp. 12-18 on the right to family reunification.

[316] ECJ, Case C-540/03 *Parliament* v. *Council* [2006] *ECR* I-05769.

fundamental right protection. In order to obtain the right of free movement, the third-country national needs to fall into the category of long-term residents, as is laid down in a specific Directive on the subject.[317] Until a third-country national falls under the requirements of this Directive, they had to ask for a separate permit for each Member State they want to reside in. This situation has changed with this Directive. Within the general boundaries set by the Persons Directive that there should not be a burden on the social benefit system of the host Member State, Member States have to recognise long-term resident status after five years' continuous legal residence. This option is not available for asylum seekers.

6.7   EVALUATION OF THE POSITION OF THIRD-COUNTRY NATIONALS

Overall, third-country nationals cannot obtain full citizenship rights, only a limited selection of them. Where some options give easier access to 'Fortress Europe', like family reunification, it is very difficult to receive the right of entry for other reasons because of the strong position the Member States have in this respect. For asylum seekers, many of their rights depend on international treaties. The cooperation between the Member States in this area is growing rapidly, shifting the emphasis from the Member States to the European level.

---

[317] Council Directive 2003/109/EC of 25 November 2003 *OJ* L 16, 23 January 2004, pp. 44-53 concerning the status of third-country nationals who are long-term residents.

Chapter 7

**LIMITATIONS BECAUSE OF THE FIGHT AGAINST
TERRORISM**

Chapter 7

LIMITATIONS BECAUSE OF THE FIGHT AGAINST TERRORISM

7.1   INTRODUCTION

Since a few years, European anti-terrorism measures cannot be left out of any discussion concerning citizens' rights in the European Union. Terrorism was, as a form of organized crime, part of the key areas of justice and home affairs, nowadays police and judicial cooperation in criminal law, in Article 29 TEU (part of Art. 67 TFEU-L). Thus, terrorism was, from an EU point of view, an element of European internal affairs. However, the main developments took place outside the EU: the first real EU measures against terrorism were taken immediately after the attacks of 11 September 2001 in the form of an action plan in the fight against terrorism.[318] Only a few measures date from before this time, from early 2000, in order to implement United Nations sanctions against the Taliban regime in Afghanistan.[319] The EU measures taken since the end of 2001 can roughly be divided into two categories: measures which are a follow-up of international obligations like the implementation of Security Council resolutions, and 'independent' EU measures. Both categories have influence on citizens' rights, mostly in a negative sense. Issues of judicial protection, privacy and human rights protection have risen in cases before the CFI and ECJ on several of these anti-terrorism measures.

---

[318] Conclusions et plan d'action du Conseil Européen extraordinaire du 21 Septembre 2001, <www.consilium.europa.eu/ueDocs/cms_Data/docs/pressData/fr/ec/ACF3B0F.pdf> (last visited on 25 March 2008).

[319] Council Regulation (EC) No. 337/2000 of 14 February 2000 *OJ* L 43, 16 February 2000, pp. 1-11 concerning a flight ban and a freeze of funds and other financial resources in respect of the Taliban of Afghanistan.

F. Goudappel, The Effects of EU Citizenship
© *2010, T·M·C·ASSER PRESS, The Hague, The Netherlands and the Author*

Since '9/11', the European Union has thus been very active in the fight against terrorism, taking many measures which have seriously affected actions by the Member States. These measures range from very broad and general framework directives entitled 'Combating terrorism'[320] to very specific Commission communications on financing terrorism and the non-profit sector.[321] Other measures were already in the process of being adopted in 2001. This has led to a 'Plan of action for the fight against terrorism',[322] leading to a system to combat terrorism by means of 'prevention, preparedness and response'.[323]

In addition, the ECJ has been very active in deciding cases concerning the list of persons, groups or entities involved in terrorist acts.[324] Many of these EU measures have severely influenced the position and rights of citizens through amendments to the criminal law systems of the Member States and adjoining measures such as the European Arrest Warrant.[325] The citizens have been affected in their fundamental rights because of the EU measures as well. The European Union anti-terrorism measures stem from a combination of international obligations (most prominently United Nations Security Council Resolutions) and original European Union measures.

7.1.1 Two examples

Two examples of situations which show the problems on citizens' rights in this respect concern Mr Sison and Mr Othman. Their cases can be summarized as follows.

---

[320] Council Framework Decision of 13 June 2002 *OJ* L 155, 14 June 2002, pp. 60-62 on combating terrorism.

[321] Commission Communication to the Council, the European Parliament and the European Economic and Social Committee of 28 November 2005 – The prevention of and fight against terrorism financing through enhanced national level coordination and greater transparency of the non-profit sector (final).

[322] Conclusions and a Plan of Action of the Extraordinary European Council Meeting on 21 September 2001, <> (last visited on 12 June 2007).

[323] Communication from the Commission to the Council and the European Parliament of 20 October 2004 Prevention, preparedness and response to terrorist attacks (COM(2004)698 final).

[324] There are a number of cases decided and still pending, which will be discussed in this book further on.

[325] Council Framework Decision 2002/584/JHA of 13 June 2002 *OJ* L 190, 18 July 2002, pp. 1-20 on the European arrest warrant and the surrender procedures between Member States, to be discussed further on in this book.

On 29 August 2007, José Maria Sison was arrested in the Netherlands on suspicion of murder: he allegedly ordered by telephone two murders on the Philippines in 2003 and 2004.[326] Soon afterwards, he was set free because of lack of evidence.[327] An asylum seeker[328] from the Philippines in the Netherlands for over twenty years, Mr Sison was already placed on the United Nations blacklist in 2002 for financing of terrorist activities.[329] Because of his inclusion in this assets freezing list, his social allowance was stopped along with his health insurance.[330] The Netherlands thus faithfully applied the prescribed financial sanctions without changing his long-standing refugee status. In fact, from the decision by the ECJ in his case can be learned that the only criminal actions brought against him at that time were recently initiated by the Philippine authorities.[331] In the ECJ decision, the profile of a hardcore terrorist is given, while Mr Sison's image in the Dutch press has that of a revolutionary and activist.[332] The ECJ ruled that the breach of his 'rights of defense is sufficiently serious for the Community to incur liability'.[333] The legal developments have not ended here; a new case was decided by the Court of First Instance (CFI) by Mr Sison in a conflict with the Council on the costs of Mr Sison to be paid by the Council for the proceedings.[334] Moreover, only on 30 September 2009, the CFI decided that Mr Sison has to be removed from the blacklist.[335]

---

[326] 'Filippijn Sison vast voor moord', *NRC Handelsblad*, 29 August 2007.

[327] 'Dutch Public Prosecutors Notice on Sison Case', <www.scribd.com/doc/13824809/Dutch-Public-Prosecutors-notice-on-Sison-case> (last visited on 9 July 2009).

[328] He was not accepted as a refugee but allowed to stay due to probable prosecution in the Philippines.

[329] See both J. Fermon, M. Beys et al., 'The Case of Prof. José Maria Sison: Dissent Labeled as "Terrorism" by the EU', 62 *Guild Prac.* 240 (2005) pp. 230-239, and J. Meijnen, 'Vanaf nu bent u "terrorist"', *NRC Handelsblad*, 1 February 2007, for a description of the situation from Mr Sison's point of view.

[330] Fermon, Beys et al., op. cit., note 329.

[331] ECJ, Case T-47/03 *Sison* v. *Council* [2007] *ECR* II-00073.

[332] J. Meijnen, 'Tot het tegendeel je bewijst', *NRC Handelsblad*, 11 July 2007; J. Fermon, 'Filipijns professor Sison totaal willekeurig op terroristenlijst gezet', <www.stopusa.be/scripts/texte.php?section=CMBA&langue=2&id=24548&PHPSESSID=361bfa01951b8da4c941112385a446f8> (last visited on 9 July 2009).

[333] *Sison* case, *supra* note 331.

[334] ECJ Order, Case T-47/03 DEP *Sison* v. *Council* [2009] *ECR* 00000.

[335] ECJ, Case T-341/07 *Sison* v. *Council II* [2009] *ECR* 00000.

A second example concerns the case of Omar Mohammed Othman. As the CFI sums up in its decision in this case,[336] his situation has developed as follows:

'46. Mr Othman is a Jordanian citizen who has lived since 1993 in the United Kingdom, where he was granted temporary political asylum in 1994. His application for indefinite leave to remain was still under consideration when the present action was brought. He has a dependent wife and five dependent children.
47. In February 2001, the applicant was arrested and held for questioning in an investigation under the Prevention of Terrorism (Temporary Provisions) Act 1989. During a search of his home, the police found and seized a substantial amount of money in cash in a number of different currencies (pounds sterling, German marks, Spanish pesetas and US dollars), the exchange value of which came to about GBP 180 000. The applicant gave no explanation of the origin of those funds. The applicant's two bank accounts, which had a credit balance of approximately GBP 1 900, were furthermore frozen in implementation of measures determined by the Sanctions Committee.
48. It is also apparent from the documents before the Court that, in December 2001, the applicant went into hiding from fear of arrest and indefinite detention under the Anti-Terrorism, Crime and Security Act 2001, which was about to be adopted by the United Kingdom Parliament. He was arrested by the police and held in Belmarsh Prison (United Kingdom) from 23 October 2002 to 13 March 2005, when he was released, under strict surveillance, following a judgment of the House of Lords holding that the United Kingdom scheme of "detention without trial", to which he was subject, was unlawful. The applicant was once more arrested on 11 August 2005 and held in Long Lartin Prison (United Kingdom), under the new anti-terrorist measures adopted by the United Kingdom Government. That government's decision to deport the applicant to Jordan and to hold him pending deportation, which was served on the applicant on 11 August 2005, has been the subject of an unsuccessful appeal before the competent national courts. That government has, nevertheless, agreed not to give effect to that decision pending the outcome of the action brought by the applicant before the European Court of Human Rights. In the meantime, the applicant was released on bail on 17 June 2008. Bail was revoked on 2 December 2008 by the Special Immigration Appeals Commission. The applicant has since then remained in detention.'

As is clear from this situation, the opinions on interpretation of anti-terrorism rules may differ at the national, European, and international level. This

---

[336] ECJ, Case T-318/01 *Othman* v. *Council and Commission* [2009] *ECR* 00000.

includes the ECHR, where a case is pending as well.[337] Different legal paths are followed concerning different fundamental rights, for instance, while the relevant legislation is being adapted at the national and European level. Different fundamental rights are being tested at different courts at different levels, all of which are ECHR fundamental rights. Ultimately, this may lead to different interpretations of the same provision in the same case. Moreover, in his British case, Othman invokes rights in a foreign case, something which has not been done before. In fact, he asks the House of Lords to protect his rights which may be under threat in another, foreign, case:

'He contends that if he is deported he will face a real risk of torture or inhuman or degrading treatment contrary to article 3 of the Convention, a real risk of a flagrant breach of his right to liberty under article 5 of the Convention and a real risk of a flagrant breach of his right to a fair trial under article 6 of the Convention, so that his deportation will infringe those three Convention rights.'[338]

It almost seems as if Mr Othman asks for a kind of subsidiary protection as it exists under the 1951 Convention relating to the Status of Refugees, as European Union law gives to refugees.[339] However, for this particular right, such a protection has not been laid down. The cases of Mr Sison and Mr Othman show the wide spectrum of problems with EU measures against terrorism.

---

[337] ECHR grants request for interim measures by Omar Othman (Abu Qatada), European Court of Human Rights, Press release issued by the Registrar, 19 February 2009, <http:// cmiskp.echr.coe.int/tkp197/view.asp?action=html&documentId=847512&portal=hbkm &source=externalbydocnumber&table=F69A27FD8FB86142BF01C1166DEA398649> (last visited on 21 September 2009).

[338] Wednesday 18 February 2009, House of Lords, Opinions of the Lords of Appeal for Judgment in the cause *RB (Algeria) (FC) and another (Appellants)* v. *Secretary of State for the Home Department (Respondent), OO (Jordan) (Original Respondent and Cross-appellant)* v. *Secretary of State for the Home Department (Original Appellant and Cross-respondent)* [2009] UKHL 10.

[339] Council Directive 2004/83/EC of 29 April 2004 *OJ* L 304, 30 September 2004, pp. 12-23 on minimum standards for the qualification and status of third-country nationals or stateless persons as refugees or as persons who otherwise need international protection and the content of the protection granted.

7.2   OVERVIEW OF EU MEASURES IN THE FIGHT AGAINST
TERRORISM

Since '9/11', the European Union has been very active in the fight against
terrorism, taking many measures which have seriously affected actions by
the Member States. These measures range from very broad and general framework directives entitled 'Combating terrorism'[340] to very specific Commission communications on financing terrorism and the non-profit sector.[341] In
fact, several measures date from before this time, from 1999, in order to
implement United Nations sanctions against the Taliban regime in Afghanistan.[342] In addition, the Court of Justice of the European Communities has
been very active in deciding cases concerning the list of persons, groups or
entities involved in terrorist acts.[343] Many of these EU measures have severely influenced the position and rights of citizens through amendments to
the criminal law systems of the Member States and adjoining measures such
as the European Arrest Warrant.[344] The citizens have been affected in their
fundamental rights because of the EU measures as well. The European Union
anti-terrorism measures stem from a combination of international obligations (most prominently United Nations Security Council Resolutions) and
original European Union measures, some already existing in 2001, others
already in the process of being adopted in 2001. This has led to a 'Plan of
action for the fight against terrorism' in 2001,[345] which in itself led up to a

---

[340] Council Framework Decision of 13 June 2002 *OJ* L 164, 22 June 2002, pp. 2-7 on
combating terrorism.

[341] Commission Communication to the Council, the European Parliament and the European Economic and Social Committee of 28 November 2005 – The prevention of and fight
against terrorism financing through enhanced national level coordination and greater transparency of the non-profit sector (final).

[342] Most recent the Common Position 2002/402/CFSP *OJ* L 139, 29 May 2002, pp. 4-5
concerning restrictive measures against Usama bin Laden, members of the Al-Qaeda
organisation and the Taliban and other individuals, groups, undertakings and entities associated with them and repealing Common Positions 96/746/CFSP, 1999/727/CFSP, 2001/154/
CFSP and 2001/771/CFSP, 27 May 2002.

[343] There are a number of cases decided and still pending, several of which will be discussed in this book further on.

[344] Council Framework Decision 2002/584/JHA of 13 June 2002 *OJ* L 190, 18 July 2002,
pp. 1-20 on the European arrest warrant and the surrender procedures between Member States,
to be discussed further on in this book.

[345] Conclusions and a Plan of Action of the Extraordinary European Council Meeting on
21 September 2001, <http://ue.eu.int/ueDocs/cms_Data/docs/pressData/en/ec/140.en.pdf> (last
visited on 12 June 2007).

system to combat terrorism by means of 'prevention, preparedness and response'.[346]

The fight against terrorism and its urgency have a backdrop of potential problems with traditional citizens' rights. As Judge Luzius Wildhaber, President of the ECHR, has expressed it:

> 'The second way in which terrorism challenges democracy and human rights law is by inciting States to take repressive measures, thereby insidiously undermining the foundations of democratic society. Our response to terrorism has accordingly to strike a balance between the need to take protective measures and the need to preserve those rights and freedoms without which there is no democracy.'[347]

This concerns not only fundamental rights, but also – from the European Union point of view – other rights that EU citizens have been given in the EU Treaty and the EC Treaty.

The ways in which the position of the citizen has been affected by the European Union involvement in the fight against terrorism will be the focal point of this article. By comparing and analyzing different levels of legislation involved (the United Nations level for the underlying Security Council resolutions, the European Union level, and the national level), the effects for the citizen can be evaluated. From the national level, examples will be taken from two contrasting legal systems in this matter: the Netherlands and the UK, as was already illustrated by the two cases sketched above. For the Netherlands, the European measures and obligations have meant a radical change in the system since not even a definition of a 'terrorist act' existed in legislation. The UK, on the other hand, had had previous experience with anti-terrorism measures and therefore already had relevant national legislation. The effects on position of the citizen in these – in final form – national measures take the form of fundamental rights, including judicial protection. From the European Union point of view, these originate both from the European Convention on Human Rights (hereafter: ECHR) and from the 'consti-

---

[346] Communication from the Commission to the Council and the European Parliament of 20 October 2004 Prevention, preparedness and response to terrorist attacks (COM(2004)698 final).

[347] L. Wildhaber, 'Balancing Necessity and Human Rights in Response in Terrorism', <www.coe.int/T/E/Com/Files/Ministerial-Conferences/2002-judicial/Disc_Wildhaber.asp> (last visited on 18 June 2007).

tutional traditions common to the Member States' as it is formulated in the present Article 6 Paragraph 2 TEU (Art. 6 TEU-L) and nowadays also originate from the EU Charter on Fundamental Rights. The European Union anti-terrorism measures and their effects in the national legal systems of Member States will thus be evaluated against the background of these fundamental rights.

7.2.1   Elements of anti-terrorism in EU legislation

As the introductory description above shows, there are many layers in the analysis of EU anti-terrorism measures. Not only can the layers of United Nations, European Union and the Member States be distinguished, the contents contain different important elements as well. First, there is the important question which rights are at stake and who has brought them in jeopardy. Second, the issue plays a part that the present-day structure of the European Union complicates it for the EU to take any actions against terrorism. Finally, the historical background of the Member States with respect to terrorism leads to different views and approaches. In a marble cake effect, these layers are all intertwined, which means that the position of the citizen in all these elements can only be discussed as part of an intricate system of anti-terrorism elements.

After the terrorist attacks on the United States on 11 September 2001, the European Union and many individual Member States were among the first to show their support to the United States, although with some hesitation.[348] A co-operation between the United States and the European Union resulted from this initial support. Part of this co-operation found its way into the Security Council Resolutions on the basis of which specific European Union measures have been taken.[349] In addition, the Council of the European Union

---

[348] M. den Boer and J. Monar, Keynote article: '11 September and the Challenge of Global Terrorism and the EU as a Security Actor' (Annual Review), 40 *JMCS* (2002) pp. 11-12. Also: Conclusions and a Plan of Action of the Extraordinary European Council Meeting on 21 September 2001, <http://ue.eu.int/ueDocs/cms_Data/docs/pressData/en/ec/140.en.pdf> (last visited on 12 June 2007).

[349] Most prominent among these UN Security Council Resolutions are: Security Council Resolution 1373 (2001) on Threats to international peace and security caused by terrorist acts, Security Council Resolution 1377 (2001) on Threats to international peace and security caused by terrorist acts, Security Council Resolution 1373 (2001) on Threats to international peace and security caused by terrorist acts.

has taken their own measures like the common definition of a terrorist act as well as improved and used existing measures and instruments like Eurojust and Europol.[350] Yet, all these measures frequently lead to a potential clash between anti-terrorism measures and human rights or citizen's rights, as has been noted by different authors[351] and by the European Union institutions in their decision-making process.[352]

7.2.2 Pillar structure and anti-terrorism measures

Important for the European Union point of view is the embedding of the fight against terrorism in the Treaty system. Yet, the legal basis of the anti-terrorism measures is not clear-cut in European Union law: the second (Common Foreign and Security Policy) and the third pillar (Police and Judicial Co-operation in Criminal Matters) both play a role, while the first pillar (containing the EC Treaty) has been used as a legal basis in specific instances (like the freezing of bank accounts)[353] as well. Terrorism as such is only mentioned once in the Treaties: in the non-exhaustive list of matters falling under the third pillar in Article 29 TEU (part of Art. 61 TFEU-L). The reason behind this is that, before 9/11, terrorism was mostly considered to be an internal matter from the European Union point of view, not so much an external matter of foreign relations.[354] Yet, this system had to be revised from September 2001 onwards because the terrorism threat came from outside the European Union with internal effects.[355]

---

[350] Council of the European Union (Justice and Home Affairs), 20 September 2001, 12156/01.

[351] For instance: T. Eicke, 'Terrorism and Human Rights', 5 *European Journal of Migration and Law* (2003) pp. 449-467; J. Hedigan, 'The European Convention on Human Rights and Counter-Terrrorism', 28 *Fordham International Law Journal* (2005) pp. 392-431; J. Wouters and F. Naert, 'The European Union and "September 11"', 13 *Ind. Int'l & Comp. L. Rev.* (2003) p. 765.

[352] See for instance Art. 1.2 of the Council Framework Decision 2002/475/JHA of 13 June 2002 *OJ* L 190, 18 July 2002, pp. 1-20 on combating terrorism.

[353] See the Council Regulation (EC) No. 2580/2001 of 27 December 2001 *OJ* L 344, 28 December 2001, pp. 70-75 on specific restrictive measures directed against certain persons and entities with a view to combating terrorism.

[354] J. Wouters and F. Naert, 'The European Union and "September 11"', 13 *Ind. Int'l & Comp. L. Rev.* (2003) pp. 723-724.

[355] M. Anderson and J. Apap, 'Changing Conceptions of Security and their Implications for EU Justice and Home Affairs Cooperation', CEPS Policy Brief No. 26/October 2002, <http://shop.ceps.eu/BookDetail.php?item_id=127> (last visited on 19 June 2007).

The question how to base anti-terrorism measures with an external dimension had to be solved for all European legislation involved. As is clear from the legislation and the cases before the ECJ on these matters, a combination of legal bases is often needed, not only to cover the subject correctly but also to be able to have the most effective instrument available. The choice of legal basis, however, can only rest on 'objective factors which are amenable to judicial review, including in particular the aim and the content of the measure' as the ECJ has decided in the *Titanium dioxide* case.[356] even if it means that criminal law measures would fall under the first pillar in a case in which environmental protection is the main aim of the legislation.[357]

If one looks at the legislation implementing the most important United Nations Security Council Resolutions, it needs to be noted that the legal basis in European Union law differs per measure: from a combination of Articles. 60, 301 and 308 EC[358] to one of Articles 15 and 34 TEU,[359] both combinations used for implementing part of Security Council Resolution 1373. In strict a strict application of the rule of the *Titanium dioxide* case, the subjects of Resolution 1373 have been split in order to allow financial measures and more general measures to be taken under both the first and the third pillar. The combinations of legal bases have, however, already been subject to ECJ case-law. This has already been labeled as 'problematic'.[360] The CFI has ruled that the combination of Articles 60, 301 and 308 EC is allowed,[361] but parties lodged for appeal with the ECJ itself against this.[362]

---

[356] ECJ, Case C-300/89 *Titanium dioxide* [1991] *ECR* I-02867.

[357] ECJ, Case C-176/03 *Commission* v. *Council* [2005] *ECR* I-07879.

[358] Council Regulation (EC) No. 2580/2001 of 27 December 2001 *OJ* L 344, 28 December 2001, pp. 70-75 on specific restrictive measures directed against certain persons and entities with a view to combating terrorism.

[359] Council Common Position of 27 December 2001 *OJ* L 344, 28 December 2001, pp. 90-92 on combating terrorism.

[360] A. Johnston, 'Frozen in Time? The ECJ Finally Rules on the Kadi Appeal', 68 *The Cambridge Law Journal* (March 2009) p. 2.

[361] ECJ, Case T-306/01 *Yusuf & Al Bakaraat* v. *Council & Commission* [2005] *ECR* II-03533.

[362] ECJ, Case C-415/05 P *Yusuf & Al Bakaraat* v. *Council & Commission* Appeal brought on 23 November 2005 by Ahmed Yusuf and Al Barakaat International Foundation against the judgment of the Court of First Instance (Second Chamber (Extended Composition)) of 21 September 2005 in Case T- 306/01 *Ahmed Yusuf and Al Barakaat International Foundation* v. the *Council of the European Union and Commission of the European Communities* (Case C-415/05 P).

The follow-up case only concerned Kadi and Al-Barakaat,[363] because Mr Yusuf was taken off the Security Council blacklist after the USA decided to support the Swedish view that Yusuf was only a bank employee of Al Barakaat bank.[364] In the *Kadi* appeal case, the ECJ decided that the wording of Article 308 TEC is crucial for the legal basis, and can only be seen in combination with the Articles 60 and 308 EC for this particular purpose. This line of reasoning has been often criticized,[365] and the argumentation of A-G Maduro is usually preferred, who states that:

'Moreover, the Court of First Instance's restrictive reading of Article 301 EC deprives this provision of much of its practical use. Within the framework of the CFSP, the Union may decide, for reasons relating to the maintenance of international peace and security, to impose economic and financial sanctions against non-State actors who are situated in third countries. I fail to see why Article 301 EC should be interpreted more narrowly. As the Court of First Instance itself recognised, "the Union and its Community pillar are not to be prevented from adapting to [threats to international peace and security] by imposing economic and financial sanctions not only on third countries, but also on associated persons, groups, undertakings or entities engaged in international terrorist activity or in any other way constituting a threat to international peace and security".'[366]

In the Lisbon Treaty, it is tried to solve this problem by creating a very specific provision in the midst of very general provisions in the Area of Freedom, Security and Justice:

'Where necessary to achieve the objectives set out in Article 67, as regards preventing and combating terrorism and related activities, the European Parliament and the Council, acting by means of regulations in accordance with the ordinary legislative procedure, shall define a framework for administrative measures with regard to capital movements and payments, such as the freezing of funds, finan-

---

[363] ECJ, Joined Cases C-402/05 P and C-415/05 P *Kadi & Barakaat* [2008] *ECR* I-06351.

[364] 'US Removes Swede from Terror List', *The Local*, 17 August 2006.

[365] For instance, Johnston, op. cit., note 360, pp. 2-3; or M. Bulterman, 'Fundamental Rights and the United Nations Financial Sanction Regime: The Kadi and Yusuf Judgments of the Court of First Instance of the European Communities', 19 *Leiden Journal of International Law* (2006) p. 763.

[366] Opinion of A-G Poiares Maduro delivered on 16 January 2008 in ECJ, C-402/05 P *Kadi* v. *Council & Commission* [2008] *ECR* I-06351.

cial assets or economic gains belonging to, or owned or held by, natural or legal persons, groups or non-State entities.'[367]

In this way, a practical, yet not very elegant solution is offered for a problem which is both the result of the then partially abolished pillar structure and relatively small role of anti-terrorism measures within the present European Union system.

The system of finding a legal basis for European Union anti-terrorism measures and its national implementation legislation has led to a series of cases before the ECJ because the legal basis under the pillar structure affects citizens' rights, most prominently the right of access to justice. In the appeal case of Gestoras Pro Amnistía,[368] for instance, the Court of Justice ruled that it has some form of jurisdiction concerning common positions taken under Article 34 TEU: although Article 35(1) TEU only directly gives the possibility for preliminary rulings on matters concerning framework decisions and decisions under Article 34 TEU, when a measure under Article 34 TEU is intended to have legal effects in relation to third parties, preliminary questions concerning the lawfulness of such acts should be indirectly possible (as well as similar actions brought by a Member State or the Commission under Art. 35(6) TEU).[369] In the opinion of the Court of Justice, this means that legal remedies are possible. However, the question remains how an organization like Gestoras Pro Amnistía – which is based in Spain and does apparently not have a conflict with the Spanish government – could force such a case to come into being. Should they start a case against the Spanish government for not voting against the relevant common position since it was a unanimously adopted measure? In any case, Article 34 TEU prescribes unanimity in adoption of such common positions, which would make the suggestion of the Court of Justice impossible that a Member State would bring a case against this common position.

7.2.3   The European Union and the United Nations

The issue is more complex than only differences in implementation of European measures at the Member State level. In many instances, there is a prior

---

[367] Art. 75 TFEU.

[368] ECJ, Case C-354/04 P *Gestoras Pro Amnistia a.o.* v. *the Council of the European Union* [2007] *ECR* I-01579.

[369] Ibid., Paras. 53-55.

international obligation via decisions of the Security Council of the United Nations. The involvement of the European Union in the United Nations combat against terrorism has a twofold basis: the co-operation between the Member States on United Nations Matters as laid down in Article 11 TEU (Art. 24 TEU-L) as well as Article 19 Paragraph 2 TEU (Art. 34 TEU-L) for the position of Member States in the Security Council, and the co-operation in the field of criminal law against terrorism, as laid down in Article 29 TEU (part of Art. 61 TFEU-L). This shows that the basis of the implementation measures is not clear-cut in European Union law: the second (Common Foreign and Security Policy) and the third pillar (Police and Judicial Co-operation in Criminal Matters) both play a role but cannot independently do so because no clear legal basis was created which contained a combination of the transatlantic and international co-operation of the European Union and the fight against terrorism with both elements laid down in different pillars with different legal instruments.

This means that the legal basis for the EU implementation legislation of Security Council Resolutions differs per specific measure to be taken. The starting-point was the pre-2001 fight against the Taliban and Al Qaida in Afghanistan.[370] The relevant Security Council Resolutions were implemented through Council Common Positions based on Article 15 TEU (Art. 29 TEU-L).[371] This general legal basis was chosen because of the role of a common position and its possible follow-up measures:

'Common positions shall define the approach of the Union to a particular matter of a geographical or thematic nature. Member States shall ensure that their national policies conform to the common positions.'[372]

A common position is therefore necessary to create follow-up measures which have a more specific nature. The Council already considers the possibility of

---

[370] See Security Council Resolution 1267 (1999) on the situation in Afghanistan and Security Council Resolution 1333 (2000) on the situation in Afghanistan.

[371] The final Common Position replacing all foregoing ones on this matter is the Council Common Position of 27 May 2002 *OJ* L 139, 29 May 2002, pp. 4-5 concerning restrictive measures against Usama bin Laden, members of the Al-Qaida organization and the Taliban and other individuals, groups, undertakings and entities associated with them and repealing Common Positions 96/746/CFSP, 1999/727/CFSP, 2001/154/CFSP and 2001/771/CFSP (2002/402/CFSP).

[372] Text of Art. 15 TEU.

follow-up measures under the first pillar in the Common Position itself.[373] A comparative study of the different, more specific, European Union measures shows that the legal basis chosen is often a mixed one. For example, as has already been discussed above, a combination of the Articles 60, 301 and 308 EC for the freezing of bank accounts,[374] Article 47(2), first and third sentences EC, together with Article 95 EC for measures against money laundering,[375] or Article 62(2)(a) EC to include biometrical features in passports.[376]

It needs to be noted that this refers to only a limited part of the EU anti-terrorism measures, several others have been taken independently from the UN obligations. Yet, the Security Council related measures were among the first to be taken by the European Union, which means that they have been very influential. It also means that it has proven more difficult to adapt blacklists which originate from the Security Council and original EU blacklists, or at least make it more difficult for citizens to get off the Security Council blacklists. Because all Member States are bound by United Nations decisions, the case-law of the CFI and of the ECJ show that this has made it very difficult to apply the tests that they simultaneously developed for the independent EU blacklists. The first case on this matter, the famous *Yusuf* decision by the ECJ,[377] shows this difficulty:

> 'From the standpoint of international law, the obligations of the Member States of the United Nations under the Charter of the United Nations clearly prevail over every other obligation of domestic law or of international treaty law including, for those of them that are members of the Council of Europe, their obligations under the ECHR and, for those that are also members of the Community, their obligations under the EC Treaty.'

---

[373] Para. 9 of the Council deliberations to Common Position 2002/402/CFSP.

[374] Council Regulation (EC) No. 2580/2001 of 27 December 2001 *OJ* L 344, 28 December 2001, pp. 70-75 on specific restrictive measures directed against certain persons and entities with a view to combating terrorism.

[375] Directive 2005/60/EC of the European Parliament and of the Council of 26 October 2005, *OJ* L 309, 25 November 2005, pp. 15-36 on the prevention of the use of the financial system for the purpose of money laundering and terrorist financing.

[376] Council Regulation (EC) No. 2252/2004 of 13 December 2004 *OJ* L 385, 29 December 2004, pp. 1-6 on standards for security features and biometrics in passports and travel documents issued by Member States.

[377] *Yusuf & Al Bakaraat* v. *Council & Commission*, op. cit., note 361.

7.2.4   Independent European Union measures against terrorism

In the course of the actions taken combating terrorism, the European Union took several measures which were not only aimed at this goal but also on combating other forms of cross-border crime.[378] Prime examples are the European Arrest Warrant,[379] and the not-yet adopted European Evidence Warrant,[380] and even Eurojust was indicated as being an important tool.[381] A good example of a broad influence of a principally anti-terrorism measure is the European Arrest Warrant.[382] A proposal which had been discussed before but not yet adopted, it was quickly adopted after '9/11' in 2001 because terrorism is one of the crimes listed for a fast surrender option between the Member States rather than the traditional extradition option between states in case an extradition treaty exists. Terrorism is only one among a list of 32 crimes[383] for which this surrender system is applicable, along with

> 'acts punishable by the law of the issuing Member State by a custodial sentence or a detention order for a maximum period of at least 12 months or, where a sentence has been passed or a detention order has been made, for sentences of at least four months'.[384]

Thus, the scope of this anti-terrorism measure is much wider within criminal law because the system of surrender only involves a marginal check, not one on contents. In the case of *Advocaten voor de Wereld*,[385] this aspect was discussed by the ECJ from the point of view of protecting citizens' rights:

---

[378] K. Lane Schleppele, 'Other People's Patriot Acts: Europe's Response to September 11', 50 *Loy. L. Rev.* 92 (2004) pp. 93-95.

[379] Council Framework Decision 2002/584/JHA of 13 June 2002 *OJ* L 190, 18 July 2002, pp. 1-20 on the European arrest warrant and the surrender procedures between Member States.

[380] Proposal for a Council framework decision on the European Evidence Warrant for obtaining objects, documents and data for use in proceedings in criminal matters, 14 November 2003, COM(2003)688 final.

[381] Council Decision of 28 February 2002 *OJ* L 63, 6 March 2002, pp. 1-13 setting up Eurojust with a view to reinforcing the fight against serious crime.

[382] Council Framework Decision 2002/584/JHA of 13 June 2002 *OJ* L 190, 18 July 2002, pp. 1-20 on the European arrest warrant and the surrender procedures between Member States.

[383] Art. 2 Para. 2 of the framework decision.

[384] Art. 2 Para. 1 of the framework decision.

[385] ECJ, Case C-303/05 *Advocaten voor de Wereld VZW* v. *Leden of de Ministerraad* [2007] *ECR* I-03633.

'Consequently, even if one were to assume that the situation of persons suspected of having committed offences featuring on the list set out in Article 2(2) of the Framework Decision or convicted of having committed such offences is comparable to the situation of persons suspected of having committed, or convicted of having committed, offences other than those listed in that provision, the distinction is, in any event, objectively justified.'

For terrorism cases, the European Arrest Warrant is not used very often. An important example was the surrender of a suspect of the London bombings by Italy. Yet, the difference between extradition and surrender can be apparent when an extradition request from a third country is compared to a European Arrest Warrant. In the case of Mr Othman, as described in the introduction above, the scrutiny of the Jordanese extradition request in the UK case shows that the protection of citizens' rights and fundamental rights is an important part of the case, which could not have been the case with a European Arrest Warrant. Moreover, the procedure itself opened the way to the ECHR because it is a national procedure which cannot happen for a European Arrest Warrant in the same manner. It is notable, by the way, that in many European anti-terrorism cases, no extradition or surrender procedure is part of the situation, and that often no criminal procedures have been started against persons on blacklists.

The question is whether the independent measures reach further than necessary to prevent terrorism because most of them were specifically mentioned in the Conclusions of the Council of the European Union in September 2001 and thus before the Security Council Resolutions were adopted.[386] The most important comprehensive measure taken so far has been the 2002 framework decision on combating terrorism.[387] This concentrates on definitions, minimum standards and co-operation, and has been evaluated by the Commission in 2004[388] and 2007.[389] In it, it is shown that many Member States have problems implementing all provisions of the framework decision. The

---

[386] Council of the European Union (Justice and Home Affairs), 20 September 2001, 12156/01.

[387] Council Framework Decision 2002/475/JHA of 13 June 2002 *OJ* L 164, 22 June 2002, pp. 3-7 on combating terrorism.

[388] Report from the Commission based on Art. 11 of the Council Framework Decision of 13 June 2002 on combating terrorism, 08 June 2004 COM(2004)409 final.

[389] Report from the Commission based on Art. 11 of the Council Framework Decision of 13 June 2002 on combating terrorism, 6 November 2007 COM(2007)681.

Netherlands, for instance, has apparently fulfilled the obligations while others have only partially done so. Based on this report, an amended framework decision has been proposed,[390] in which new offenses are proposed to be part of the system.

On top, the European Union has added persons and entities to the UN blacklists who are not on the UN list. Thus, the conflict between those on the list and the European Union is a direct one without United Nations involvement which means that the European institutions can be held directly responsible for the listing and de-listing of these persons and entities. It has given rise to a series of cases on de-listings in which it was easier for the ECJ to decide. The most important ones are the *OMPI* case[391] and the *Sison* case described above. In these cases, the ECJ did not only decide on the admissibility of the claims but also on grounds for de-listing.

At present, the EU fight against terrorism is planned to continue as a matter independent of UN measures. In 2007, a package of measures was proposed by the Commission,[392] which includes passenger name records (PNR), practical actions, and measures against those who support terrorism. This package follows directly from the Hague Programme and the accompanying Action Plan,[393] in which as an aim of anti-terrorism measures was formulated that:

> 'The European Council underlines that effective prevention and combating of terrorism in full compliance with fundamental rights requires Member States not to confine their activities to maintaining their own security, but to focus also on the security of the Union as a whole.'

In addition, this Hague Programme will be followed by a new Stockholm Programme, for which at the moment of writing proposals have already been

---

[390] Proposal for a Council Framework Decision of 6 November 2007 amending Framework Decision 2002/475/JHA on combating terrorism (COM(2007)650 final).

[391] ECJ, Case T-228/02 *Organisation des Modjahedines du peuple d'Iran* v. *Council* [2006] *ECR* II-04665.

[392] European Commission, 6 November 2007.

[393] The Hague Programme: strengthening freedom, security and justice in the European Union, European Council of 5 November 2004, and European Commission, Action Plan for Freedom, Justice and Security, 10 May 2005.

published.[394] Under this programme, a core of common standards in the fight against terrorism should be developed.

7.3   ACCESS TO JUSTICE

One aspect of citizens' rights needs to be discussed in more detail: access to justice. In different ways, access to justice has been the subject of discussion when it concerns measures against terrorism by the European Union. It first needs to be pointed out that the different legal bases for the European Union measures as described above lead to differences in access to justice. The most comprehensive access to justice is of course available for first pillar measures like the freezing of bank accounts[395] where the ECJ has the most comprehensive powers. However, under the third pillar, the jurisdiction of the ECJ is limited[396] while it has no jurisdiction at all under the second pillar. The position of the European Parliament as a democratic control institution resembles the position of the ECJ: under the first pillar, the competences of the European Parliament in the decision-making procedure can lead to extensive influence on the contents of measures, while the European Parliament has only an advisory role under the third pillar[397] and is not mentioned as such in the second pillar.[398]

Access to justice was also at the forefront in several cases concerning the Security Council blacklists as decided by the Court of Justice of the European Communities. As described above, the case of Gestoras Pro Amnistía[399] is a good example of a case in which the Court of Justice discussed access to justice for third parties affected by third-pillar measures. Interestingly, the Court of Justice suggests that it is against a narrow interpretation of its pow-

---

[394] Communication from the Commission to the European Parliament and the Council; an area of freedom, security and justice serving the citizen, 10 June 2009.

[395] For a detailed analysis of first pillar measures by the ECJ itself, see for instance the *Yusuf* case: ECJ, Case T-306/01 *Yusuf & Al Bakaraat* v. *Council & Commission* [2005] *ECR* II-03533.

[396] Art. 35 TEU.

[397] Art. 39 TEU.

[398] Wouters and Naert, op. cit., note 354, p. 767.

[399] ECJ, Case C-354/04 P *Gestoras Pro Amnistía a.o.* v. *the Council of the European Union* [2007] *ECR* I-01579.

ers under Article 35 TEU[400] but practical application of its broad interpretation leaves many questions unanswered. Firstly, there is the question how a case concerning the Security Council blacklists and its implementation measures in the third pillar would come before a national court. Secondly, the suggestion that Member States could bring a case to the Court of Justice against the lawfulness of a third-pillar common position does not seem to take into account that Article 34 TEU prescribes unanimity for such common positions, which would lead to a Member State bringing a case against its own voting in favour of it in the past. Yet, the underlying idea that national courts have jurisdiction when the Court of Justice does not is in harmony with both the system of the Treaties (Art. 5 EC) and the steady case-law of the Court of Justice on this matter.

The first cases in which the access to justice concerning placing on Security Council blacklists was discussed were the cases of *Yusuf*[401] and of *Kadi* of the CFI.[402] In these cases, the CFI discusses in detail how there is (limited) access to justice possible when a person or legal entity is placed on a Security Council blacklist: a state proposes the placement on the list, after which a Security Council committee decides. Yet, all members of the Security Council have to agree on de-listing after a request by a state. In this way, the individuals are placed outside the system and are dependent on their states to safeguard their rights. In the case of Mr Yusuf, it is clear that his state, Sweden, had been successful in the de-listing of two other Swedes but failed in his case until 2006.[403] However, someone like Mr Kadi is in a different situation. He is not a national of the state who has to freeze his bank account, he does not even reside in that state. This makes it more difficult for an individual to have his rights defended by a state.

This line of reasoning has resulted in maneuvering by the European courts in order to test the Security Council resolutions against fundamental rights standards. The final result in the *Kadi* appeal case shows that a way was tried to be found by the ECJ to avoid directly testing UN sanctions against European fundamental rights. Because the ECJ took the standpoint that it was allowed to perform this test, citizens' rights were placed up front. This has

---

[400] Ibid, Para. 53.

[401] ECJ, Case T-306/01 *Yusuf & Al Bakaraat* v. *Council & Commission* [2005] *ECR* II-03533.

[402] ECJ, Case T-315/01 *Kadi* v. *Council & Commission* [2005] *ECR* II-03649.

[403] 'US Removes Swede from Terror List', *The Local*, 17 August 2006.

been viewed as showing 'contempt for UN law, at least when fundamental rights are affected'.[404] Yet, the result has been that a similar test could be applied to UN measures within European law as to independent European measures.

In the so-called *OMPI* case,[405] the ECJ defined standards for access to justice from the point of EU list cases:

'In the case of an initial decision to freeze funds, the notification of the evidence requires, in principle, first, that the party concerned be informed by the Council of the specific information or material in the file which indicates that a decision meeting the definition given in Article 1(4) of Common Position 2001/931 on the application of specific measures to combat terrorism has been taken in respect of it by a competent authority of a Member State, and also, where applicable, any new material resulting from information or evidence communicated to the Council by representatives of the Member States without it having been assessed by the competent national authority and, second, that it must be placed in a position in which it can effectively make known its view on the information or material in the file.

In the case of a subsequent decision to freeze funds, observance of the right to a fair hearing similarly requires, first, that the party concerned be informed of the information or material in the file which, in the view of the Council, justifies maintaining it in the disputed lists, and also, where applicable, of any new material referred to above and, second, that it must be afforded the opportunity effectively to make known its view on the matter.'

On the basis of this line of reasoning, many others have been de-listed since, referring to the *OMPI* case. It has been a basic decision in which a test was laid down by the ECJ. In the *Kadi* case, a similar line of reasoning was followed for UN originating listings, although first the possibility of applying such rights had to be proven by the ECJ. In the latest *Sison* case, the ECJ added to this the way in which the Council should handle requests to place persons on a blacklist:

'In any event, it is to be stressed that the Council, when contemplating adopting or maintaining, after review, a fund-freezing measure pursuant to Regulation No

---

[404] L.M. Hinojosa Martínez, 'Bad Law for Good Reasons: The Contradictions of the Kadi Judgment', 5 *International Organizations Law Review* (2008) p. 342.
[405] ECJ, Case T-228/02 *Organisation des Modjahedines du peuple d'Iran* v. *Council* [2006] *ECR* II-04665.

2580/2001, on the basis of a national decision for the "instigation of investigations or prosecution" for an act of terrorism, may not disregard subsequent developments arising out of those investigations or that prosecution (see, to that effect, PMOI I and PMOI II). It may thus happen that police or security enquiries are closed without giving rise to any judicial consequences, because it proved impossible to gather sufficient evidence, or that measures of investigation ordered by the investigating judge do not lead to proceedings going to judgment for the same reasons. Similarly, a decision to prosecute may end in the abandoning of the prosecution or in acquittal in the criminal proceedings. It would be unacceptable for the Council not to take account of such matters, which form part of the body of information having to be taken into account in order to assess the situation (see paragraph 98 above). To decide otherwise would be tantamount to giving the Council and the Member States the excessive power to freeze a person's funds indefinitely, beyond review by any court and whatever the result of any judicial proceedings taken.'

All this shows clearly the way in which the ECJ has managed to uphold this fundamental right against all arguments by different parties to the contrary.

In the *Selmani* case,[406] the implications of the choice between legal bases in the different pillars came to the forefront. In this case, in which an Algerian refugee in Ireland asks for annulment of the placing of his name on the UN and therefore also EU blacklist, one of the key elements is the discussion concerned the question when and against which measure Mr Selmani could bring actions. There was the problem of a decision under the first pillar[407] which was linked to a Common Position under the second pillar.[408] In the Selmani decision the CFI points out that Article 46 TEU does not offer the ECJ the possibility to give legal remedies in the second pillar. For the first pillar decision, the CFI points out the time-limit of two months (with extensions according to the Rules of Procedure) that is laid down in Article 230(5) TEC (Art. 263 TFEU-L). Yet, in the case concerning security in the Philippines,[409] the ECJ agreed with The European Parliament that the moment of gaining of precise knowledge of the contents was the starting point for the

---

[406] ECJ, Case T-299/04 *Abdelghani Selmani* v. *Council & Commission* [2005] *ECR* II-00020.

[407] Decision 2004/306 of 2 April 2004 *OJ* L 99, 3 April 2004, pp. 28-29 implementing Art. 2(3) of Regulation No. 2580/2001 and repealing Decision 2003/902/EC.

[408] Common Position 2001/931/CFSP *OJ* L 344, 28 December 2001, pp. 93-96 on the application of specific measures to combat terrorism.

[409] ECJ, Case C-403/05 *European Parliament* v. *Commission* [2007] *ECR* I-09045.

running of the time period in which to bring an action to the ECJ. For Mr Selmani, who claims to speak little English, it was much more difficult to prove that he gained such knowledge.

7.3.1   Judicial protection and access to justice

Issues concerning the judicial protection of citizens have all in a way followed from the limitations of the powers of the ECJ under the second and third pillar. The ECJ has maintained that Article 35 TEU provides for the following situations under the third pillar:

> 'That article provides that the Court of Justice has jurisdiction in three situations. First, by virtue of Article 35(1) EU, it has jurisdiction to give preliminary rulings on the validity and interpretation of framework decisions and decisions, on the interpretation of conventions established under Title VI of the EU Treaty and on the validity and interpretation of the measures implementing them. Second, Article 35(6) EU provides also for the Court of Justice to have jurisdiction to review the legality of framework decisions and decisions in actions brought by a Member State or the Commission of the European Communities on grounds of lack of competence, infringement of an essential procedural requirement, infringement of the EU Treaty or of any rule of law relating to its application, or misuse of powers. Last, Article 35(7) EU provides for the Court of Justice to have jurisdiction to rule on any dispute between Member States regarding the interpretation or the application of acts adopted under Article 34(2) EU whenever such dispute cannot be settled by the Council within six months of its being referred to the latter by one of its members.
> 46. In contrast, Article 35 EU confers no jurisdiction on the Court of Justice to entertain any action for damages whatsoever.'[410]

On the basis of the Treaty text, the ECJ therefore concludes that it has – although limited – jurisdiction under the third pillar, and that judicial protection should be available. For anti-terrorism cases this leads to the following system.

The relevant cases fall into one of two different categories: cases concerning the (Security Council) blacklists and cases against independent EU measures.

---

[410] ECJ, Case C-354/04 P *Gestoras Pro Amnistía a.o.* v. *the Council of the European Union* [2007] *ECR* I-01579 Nos. 45 and 46.

Access to justice was also at the forefront in several cases concerning the (Security Council) blacklists as decided by the Court of Justice of the European Communities. When implementing the Security Council blacklists at the European Union level, the Council had specifically stated that access to justice needed to be possible: '(…) that in the event of any error in respect of the persons, groups or entities referred to, the injured party shall have the right to seek judicial redress.'[411]

Especially where the freezing of an individual's bank account is concerned, judicial redress proves to be very difficult. Although it is in fact the Member State who needs to freeze the bank account as such, this is only a material act following from an obligation under a first pillar Regulation. Seeking judicial redress at the national level is therefore not an option. As A-G Maduro explains[412] and as the CFI earlier discussed in its famous cases of *Yusuf*[413] and *Kadi*,[414] only states have been given the option to ask for de-listing of a person or entity at the UN Security Council level.[415] Maduro rightly concluded from this that this represents intergovernmental consultation and not any direct right for a defendant.[416] Thus, it is impossible for anyone on this blacklist to have access to justice at the Security Council level. This only leaves the EU level for access to justice. In the first decisions[417] regarding this element, the CFI has much difficulty declaring itself competent to hear the case. The CFI considered this not only part of the system of fundamental rights but also of ius cogens – necessary because of the supremacy of UN law over EU law in the eyes of the CFI – over which it decided it did possess competence.

---

[411] Case *Gestoras Pro Amnistia*, op. cit., note 410.

[412] Opinion of A-G Poiares Maduro, delivered on 23 January 2008, in ECJ, Case C-415/05 P *Kadi & Al Barakaat* [2008] *ECR* I-06351 No. 51.

[413] ECJ, Case T-306/01 *Yusuf & Al Bakaraat* v. *Council & Commission* [2005] *ECR* II-03533. Please note that on the request of the Swedish government, Mr Yusuf was finally removed from the Security Council blacklist. See the opinion of A-G Poiares Maduro in ECJ, Case C-415/05 P *Al Barakaat* [2008] *ECR* I-06351 sub 9.

[414] ECJ, Case T-315/01 *Kadi* v. *Council & Commission* [2005] *ECR* II-03649.

[415] Security Council Resolution 1730 (2006), adopted by the Security Council at its 5599th meeting, on 19 December 2006. See <http://daccessdds.un.org/doc/UNDOC/GEN/N06/671/31/PDF/N0667131.pdf?OpenElement> (last visited on 1 April 2008).

[416] Conclusion A-G Maduro, op. cit., note 412, No. 51.

[417] *Yusuf* and *Kadi* cases, op. cit., note 401 and 402.

This argument has caused much debate[418] and did not seem to be very convincing: because Article 11 TEU (Art. 24 TEU-L) expresses loyalty to the United Nations Charter, also because all Member States are party to it. Because the subjects covered in the second pillar mostly also fall under the United Nations Charter, it can be argued that the UN Security Council obligations need to be implemented under the EU Treaty. However, the question then needed to be answered what this supremacy of UN law means for access to justice, which should be available according to the Council. The CFI argues in the *Yusuf* and *Kadi* cases that a regional organization like the EU (and the Council of Europe for that matter) cannot test the decisions taken by a global organization like the UN and its Security Council against the principles laid down in Treaties of that global organization, based on Article 27 of the Vienna Convention of the Law of Treaties. Yet, it has convincingly been argued that, from an EU internal point of view, this line of reasoning makes the EU legal order indirectly a 'monist system'.[419]

'The only way around this problem lies in a test against the rules of jus cogens, which has only been done once before by any international court.[420] Yet, the argumentation of the CFI seems to ignore the fact that jus cogens is usually not used in decisions by (international) courts. In the appeal ruling, however, the ECJ commented on this that:

It follows from the foregoing that the Community judicature must, in accordance with the powers conferred on it by the EC Treaty, ensure the review, in principle the full review, of the lawfulness of all Community acts in the light of the fundamental rights forming an integral part of the general principles of Community law, including review of Community measures which, like the contested regulation, are designed to give effect to the resolutions adopted by the Security Council under Chapter VII of the Charter of the United Nations.

---

[418] For instance: M. Bulterman, 'Fundamental Rights and the United Nations Financial Sanction Regime: The Kadi and Yusuf Judgments of the Court of First Instance of the European Communities', 19 *Leiden Journal of International Law* (2006) pp. 753-772. Also the opinion of A-G Poiares Maduro, delivered on 23 January 2008, in ECJ, Case C-415/05 P *Kadi & Al Barakaat* [2008] *ECR* I-06351 No. 51.

[419] A. Garde, 'Is It Really for the European Community to Implement Anti-Terrorism UN Security Council Resolutions?', 65 *The Cambridge Law Journal* (2006) p. 284.

[420] Case Concerning Armed Activities on the Territory of the Congo (*Congo* v. *Rwanda*), Judgment of the International Court of Justice of 3 February 2006, General List No. 126, <www.icj-cij.org/docket/files/126/10435.pdf> (last visited on 2 April 2008). See also Bulterman, op. cit., note 418, pp. 768-769.

The Court of First Instance erred in law, therefore, when it held, in paragraphs 212 to 231 of Kadi and 263 to 282 of Yusuf and Al Barakaat, that it followed from the principles governing the relationship between the international legal order under the United Nations and the Community legal order that the contested regulation, since it is designed to give effect to a resolution adopted by the Security Council under Chapter VII of the Charter of the United Nations affording no latitude in that respect, must enjoy immunity from jurisdiction so far as concerns its internal lawfulness save with regard to its compatibility with the norms of jus cogens.'

7.4   Concluding Remarks

Overall, it needs to be concluded that EU measures in the fight against terrorism potentially threaten to diminish the citizenship rights for anyone residing in the European Union. The emphasis lies on protection of fundamental rights and access to justice. However, the ECJ has so far managed to protect these rights. Yet, there is a difference between EU nationals and others. The status of EU citizens seems to give more options for protection. Within the EU on the basis of the European arrest warrant, for the Member States to stand for their own citizens in the Security Council and other elements. It appears to be easier for the ECJ to protect rights on the basis of European legislation than on indirect international obligations.

Chapter 8

AN EVALUATION

Chapter 8

AN EVALUATION

INTRODUCTION

Taking all the information from the preceding chapters together, it is possible to evaluate the position of the citizen in the European Union. This evaluation is divided into two parts. The most general group of citizens whose citizenship rights may have been affected by European Union law are the nationals of the Member States who have not left their own Member State. After all, only a relatively small percentage of EU nationals uses their right to free movement and relocate to another Member State. Assuming that the Member States themselves offer full citizenship rights to their own citizens (after all, they all have signed the EU Treaty, including Art. 6 TEU), the influence of European law should not have lessened these citizenship rights, but either kept them at the same level or increased the citizenship rights. Of course, this evaluation will only look at the European Union point of view of citizenship rights without discussing the impact in the different Member States.

In addition, the position of all other legal citizens in the EU needs to be evaluated in order to obtain a full overview of the citizenship rights in the EU. Not only the citizenship rights of EU citizens who have moved to another Member State will be assessed but also those of legal third-country nationals in the EU.

For new Member States, it needs to be highlighted that they must all fulfill the Kopenhagen criteria upon accession to the EU, which means that the citizens of these new Member States who have not moved to another Member State have the same citizenship rights as the citizens of the old Member States because democratic rights are included as well as the acceptance of the acquis communautaire, of which the economic and social rights are part.

F. Goudappel, The Effects of EU Citizenship
© 2010, T·M·C·ASSER PRESS, *The Hague, The Netherlands and the Author*

Part I.   EU CITIZENS IN THEIR OWN MEMBER STATE

EU citizens who have not used the right of free movement and have thus
stayed in their own Member State only feel the effect of the direct effect of
primary and secondary European legislation and implemented directives. This
means firstly that the economic rights as given form through free movement
rights, do not affect this category of citizens and is solely national law. Yet,
for political rights, there is European influence. On the one hand, there is the
question whether The European Parliament is a 'real' parliament. Of course,
it does not possess the right of initiative and some other control powers are
limited, but it has gained much power over the decades. This is most important because by signing the EC and EU Treaties, the Member States have
transposed powers to the European level, which means that political control
should have moved to the European level as well. If the political power at the
European level does not fulfill the criteria of the national level, there truly is
a democratic deficit. The citizen thus looses political power because his
Member State joined the European Union. Yet, in a more indirect way, the
Council plays a role in the exercise of the political rights of the citizens. As
the members of the Council (and the European Council) represent the governments of their Member States, they indirectly represent the citizens at the
European level and are checked by the national parliaments. In this way, part
of the democratic deficit at the parliamentary level is being taken care of via
the Council. In addition, the Treaty of Lisbon offers more safety nets for the
political rights of the citizens by giving control options to national parliaments. Thus it can be maintained that political rights of EU citizens have
been negatively affected by EU membership although these negative effects
have been partially counterbalanced by the powers of the Council and the
national parliaments.
    For social rights, it needs to be concluded that there have been mostly
positive effects of EU membership for the nationals of the Member States
who have not moved to another Member State. From the early days of the
EEC, the Treaty itself has given rights, most notably the right to equal pay
for men and women, to the citizens and all legal inhabitants of the Member
States without the necessity of a cross-border element in the relationship
between citizen and state. On top of this, a European social policy has been
developed which directly gives social rights to the citizens. This means that
social rights have a direct effect for all citizens, independent of the way in
which they have become citizen in a Member State. The ECJ has added to

this a wide application of social rights. In the EU Charter of Fundamental Rights, to be made binding in most Member States in the Treaty of Lisbon, these social rights are considered fundamental European rights, which may lead to a further development of social rights in the future.

On the other hand, if we look at some other case-law of the ECJ, it seems that the own citizens have, in total, less rights than the nationals of other Member States. Several cases of the ECJ have given rights to the citizens of other Member States, but if we look at these cases not from the point of view of the parties in the underlying national cases (who are all nationals of other Member States) but from the point of view of the nationals of the Member States in question, the second category cannot fall under the rules of the case-law because the cross-border element in the cases is crucial. Therefore, it can easily be concluded that there is a difference in citizenship rights. This means that in cases like *Carpenter* and *Metock* on the one hand and *Garcia Avello* and *Grunkin et Paul* have shown that EU nationals who have moved to another Member State have been given more rights under European law than the nationals who have not moved have because this latter group can only refer to national law under the same circumstances. The relevant rights mostly concern the right to have an illegal third-country national as a spouse not extradited or move with you to another Member State or the right to have a name registered differently from national traditions.

Does this mean that the citizens who have not used the right of free move-ment have less citizenship rights or do the others have a kind of bonus rights? If the starting point is the fact that the legislation of the Member States at the national level reflects full citizenship rights (as is required for membership of the EU), the latter argument shows a bonus because it is on top of some-thing that is similar in the Member States and therefore not an integral part of citizenship rights. It represents an element of free movement that any citizen may obtain after using free movement rights. It can even be said that the rights themselves often do not differ but that the contents given to these rights may slightly vary.

Apart from this analysis, a second element that needs to be taken into consideration when evaluating the position of EU citizens who have remained in their own Member State, is the role of EU legislation which affects or may affect citizenship rights in the Member States although these rights tradition-ally are national citizenship rights whose existence is independent of Euro-pean law. Where the foregoing analysis started from the point of view that European law could add elements to existing citizenship rights, European law also seems to have a negative impact on the existing citizenship rights in the Member States. Especially measures in the field of Justice and Home Affairs may, after implementation in the legislative systems of the Member States, have such an effect. Where the fight against terrorism is concerned, this is a very delicate balance between security and the protection of human rights.

As an overall conclusion, it needs to be noted that European law has improved social rights for the citizens who have not left their Member State. However, there is a (limited) negative impact when political control rights and measures against terrorism are concerned.

Part II.   OTHER SITUATIONS

A.   Nationals of other Member States

Although most of the evaluation above concerning EU citizens who have stayed in their own Member State can be applied to the nationals of Member States who have moved to another Member States (such as the social rights and the negative effects of anti-terrorism measures), the situation of this latter category differs in many aspects when one looks at the overall picture of citizenship rights. Especially the application of economic rights, but also of political rights, differs for them and seems to give them more or additional rights.

As Article 12 TEC (Art. 18 TFEU-L) indicates that the Member States should not discriminate between their own nationals and the nationals of the other Member States, the latter category of nationals should have similar rights as the citizens described above. This ECJ has maintained this prohibition of discrimination in extensive case-law. Especially concerning economic rights (free movement of workers, freedom of establishment and free movement of services) the ECJ has given form and substance to the citizenship right of free movement. Apart from defining who is a worker, for instance, and therefore has free movement rights, the ECJ has defined the scope of those rights. By considering the free movement rights as a large umbrella under which many rights can be maintained by the citizens concerned, economic citizenship rights have been enlarged by the ECJ.

A more or less similar line of reasoning can be given for basic rights protection and social rights protection. Although within the Member States, these two sets of rights are protected at a similar level for all citizens, whether the citizens of that particular Member State or not, there appears to be additional protection for these rights from the ECJ for nationals of other Member States. For the application of fundamental rights, the ECJ can judge when there is an EU element in the case, as it did for instance in the cases of *Internationale Handelsgesellschaft* and *Carpenter*. For purely internal situations, the Member States themselves are responsible because the situation does not have a EU dimension, while for cross-border situations, the EU dimension is very much present. This is different for social rights because the EU protects both categories of social rights: both the purely internal social rights and the cross-border social rights. However, the aim seems to be that these two categories should have similar social rights, whether an EU national stays in his own Member State or moves to another.

This shows that there is at least the impression that the nationals of other Member States have been given some citizenship rights which are an addition to the rights of the own nationals. The additional rights have mostly been given by the ECJ while interpreting the text of the Treaties, thus not overstepping the boundaries of the Treaties but instead making the most of the possibilities the Treaties offer. As already stated above, this is a kind of bonus for the EU nationals living in another Member State and gives a different kind of flavor to the existing citizenship rights.

B.   Nationals of new Member States

A separate category is formed by the free movement rights of the nationals of new Member States. Free movement rights are at the basis of citizenship rights for the European Union but are not directly given in all circumstances to all citizens of new Member States at the moment of accession. In the most recent Treaties of Accession, not all old Member States immediately give free movement rights to all citizens of these new Member States but rather temporarily put quota and other limitations in place. This means that this element of citizenship is not immediately given to all EU citizens during transitional periods. Yet, all other citizenship rights are given to them, including the rights of EU citizens in other Member States once a national of a new Member State has gained entrance into another Member State. Therefore, it needs to be concluded that the evaluation of EU citizens in another Member State is not fully valid for the nationals of new Member State at the moment of accession.

C. Third-country nationals married to an EU national and family reunifications

The citizenship rights of third-country nationals who are married to an EU national are in a way dependent upon the citizenship rights of the categories described above. Apart from the fact that some citizenship rights depend upon nationality (like the right to vote in national elections) and can therefore not be exercised by third-country nationals unless they decide to adopt the nationality of the Member State, they have all other citizenship rights. Directive 2004/38/EC gives these third-country nationals similar rights to EU nationals while they are dependent upon the status of their spouse: if the spouse has moved to another Member State, the third-country national obtains the rights under the Directive. The main difference for this category of third-country nationals lies in their options to move to the Member State and thus exercise the right to move and reside freely in the territory of the Member State(s). For this, there is a large difference between those married to an EU national living in his or her own Member State and those married to an EU national living in another Member State. European Union law only governs the position of third-country nationals if they marry an EU citizen who is living in another Member State. If not, the rules are completely national and form part of the internal legal system of the relevant Member State.

Special attention needs to be paid to third-country nationals who come to the EU because of family reunification. Their position and options have been laid down in a specific Directive which has been under scrutiny by the ECJ. Member States have freedom of choice in many instances and one Member State even refuses to implement the Directive. It is therefore at the time of writing unknown what the consequences of this Directive will be.

D. Third-country nationals working in the EU for less than five years

Although the group with the most limited set of citizenship rights consists of illegal third-country nationals (they only have basic fundamental rights protection), the third-country nationally legally working in the EU for less than five years has very limited citizenship rights. The fundamental rights protection is valid for them, and they have the right to reside in the Member State which has given them a work permit. Yet, here it halts. No other citizenship rights are given to them via European Union law. Secondary European legislation gives more and more options for specific groups of third-country nationals to work (for a limited period) in the EU but does not add citizenship rights to these options.

E. Third-country nationals working in the EU for more than five years

Third-country nationals long-term residents have a slightly better position concerning citizenship rights than those working for less than five years. The specific directive for their position gives them limited citizenship rights. Because they have been legally resident in one of the Member States and have been economically active, they of course have the right to reside in that particular Member State and have a basic fundamental rights protection. To this is added the right to move and reside freely within the territory of the Member States. Yet, this completes the rights they are given based on European Union law. Individual Member States may for instance grant them the right to vote in local elections but a right like this does not follow from European obligations. In order to obtain any more citizenship rights, the nationality of one of the Member States is required.

Influence of the Treaty of Lisbon

Will the Treaty of Lisbon change much for these citizenship rights? It might. Firstly, the provision on the prohibition of discrimination based on nationality will be in the chapter on EU citizenship. The consequences of this move are not clear. Yet, at least citizenship rights will be one-on-one linked to this prohibition of discrimination. Secondly, there is the possibility of a different and faster development of both the position of third-country nationals and police and judicial cooperation in criminal matters because the Community method with a co-decision procedure will be applicable on all elements of the Area of Freedom, Security and Justice. This means that there will be more options for adopting new legislation in these fields without the consent of all Member States. Moreover, for some Member States there is an opt-out or opt-in possibility if they decide against participation in a certain measure, which will make it possible for the other Member States to go ahead with the measure.

IN CONCLUSION

Indeed, the descriptions and analyses above show that the citizenship rights of persons residing in Member States of the European Union have not been influenced in a negative sense by the influence of European Union law. It seems that the citizenship rights as they are considered to have to exist in a state are for the overall part still in place, and have even been expanded through the European influence. Although these rights have not developed in the way they have usually developed in independent states, they contain the basic economic, social and political rights as they are distinguished by Marshall. Some citizenship rights, like the right to equal treatment in the workplace for men and women, has been given a boost by European Union law. Other citizenship rights, like parliamentary representation (the democratic deficit), do not exist in the same way as it would at a national level.

Although the European Union system did initially not contain many of these citizenship rights, they have either developed through secondary legislation or, most importantly, through the case-law of the ECJ. Influential in recent development have been both the introduction of the notion of EU citizenship in the Treaty of Maastricht and the link to fundamental right protection. In this way, several citizenship rights have been created which are not common or universal: most notably the right to bring family members along to the host Member State and the right of these family members to develop individual citizenship rights this way, and the right to vote in local elections in the host Member State. In addition, quasi-citizenship rights or partial citizenship rights are given to third-country nationals.

LIST OF LEGISLATION

TREATIES

Consolidated versions of the Treaty on European Union and of the Treaty establishing the European Community (consolidated text), *Official Journal C 321E of 29 December 2006*

EU Charter on Fundamental Rights, 2000 *OJ* C 364 1, 7 December 2000.

Treaty between the Kingdom of Belgium, the Czech Republic, the Kingdom of Denmark, the Federal Republic of Germany, the Republic of Estonia, the Hellenic Republic, the Kingdom of Spain, the French Republic, Ireland, the Italian Republic, the Republic of Cyprus, the Republic of Latvia, the Republic of Lithuania, the Grand Duchy of Luxembourg, the Republic of Hungary, the Republic of Malta, the Kingdom of the Netherlands, the Republic of Austria, the Republic of Poland, the Portuguese Republic, the Republic of Slovenia, the Slovak Republic, the Republic of Finland, the Kingdom of Sweden, the United Kingdom of Great Britain and Northern Ireland (Member States of the European Union) and the Republic of Bulgaria and Romania, concerning the accession of the Republic of Bulgaria and Romania to the European Union, 25 April 2005

Treaty of Lisbon amending the Treaty on European Union and the Treaty establishing the European Community, Brussels 3 December 2007, CIG 14/07 *OJ C* 306 of 17 December 2007.

REGULATIONS

Regulation (EEC) No. 1408/71 of the Council of 14 June 1971 *OJ* L 149, 5 July 1971, pp. 2-50 on the application of social security schemes to employed persons and their families moving within the Community, and amending acts.

Council Regulation (EC) No. 337/2000 of 14 February 2000 *OJ* L 43, 16 February 2000, pp. 1-11 concerning a flight ban and a freeze of funds and other financial resources in respect of the Taliban of Afghanistan.

Council Regulation (EC) No. 539/2001 of 15 March 2001 *OJ* L 81, 21 March 2001, pp. 1-7 listing the third countries whose nationals must be in possession of visas when crossing the external borders and those whose nationals are exempt from that requirement.

Regulation (EC) 1049/2001 of the European Parliament and of the Council of 30 May 2001 *OJ* L 145, 31 May 2001, pp. 43-48 regarding public access to European Parliament, Council and Commission documents.

Council Regulation (EC) No. 2580/2001 of 27 December 2001 *OJ* L 344, 28 December 2001, pp. 70-75 on specific restrictive measures directed against certain persons and entities with a view to combating terrorism.

Council Regulation (EC) No. 343/2003 of 18 February 2003 *OJ* L 50, 25 February 2003, pp. 1-10 establishing the criteria and mechanisms for determining the Member State responsible for examining an asylum application lodged in one of the Member States by a third-country national.

Council Regulation (EC) No. 2252/2004 of 13 December 2004 *OJ* L 385, 29 December 2004, pp. 1-6 on standards for security features and biometrics in passports and travel documents issued by Member States.

Regulation (EC) No. 810/2009 of the European Parliament and of the Council of 13 July 2009 establishing a Community Code on Visas *OJ* L 243, 15 September 2009, pp. 1-58.

DIRECTIVES

Regulation (EEC) No. 1612/68 of 15 October 1968 *OJ* L 257, 19 October 1968, pp. 2-12 on the free movement of workers within the Community, lastly partially amended by the Persons Directive.

Council Directive 76/207/EEC of 9 February 1976 *OJ* L 39, 14 February 1976, pp. 40-42 on the implementation of the principle of equal treatment for men and women as regards access to employment, vocational training and promotion, and working conditions.

Council Directive 79/7/EEC of 19 December 1978 *OJ* L 6, 10 January 1979, pp. 24-25 on the progressive implementation of the principle of equal treatment for men and women in matters of social security.

Council Directive 89/48/EEC of 21 December 1988 *OJ* L 19, 24 January 1989, pp. 16-23 on a general system for the recognition of higher-education diplomas awarded on completion of professional education and training of at least three years' duration.

Council Directive 98/59/EC of 20 July 1998 *OJ* L 225, 12 August 1998, pp. 16-21 on the approximation of the laws of the Member States relating to collective redundancies.

Council Directive 93/104/EC of 23 November 1993 *OJ* L 307, 13 December 1993, pp. 18-24 concerning certain aspects of the organization of working time.

Council Directive 2000/43/EC of 29 June 2000 *OJ* L 180, 19 July 2000, pp. 22-26 implementing the principle of equal treatment between persons irrespective of racial or ethnic origin.

Council Directive 2001/40/EC of 28 May 2001 *OJ* L 149, 2 June 2001, pp. 34-36 on the mutual recognition of decisions on the expulsion of third-country nationals.

Council Directive 2003/86/EC of 22 September 2003 on the right to family reunification. *OJ PB* L 251 of 3 October 2003, pp. 12-18.

Council Directive 2003/109/EC of 25 November 2003 *OJ L* 16 of 23 January 2004, pp. 44-53 concerning the status of third-country nationals who are long-term residents.

European Parliament and Council Directive 2004/38/EC of 29 April 2004 on the right of citizens of the Union and their family members to move and reside freely within the territory of the Member States amending Regulation (EEC) No. 1612/68 and repealing Directives 64/221/EEC, 68/360/EEC, 72/194/EEC, 73/148/EEC, 75/34/EEC, 75/35/EEC, 90/364/EEC, 90/365/EEC and 93/96/EEC, OJ PB L 158 of 30 April 2004, rectified in PB L 229 of 29 June 2004.

Council Directive 2004/83/EC of 29 April 2004 *OJ* L 304, 30 September 2004, pp. 12-23 on minimum standards for the qualification and status of third-country nationals or stateless persons as refugees or as persons who otherwise need international protection and the content of the protection granted.

Directive 2005/36/EC of the European Parliament and of the Council of 7 September 2005 on the recognition of professional qualifications.

Directive 2005/60/EC of the European Parliament and of the Council of 26 October 2005 *OJ* L 309, 25 November 2005, pp. 15-36 on the prevention of the use of the financial system for the purpose of money laundering and terrorist financing.

Council Directive 2005/71/EC *OJ* L 289, 3 November 2005, pp. 15-22 on a specific procedure for admitting third-country nationals for the purposes of scientific research.

Directive 2006/123/EC of the European Parliament and of the Council of 12 December 2006 *OJ* L 376, 27 December 2006, pp. 36-68 on services in the internal market.

DECISIONS

Council Decision 93/731/EC on public access to Council documents, *OJ* L 340 31 December 1993.

Decision 94/90/ECSC, EC, Euratom on public access to Commission documents, *OJ* L 46, 18 February 1994.

97/632/EC, ECSC, Euratom Decision of the European Parliament of 10 July 1997 on public access to document of the European Parliament *OJ* L 263 25 September 1997.

Council Decision of 28 February 2002 *OJ* L 63, 6 March 2002, pp. 1-13 setting up Eurojust with a view to reinforcing the fight against serious crime.

Decision 2004/306 of 2 April 2004 *OJ* L 99, 3 April 2004, pp. 28-29 implementing Art. 2(3) of Regulation No. 2580/2001 and repealing Decision 2003/902/EC.

2004/573/EC, Council Decision of 29 April 2004 *OJ* L 261, 6 August 2004, pp. 28-35 on the organisation of joint flights for removals from the territory of two or more Member States, of third-country nationals who are subjects of individual removal orders.

Council Decision of 15 September 2006 *OJ* L 285, 16 October 2006, pp. 47-71 adopting the Council's Rules of Procedure (2006/683/EC, Euratom).

COMMON POSITIONS

Council Common Position 2001/931/CFSP of 27 December 2001 on the application of specific measures to combat terrorism *OJ PB L* 344 of 28 December 2001, pp. 93-96.

Common Position 2002/402/CFSP *OJ* L 139, 29 May 2002, pp. 4-5 concerning restrictive measures against Usama bin Laden, members of the Al-Qaeda organisation and the Taliban and other individuals, groups, undertakings and entities associated with them and repealing Common Positions 96/746/CFSP, 1999/727/CFSP, 2001/154/CFSP and 2001/771/CFSP, 27 May 2002.

FRAMEWORK DECISIONS

Council Framework Decision 2002/475/JHA of 13 June 2002 *OJ* L 155, 14 June 2002, pp. 60-62 on combating terrorism.

Council Framework Decision 2002/584/JHA of 13 June 2002 *OJ* L 190, 18 July 2002, pp. 1-20 on the European arrest warrant and the surrender procedures between Member States.

TABLE OF CASES OF THE COURT OF JUSTICE OF THE EUROPEAN UNION (ECJ)

Case 25/62 *Plaumann* [1963] *ECR* 207.

Case 26/62 *Van Gend & Loos* [1963] *ECR* 3.

Case 32/75 *Fiorinin* [1975] *ECR* 01085.

Case 43/75 *Defrenne* [1976] *ECR* 00455.

Case 207/78 *Criminal Proceedings against Gilbert Even* [1979] *ECR* 02019.

Case 53/81 *Levin* [1982] *ECR* 01035.

Joined Cases 115 and 116/81 *Adoui and Cornuaille* [1982] *ECR* 01665.

Case 66/85 *Lawrie-Blum* [1986] *ECR* 02121.

Case 196/87 *Steymann* [1988] *ECR* 06159.

Case 344/87 *Bettray* [1989] *ECR* 01621.

Case C-379/87 *Groener* [1989] *ECR* 03967.

Case C-340/89 *Vlassopoulou* [1991] *ECR* I-02663.

Case C-357/89 *Raulin* [1992] *ECR* I-01027.

Case C-3/90 *Bernini* [1992] *ECR* I-01071.

Case 159/90 *SPUC* v. *Grogan* [1991] *ECR* I-04685.

Case C-370/90 *Singh* [1992] *ECR* I-04265.

Case C-271/91 *Marshall* [1993] *ECR* I-04367.

Case C-37/93 *Commission* v. *Belgium* [1993] *ECR* I-06295.

Case C-55/94 *Gebhard* [1995] *ECR* I-04165.

Case C-265/95 *Spanish strawberries* [1997] *ECR* I-06959.

Case C-409/95 *Marschall* [1997] *ECR* I-06363.

Joined Cases C-51/96 and C-191/97 *Deliège* [2000] *ECR* I-02549.

Case C-101/04 *Noteboom* [2005] *ECR* I-00771.

Case C-109/04 *Kranemann* [2005] *ECR* I-02421.

Case C-142/04 *Aslanidou* [2005] *ECR* I-07181.

Case C-145/04 *Spain* v. *United Kingdom* [2006] *ECR* I-07917.

Case C-207/04 *Vergani* [2005] *ECR* I-07453.

Case T-299/04 *Abdelghani Selmani* v. *Council & Commission* [2005] *ECR* II-00020.

Case C-354/04 P *Gestoras Pro Amnistía a.o.* v. *the Council of the European Union* [2007] *ECR* I-01579.

Case C-300/04 *Eman & Sevinger* [2006] *ECR* I-08055.

Case C-423/04 *Richards* [2006] *ECR* I-03585.

Case C-1/05 *Jia* [2007] *ECR* I-00001.

Case C-192/05 *Tas-Hagen & Tas* [2006] *ECR* I-10451.

Case C-303/05 *Advocaten voor de Wereld VZW* v. *Leden of de Ministerraad* [2007] *ECR* I-03633.

Joined Cases C-402/05 P and C-415/05 P *Kadi and Barakaat* [2008] *ECR* I-06351.

Case C-403/05 *European Parliament* v. *Commission* [2007] *ECR* I-09045.

Case C-438/05 *Viking Line* [2007] *ECR* I-10779.

Case C-294/06 *Payir et al.* [2008] *ECR* I-00203.

Case C-33/07 *Jipa* [2008] *ECR* I-05157.

Case C-155/07 *Sahin* [2008] *ECR* 00000.

Case C-221/07 *Zablocka-Weyhermüller* [2008] *ECR* 00000.

Case T-341/07 *Sison* v. *Council II* [2009] *ECR* 00000.

Case C-465/07 *Elgafaji* [2009] *ECR* 00000.

Case C-127/08 *Metock and Others* [2008] *ECR* I-06241.

INDEX

Annexes

Annex I

RELEVANT PROVISIONS FROM THE TREATY ESTABLISHING THE EUROPEAN COMMUNITY

Article 17

1. Citizenship of the Union is hereby established. Every person holding the nationality of a Member State shall be a citizen of the Union. Citizenship of the Union shall complement and not replace national citizenship.
2. Citizens of the Union shall enjoy the rights conferred by this Treaty and shall be subject to the duties imposed thereby.

Article 18

1. Every citizen of the Union shall have the right to move and reside freely within the territory of the Member States, subject to the limitations and conditions laid down in this Treaty and by the measures adopted to give it effect.
2. The Council may adopt provisions with a view to facilitating the exercise of the rights referred to in paragraph 1; save as otherwise provided in this Treaty, the Council shall act in accordance with the procedure referred to in Article 251. The Council shall act unanimously throughout this procedure.

Article 19

1. Every citizen of the Union residing in a Member State of which he is not a national shall have the right to vote and to stand as a candidate at municipal elections in the Member State in which he resides, under the same conditions as nationals of that State. This right shall be exercised subject to detailed arrangements adopted by the Council, acting unanimously on a proposal from the Commission and after consulting the European Parliament; these arrangements may provide for derogations where warranted by problems specific to a Member State.
2. Without prejudice to Article 190(4) and to the provisions adopted for its implementation, every citizen of the Union residing in a Member State of which he is not a national shall have the right to vote and to stand as a candidate in elections to the European Parliament in the Member State in which he resides, under the same conditions as nationals of that State. This right shall be exercised subject to detailed arrangements adopted by the Council, acting unanimously on a proposal from the

Commission and after consulting the European Parliament; these arrangements may provide for derogations where warranted by problems specific to a Member State.

Article 20

Every citizen of the Union shall, in the territory of a third country in which the Member State of which he is a national is not represented, be entitled to protection by the diplomatic or consular authorities of any Member State, on the same conditions as the nationals of that State. Member States shall establish the necessary rules among themselves and start the international negotiations required to secure this protection.

Article 21

Every citizen of the Union shall have the right to petition the European Parliament in accordance with Article 194.
Every citizen of the Union may apply to the Ombudsman established in accordance with Article 195.
Every citizen of the Union may write to any of the institutions or bodies referred to in this Article or in Article 7 in one of the languages mentioned in Article 314 and have an answer in the same language.

Article 39

1. Freedom of movement for workers shall be secured within the Community.
2. Such freedom of movement shall entail the abolition of any discrimination based on nationality between workers of the Member States as regards employment, remuneration and other conditions of work and employment.
3. It shall entail the right, subject to limitations justified on grounds of public policy, public security or public health:
(a) to accept offers of employment actually made;
(b) to move freely within the territory of Member States for this purpose;
(c) to stay in a Member State for the purpose of employment in accordance with the provisions governing the employment of nationals of that State laid down by law, regulation or administrative action;
(d) to remain in the territory of a Member State after having been employed in that State, subject to conditions which shall be embodied in implementing regulations to be drawn up by the Commission.
4. The provisions of this Article shall not apply to employment in the public service.

Article 43

Within the framework of the provisions set out below, restrictions on the freedom of establishment of nationals of a Member State in the territory of another Member State shall be prohibited. Such prohibition shall also apply to restrictions on the setting-up of agencies, branches or subsidiaries by nationals of any Member State established in the territory of any Member State.

Freedom of establishment shall include the right to take up and pursue activities as self-employed persons and to set up and manage undertakings, in particular companies or firms within the meaning of the second paragraph of Article 48, under the conditions laid down for its own nationals by the law of the country where such establishment is effected, subject to the provisions of the Chapter relating to capital.

Article 47

1. In order to make it easier for persons to take up and pursue activities as self-employed persons, the Council shall, acting in accordance with the procedure referred to in Article 251, issue directives for the mutual recognition of diplomas, certificates and other evidence of formal qualifications.

2. For the same purpose, the Council shall, acting in accordance with the procedure referred to in Article 251, issue directives for the coordination of the provisions laid down by law, regulation or administrative action in Member States concerning the taking-up and pursuit of activities as self-employed persons. The Council, acting unanimously throughout the procedure referred to in Article 251, shall decide on directives the implementation of which involves in at least one Member State amendment of the existing principles laid down by law governing the professions with respect to training and conditions of access for natural persons. In other cases the Council shall act by qualified majority.

3. In the case of the medical and allied and pharmaceutical professions, the progressive abolition of restrictions shall be dependent upon coordination of the conditions for their exercise in the various Member States.

Article 49

Within the framework of the provisions set out below, restrictions on freedom to provide services within the Community shall be prohibited in respect of nationals of Member States who are established in a State of the Community other than that of the person for whom the services are intended.

The Council may, acting by a qualified majority on a proposal from the Commission, extend the provisions of the Chapter to nationals of a third country who provide services and who are established within the Community.

Article 50

Services shall be considered to be 'services' within the meaning of this Treaty where they are normally provided for remuneration, insofar as they are not governed by the provisions relating to freedom of movement for goods, capital and persons.
'Services' shall in particular include:
(a) activities of an industrial character;
(b) activities of a commercial character;
(c) activities of craftsmen;
(d) activities of the professions.
Without prejudice to the provisions of the Chapter relating to the right of establishment, the person providing a service may, in order to do so, temporarily pursue his activity in the State where the service is provided, under the same conditions as are imposed by that State on its own nationals.

Article 60

1. If, in the cases envisaged in Article 301, action by the Community is deemed necessary, the Council may, in accordance with the procedure provided for in Article 301, take the necessary urgent measures on the movement of capital and on payments as regards the third countries concerned.
2. Without prejudice to Article 297 and as long as the Council has not taken measures pursuant to paragraph 1, a Member State may, for serious political reasons and on grounds of urgency, take unilateral measures against a third country with regard to capital movements and payments. The Commission and the other Member States shall be informed of such measures by the date of their entry into force at the latest. The Council may, acting by a qualified majority on a proposal from the Commission, decide that the Member State concerned shall amend or abolish such measures. The President of the Council shall inform the European Parliament of any such decision taken by the Council.

Article 63

The Council, acting in accordance with the procedure referred to in Article 67, shall, within a period of five years after the entry into force of the Treaty of Amsterdam, adopt:
(1) measures on asylum, in accordance with the Geneva Convention of 28 July 1951 and the Protocol of 31 January 1967 relating to the status of refugees and other relevant treaties, within the following areas:
(a) criteria and mechanisms for determining which Member State is responsible for considering an application for asylum submitted by a national of a third country in one of the Member States,
(b) minimum standards on the reception of asylum seekers in Member States,

(c) minimum standards with respect to the qualification of nationals of third countries as refugees,

(d) minimum standards on procedures in Member States for granting or withdrawing refugee status;

(2) measures on refugees and displaced persons within the following areas:

(a) minimum standards for giving temporary protection to displaced persons from third countries who cannot return to their country of origin and for persons who otherwise need international protection,

(b) promoting a balance of effort between Member States in receiving and bearing the consequences of receiving refugees and displaced persons;

(3) measures on immigration policy within the following areas:

(a) conditions of entry and residence, and standards on procedures for the issue by Member States of long term visas and residence permits, including those for the purpose of family reunion,

(b) illegal immigration and illegal residence, including repatriation of illegal residents;

(4) measures defining the rights and conditions under which nationals of third countries who are legally resident in a Member State may reside in other Member States.

Measures adopted by the Council pursuant to points 3 and 4 shall not prevent any Member State from maintaining or introducing in the areas concerned national provisions which are compatible with this Treaty and with international agreements.

Measures to be adopted pursuant to points 2(b), 3(a) and 4 shall not be subject to the five year period referred to above.

Article 136

The Community and the Member States, having in mind fundamental social rights such as those set out in the European Social Charter signed at Turin on 18 October 1961 and in the 1989 Community Charter of the Fundamental Social Rights of Workers, shall have as their objectives the promotion of employment, improved living and working conditions, so as to make possible their harmonisation while the improvement is being maintained, proper social protection, dialogue between management and labour, the development of human resources with a view to lasting high employment and the combating of exclusion.

To this end the Community and the Member States shall implement measures which take account of the diverse forms of national practices, in particular in the field of contractual relations, and the need to maintain the competitiveness of the Community economy.

They believe that such a development will ensue not only from the functioning of the common market, which will favour the harmonisation of social systems, but also from the procedures provided for in this Treaty and from the approximation of provisions laid down by law, regulation or administrative action.

Article 137

1. With a view to achieving the objectives of Article 136, the Community shall support and complement the activities of the Member States in the following fields:
– improvement in particular of the working environment to protect workers' health and safety;
– working conditions;
– the information and consultation of workers;
– the integration of persons excluded from the labour market, without prejudice to Article 150;
– equality between men and women with regard to labour market opportunities and treatment at work.

2. To this end, the Council may adopt, by means of directives, minimum requirements for gradual implementation, having regard to the conditions and technical rules obtaining in each of the Member States. Such directives shall avoid imposing administrative, financial and legal constraints in a way which would hold back the creation and development of small and medium-sized undertakings.

The Council shall act in accordance with the procedure referred to in Article 251 after consulting the Economic and Social Committee and the Committee of the Regions.

The Council, acting in accordance with the same procedure, may adopt measures designed to encourage cooperation between Member States through initiatives aimed at improving knowledge, developing exchanges of information and best practices, promoting innovative approaches and evaluating experiences in order to combat social exclusion.

3. However, the Council shall act unanimously on a proposal from the Commission, after consulting the European Parliament, the Economic and Social Committee and the Committee of the Regions in the following areas:
– social security and social protection of workers;
– protection of workers where their employment contract is terminated;
– representation and collective defence of the interests of workers and employers, including co-determination, subject to paragraph 6;
– conditions of employment for third-country nationals legally residing in Community territory;
– financial contributions for promotion of employment and job-creation, without prejudice to the provisions relating to the Social Fund.

4. A Member State may entrust management and labour, at their joint request, with the implementation of directives adopted pursuant to paragraphs 2 and 3.

In this case, it shall ensure that, no later than the date on which a directive must be transposed in accordance with Article 249, management and labour have introduced the necessary measures by agreement, the Member State concerned being required to take any necessary measure enabling it at any time to be in a position to guarantee the results imposed by that directive.

5. The provisions adopted pursuant to this Article shall not prevent any Member State from maintaining or introducing more stringent protective measures compatible with this Treaty.

6. The provisions of this Article shall not apply to pay, the right of association, the right to strike or the right to impose lock-outs.

Article 141

1. Each Member State shall ensure that the principle of equal pay for male and female workers for equal work or work of equal value is applied.

2. For the purpose of this Article, 'pay' means the ordinary basic or minimum wage or salary and any other consideration, whether in cash or in kind, which the worker receives directly or indirectly, in respect of his employment, from his employer.

Equal pay without discrimination based on sex means:

(a) that pay for the same work at piece rates shall be calculated on the basis of the same unit of measurement;

(b) that pay for work at time rates shall be the same for the same job.

3. The Council, acting in accordance with the procedure referred to in Article 251, and after consulting the Economic and Social Committee, shall adopt measures to ensure the application of the principle of equal opportunities and equal treatment of men and women in matters of employment and occupation, including the principle of equal pay for equal work or work of equal value.

4. With a view to ensuring full equality in practice between men and women in working life, the principle of equal treatment shall not prevent any Member State from maintaining or adopting measures providing for specific advantages in order to make it easier for the under-represented sex to pursue a vocational activity or to prevent or compensate for disadvantages in professional careers.

Article 190

1. The representatives in the European Parliament of the peoples of the States brought together in the Community shall be elected by direct universal suffrage.

2. The number of representatives elected in each Member State shall be as follows:

Belgium	25
Denmark	16
Germany	99
Greece	25
Spain	64
France	87
Ireland	15

Italy   87
Luxembourg   6
Netherlands   31
Austria   21
Portugal   25
Finland   16
Sweden   22
United Kingdom   87.

In the event of amendments to this paragraph, the number of representatives elected in each Member State must ensure appropriate representation of the peoples of the States brought together in the Community.
3. Representatives shall be elected for a term of five years.
4. The European Parliament shall draw up a proposal for elections by direct universal suffrage in accordance with a uniform procedure in all Member States or in accordance with principles common to all Member States.
The Council shall, acting unanimously after obtaining the assent of the European Parliament, which shall act by a majority of its component members, lay down the appropriate provisions, which it shall recommend to Member States for adoption in accordance with their respective constitutional requirements.
5. The European Parliament shall, after seeking an opinion from the Commission and with the approval of the Council acting unanimously, lay down the regulations and general conditions governing the performance of the duties of its Members.

Article 191

Political parties at European level are important as a factor for integration within the Union. They contribute to forming a European awareness and to expressing the political will of the citizens of the Union.

Article 192

Insofar as provided in this Treaty, the European Parliament shall participate in the process leading up to the adoption of Community acts by exercising its powers under the procedures laid down in Articles 251 and 252 and by giving its assent or delivering advisory opinions.
The European Parliament may, acting by a majority of its Members, request the Commission to submit any appropriate proposal on matters on which it considers that a Community act is required for the purpose of implementing this Treaty.

Article 194

Any citizen of the Union, and any natural or legal person residing or having its registered office in a Member State, shall have the right to address, individually or in association with other citizens or persons, a petition to the European Parliament on a matter which comes within the Community's fields of activity and which affects him, her or it directly.

Article 195

1. The European Parliament shall appoint an Ombudsman empowered to receive complaints from any citizen of the Union or any natural or legal person residing or having its registered office in a Member State concerning instances of maladministration in the activities of the Community institutions or bodies, with the exception of the Court of Justice and the Court of First Instance acting in their judicial role.
In accordance with his duties, the Ombudsman shall conduct inquiries for which he finds grounds, either on his own initiative or on the basis of complaints submitted to him direct or through a Member of the European Parliament, except where the alleged facts are or have been the subject of legal proceedings. Where the Ombudsman establishes an instance of maladministration, he shall refer the matter to the institution concerned, which shall have a period of three months in which to inform him of its views. The Ombudsman shall then forward a report to the European Parliament and the institution concerned. The person lodging the complaint shall be informed of the outcome of such inquiries.
The Ombudsman shall submit an annual report to the European Parliament on the outcome of his inquiries.
2. The Ombudsman shall be appointed after each election of the European Parliament for the duration of its term of office. The Ombudsman shall be eligible for reappointment.
The Ombudsman may be dismissed by the Court of Justice at the request of the European Parliament if he no longer fulfils the conditions required for the performance of his duties or if he is guilty of serious misconduct.
3. The Ombudsman shall be completely independent in the performance of his duties. In the performance of those duties he shall neither seek nor take instructions from any body. The Ombudsman may not, during his term of office, engage in any other occupation, whether gainful or not.
4. The European Parliament shall, after seeking an opinion from the Commission and with the approval of the Council acting by a qualified majority, lay down the regulations and general conditions governing the performance of the Ombudsman's duties.

Article 202

To ensure that the objectives set out in this Treaty are attained the Council shall, in accordance with the provisions of this Treaty:
– ensure coordination of the general economic policies of the Member States;
– have power to take decisions;

– confer on the Commission, in the acts which the Council adopts, powers for the implementation of the rules which the Council lays down. The Council may impose certain requirements in respect of the exercise of these powers. The Council may also reserve the right, in specific cases, to exercise directly implementing powers itself. The procedures referred to above must be consonant with principles and rules to be laid down in advance by the Council, acting unanimously on a proposal from the Commission and after obtaining the Opinion of the European Parliament.

Article 203

The Council shall consist of a representative of each Member State at ministerial level, authorised to commit the government of that Member State.
The office of President shall be held in turn by each Member State in the Council for a term of six months in the order decided by the Council acting unanimously.

Article 205

1. Save as otherwise provided in this Treaty, the Council shall act by a majority of its members.
2. Where the Council is required to act by a qualified majority, the votes of its members shall be weighted as follows:

Belgium	5
Denmark	3
Germany	10
Greece	5
Spain	8
France	10
Ireland	3
Italy	10
Luxembourg	2
Netherlands	5
Austria	4
Portugal	5
Finland	3
Sweden	4
United Kingdom	10.

For their adoption, acts of the Council shall require at least:
– 62 votes in favour where this Treaty requires them to be adopted on a proposal from the Commission,
– 62 votes in favour, cast by at least 10 members, in other cases.
3. Abstentions by members present in person or represented shall not prevent the adoption by the Council of acts which require unanimity.

Article 301

Where it is provided, in a common position or in a joint action adopted according to the provisions of the Treaty on European Union relating to the common foreign and security policy, for an action by the Community to interrupt or to reduce, in part or completely, economic relations with one or more third countries, the Council shall take the necessary urgent measures. The Council shall act by a qualified majority on a proposal from the Commission.

Article 308

If action by the Community should prove necessary to attain, in the course of the operation of the common market, one of the objectives of the Community and this Treaty has not provided the necessary powers, the Council shall, acting unanimously on a proposal from the Commission and after consulting the European Parliament, take the appropriate measures.

Annex II

RELEVANT PROVISIONS FROM THE TREATY OF LISBON

Treaty on European Union

Article 9

In all its activities, the Union shall observe the principle of the equality of its citizens, who shall receive equal attention from its institutions, bodies, offices and agencies. Every national of a Member State shall be a citizen of the Union. Citizenship of the Union shall be additional to national citizenship and shall not replace it.

Article 10

1. The functioning of the Union shall be founded on representative democracy.

2. Citizens are directly represented at Union level in the European Parliament.

Member States are represented in the European Council by their Heads of State or Government and in the Council by their governments, themselves democratically accountable either to their national Parliaments, or to their citizens.

3. Every citizen shall have the right to participate in the democratic life of the Union. Decisions shall be taken as openly and as closely as possible to the citizen.

4. Political parties at European level contribute to forming European political awareness and to expressing the will of citizens of the Union.

Article 11

1. The institutions shall, by appropriate means, give citizens and representative associations the opportunity to make known and publicly exchange their views in all areas of Union action.

2. The institutions shall maintain an open, transparent and regular dialogue with representative associations and civil society.

3. The European Commission shall carry out broad consultations with parties concerned in order to ensure that the Union's actions are coherent and transparent.

4. Not less than one million citizens who are nationals of a significant number of Member States may take the initiative of inviting the European Commission, within

the framework of its powers, to submit any appropriate proposal on matters where citizens consider that a legal act of the Union is required for the purpose of implementing the Treaties.

The procedures and conditions required for such a citizens' initiative shall be determined in accordance with the first paragraph of Article 24 of the Treaty on the Functioning of the European Union.

Article 12

National Parliaments contribute actively to the good functioning of the Union:

(a) through being informed by the institutions of the Union and having draft legislative acts of the Union forwarded to them in accordance with the Protocol on the role of national Parliaments in the European Union;

(b) by seeing to it that the principle of subsidiarity is respected in accordance with the procedures provided for in the Protocol on the application of the principles of subsidiarity and proportionality;

(c) by taking part, within the framework of the area of freedom, security and justice, in the evaluation mechanisms for the implementation of the Union policies in that area, in accordance with Article 70 of the Treaty on the Functioning of the European Union, and through being involved in the political monitoring of Europol and the evaluation of Eurojust's activities in accordance with Articles 88 and 85 of that Treaty;

(d) by taking part in the revision procedures of the Treaties, in accordance with Article 48 of this Treaty;

(e) by being notified of applications for accession to the Union, in accordance with Article 49 of this Treaty;

(f) by taking part in the inter-parliamentary cooperation between national Parliaments and with the European Parliament, in accordance with the Protocol on the role of national Parliaments in the European Union.

Article 14

1. The European Parliament shall, jointly with the Council, exercise legislative and budgetary functions. It shall exercise functions of political control and consultation as laid down in the Treaties. It shall elect the President of the Commission.

2. The European Parliament shall be composed of representatives of the Union's citizens. They shall not exceed seven hundred and fifty in number, plus the President. Representation of citizens shall be degressively proportional, with a minimum threshold of six members per Member State. No Member State shall be allocated more than ninety-six seats.

The European Council shall adopt by unanimity, on the initiative of the European Parliament and with its consent, a decision establishing the composition of the European Parliament, respecting the principles referred to in the first subparagraph.

3. The members of the European Parliament shall be elected for a term of five years by direct universal suffrage in a free and secret ballot.

4. The European Parliament shall elect its President and its officers from among its members.

Article 16

1. The Council shall, jointly with the European Parliament, exercise legislative and budgetary functions. It shall carry out policy-making and coordinating functions as laid down in the Treaties.

2. The Council shall consist of a representative of each Member State at ministerial level, who may commit the government of the Member State in question and cast its vote.

3. The Council shall act by a qualified majority except where the Treaties provide otherwise.

4. As from 1 November 2014, a qualified majority shall be defined as at least 55 % of the members of the Council, comprising at least fifteen of them and representing Member States comprising at least 65 % of the population of the Union.

A blocking minority must include at least four Council members, failing which the qualified majority shall be deemed attained.

The other arrangements governing the qualified majority are laid down in Article 238(2) of the Treaty on the Functioning of the European Union.

5. The transitional provisions relating to the definition of the qualified majority which shall be applicable until 31 October 2014 and those which shall be applicable from 1 November 2014 to 31 March 2017 are laid down in the Protocol on transitional provisions.

6. The Council shall meet in different configurations, the list of which shall be adopted in accordance with Article 236 of the Treaty on the Functioning of the European Union.

The General Affairs Council shall ensure consistency in the work of the different Council configurations. It shall prepare and ensure the follow-up to meetings of the European Council, in liaison with the President of the European Council and the Commission.

The Foreign Affairs Council shall elaborate the Union's external action on the basis of strategic guidelines laid down by the European Council and ensure that the Union's action is consistent.

7. A Committee of Permanent Representatives of the Governments of the Member States shall be responsible for preparing the work of the Council.

8. The Council shall meet in public when it deliberates and votes on a draft legislative act. To this end, each Council meeting shall be divided into two parts, dealing respectively with deliberations on Union legislative acts and non-legislative activities.

9. The Presidency of Council configurations, other than that of Foreign Affairs, shall be held by Member State representatives in the Council on the basis of equal rotation, in accordance with the conditions established in accordance with Article 236 of the Treaty on the Functioning of the European Union.

THE TREATY ON THE FUNCTIONING OF THE EUROPEAN UNION

Article 15

(ex Article 255 TEC)

1. In order to promote good governance and ensure the participation of civil society, the Union institutions, bodies, offices and agencies shall conduct their work as openly as possible.

2. The European Parliament shall meet in public, as shall the Council when considering and voting on a draft legislative act.

3. Any citizen of the Union, and any natural or legal person residing or having its registered office in a Member State, shall have a right of access to documents of the Union institutions, bodies, offices and agencies, whatever their medium, subject to the principles and the conditions to be defined in accordance with this paragraph.

General principles and limits on grounds of public or private interest governing this right of access to documents shall be determined by the European Parliament and the Council, by means of regulations, acting in accordance with the ordinary legislative procedure.

Each institution, body, office or agency shall ensure that its proceedings are transparent and shall elaborate in its own Rules of Procedure specific provisions regarding access to its documents, in accordance with the regulations referred to in the second subparagraph.

The Court of Justice of the European Union, the European Central Bank and the European Investment Bank shall be subject to this paragraph only when exercising their administrative tasks.

The European Parliament and the Council shall ensure publication of the documents relating to the legislative procedures under the terms laid down by the regulations referred to in the second subparagraph.

Article 19

(ex Article 13 TEC)

1. Without prejudice to the other provisions of the Treaties and within the limits of the powers conferred by them upon the Union, the Council, acting unanimously in accordance with a special legislative procedure and after obtaining the consent of the European Parliament, may take appropriate action to combat discrimination based on sex, racial or ethnic origin, religion or belief, disability, age or sexual orientation.

2. By way of derogation from paragraph 1, the European Parliament and the Council, acting in accordance with the ordinary legislative procedure, may adopt the basic principles of Union incentive measures, excluding any harmonisation of the laws and regulations of the Member States, to support action taken by the Member States in order to contribute to the achievement of the objectives referred to in paragraph 1.

Article 20

(ex Article 17 TEC)

1. Citizenship of the Union is hereby established. Every person holding the nationality of a Member State shall be a citizen of the Union. Citizenship of the Union shall be additional to and not replace national citizenship.

2. Citizens of the Union shall enjoy the rights and be subject to the duties provided for in the Treaties. They shall have, inter alia:

(a) the right to move and reside freely within the territory of the Member States;

(b) the right to vote and to stand as candidates in elections to the European Parliament and in municipal elections in their Member State of residence, under the same conditions as nationals of that State;

(c) the right to enjoy, in the territory of a third country in which the Member State of which they are nationals is not represented, the protection of the diplomatic and consular authorities of any Member State on the same conditions as the nationals of that State;

(d) the right to petition the European Parliament, to apply to the European Ombudsman, and to address the institutions and advisory bodies of the Union in any of the Treaty languages and to obtain a reply in the same language.

These rights shall be exercised in accordance with the conditions and limits defined by the Treaties and by the measures adopted thereunder.

Article 21

(ex Article 18 TEC)

1. Every citizen of the Union shall have the right to move and reside freely within the territory of the Member States, subject to the limitations and conditions laid down in the Treaties and by the measures adopted to give them effect.

2. If action by the Union should prove necessary to attain this objective and the Treaties have not provided the necessary powers, the European Parliament and the Council, acting in accordance with the ordinary legislative procedure, may adopt provisions with a view to facilitating the exercise of the rights referred to in paragraph 1.

3. For the same purposes as those referred to in paragraph 1 and if the Treaties have not provided the necessary powers, the Council, acting in accordance with a special legislative procedure, may adopt measures concerning social security or social protection. The Council shall act unanimously after consulting the European Parliament.

Article 22

(ex Article 19 TEC)

1. Every citizen of the Union residing in a Member State of which he is not a national shall have the right to vote and to stand as a candidate at municipal elections in the Member State in which he resides, under the same conditions as nationals of that State. This right shall be exercised subject to detailed arrangements adopted by the Council, acting unanimously in accordance with a special legislative procedure and after consulting the European Parliament; these arrangements may provide for derogations where warranted by problems specific to a Member State.

2. Without prejudice to Article 223(1) and to the provisions adopted for its implementation, every citizen of the Union residing in a Member State of which he is not a national shall have the right to vote and to stand as a candidate in elections to the European Parliament in the Member State in which he resides, under the same conditions as nationals of that State. This right shall be exercised subject to detailed arrangements adopted by the Council, acting unanimously in accordance with a special legislative procedure and after consulting the European Parliament; these arrangements may provide for derogations where warranted by problems specific to a Member State.

Article 23

(ex Article 20 TEC)

Every citizen of the Union shall, in the territory of a third country in which the Member State of which he is a national is not represented, be entitled to protection by the diplomatic or consular authorities of any Member State, on the same conditions as the nationals of that State. Member States shall adopt the necessary provisions and start the international negotiations required to secure this protection.

The Council, acting in accordance with a special legislative procedure and after consulting the European Parliament, may adopt directives establishing the coordination and cooperation measures necessary to facilitate such protection.

Article 24

(ex Article 21 TEC)

The European Parliament and the Council, acting by means of regulations in accordance with the ordinary legislative procedure, shall adopt the provisions for the procedures and conditions required for a citizens' initiative within the meaning of Article 11 of the Treaty on European Union, including the minimum number of Member States from which such citizens must come.

Every citizen of the Union shall have the right to petition the European Parliament in accordance with Article 227.

Every citizen of the Union may apply to the Ombudsman established in accordance with Article 228.

Every citizen of the Union may write to any of the institutions, bodies, offices or agencies referred to in this Article or in Article 13 of the Treaty on European Union in one of the languages mentioned in Article 55(1) of the Treaty on European Union and have an answer in the same language.

Article 45

(ex Article 39 TEC)

1. Freedom of movement for workers shall be secured within the Union.

2. Such freedom of movement shall entail the abolition of any discrimination based on nationality between workers of the Member States as regards employment, remuneration and other conditions of work and employment.

3. It shall entail the right, subject to limitations justified on grounds of public policy, public security or public health:

(a) to accept offers of employment actually made;

(b) to move freely within the territory of Member States for this purpose;

(c) to stay in a Member State for the purpose of employment in accordance with the provisions governing the employment of nationals of that State laid down by law, regulation or administrative action;

(d) to remain in the territory of a Member State after having been employed in that State, subject to conditions which shall be embodied in regulations to be drawn up by the Commission.

4. The provisions of this Article shall not apply to employment in the public service.

Article 49

(ex Article 43 TEC)

Within the framework of the provisions set out below, restrictions on the freedom of establishment of nationals of a Member State in the territory of another Member State shall be prohibited. Such prohibition shall also apply to restrictions on the setting-up of agencies, branches or subsidiaries by nationals of any Member State established in the territory of any Member State.

Freedom of establishment shall include the right to take up and pursue activities as self-employed persons and to set up and manage undertakings, in particular companies or firms within the meaning of the second paragraph of Article 54, under the conditions laid down for its own nationals by the law of the country where such establishment is effected, subject to the provisions of the Chapter relating to capital.

Article 53

(ex Article 47 TEC)

1. In order to make it easier for persons to take up and pursue activities as self-employed persons, the European Parliament and the Council shall, acting in accordance with the ordinary legislative procedure, issue directives for the mutual recognition of diplomas, certificates and other evidence of formal qualifications and for the coordination of the provisions laid down by law, regulation or administrative action in Member States concerning the taking-up and pursuit of activities as self-employed persons.

2. In the case of the medical and allied and pharmaceutical professions, the progressive abolition of restrictions shall be dependent upon coordination of the conditions for their exercise in the various Member States.

Article 56

(ex Article 49 TEC)

Within the framework of the provisions set out below, restrictions on freedom to provide services within the Union shall be prohibited in respect of nationals of Member States who are established in a Member State other than that of the person for whom the services are intended.

The European Parliament and the Council, acting in accordance with the ordinary legislative procedure, may extend the provisions of the Chapter to nationals of a third country who provide services and who are established within the Union.

Article 57

(ex Article 50 TEC)

Services shall be considered to be "services" within the meaning of the Treaties where they are normally provided for remuneration, in so far as they are not governed by the provisions relating to freedom of movement for goods, capital and persons.

"Services" shall in particular include:

(a) activities of an industrial character;

(b) activities of a commercial character;

(c) activities of craftsmen;

(d) activities of the professions.

Without prejudice to the provisions of the Chapter relating to the right of establishment, the person providing a service may, in order to do so, temporarily pursue his activity in the Member State where the service is provided, under the same conditions as are imposed by that State on its own nationals.

Article 75

(ex Article 60 TEC)

Where necessary to achieve the objectives set out in Article 67, as regards preventing and combating terrorism and related activities, the European Parliament and the Council, acting by means of regulations in accordance with the ordinary legislative procedure, shall define a framework for administrative measures with regard to capital movements and payments, such as the freezing of funds, financial assets or economic gains belonging to, or owned or held by, natural or legal persons, groups or non-State entities.

The Council, on a proposal from the Commission, shall adopt measures to implement the framework referred to in the first paragraph.

The acts referred to in this Article shall include necessary provisions on legal safeguards.

Article 78

(ex Articles 63, points 1 and 2, and 64(2) TEC)

1. The Union shall develop a common policy on asylum, subsidiary protection and temporary protection with a view to offering appropriate status to any third-country national requiring international protection and ensuring compliance with the principle of non-refoulement. This policy must be in accordance with the Geneva Convention of 28 July 1951 and the Protocol of 31 January 1967 relating to the status of refugees, and other relevant treaties.

2. For the purposes of paragraph 1, the European Parliament and the Council, acting in accordance with the ordinary legislative procedure, shall adopt measures for a common European asylum system comprising:

(a) a uniform status of asylum for nationals of third countries, valid throughout the Union;

(b) a uniform status of subsidiary protection for nationals of third countries who, without obtaining European asylum, are in need of international protection;

(c) a common system of temporary protection for displaced persons in the event of a massive inflow;

(d) common procedures for the granting and withdrawing of uniform asylum or subsidiary protection status;

(e) criteria and mechanisms for determining which Member State is responsible for considering an application for asylum or subsidiary protection;

(f) standards concerning the conditions for the reception of applicants for asylum or subsidiary protection;

(g) partnership and cooperation with third countries for the purpose of managing inflows of people applying for asylum or subsidiary or temporary protection.

3. In the event of one or more Member States being confronted by an emergency situation characterised by a sudden inflow of nationals of third countries, the Council, on a proposal from the Commission, may adopt provisional measures for the benefit of the Member State(s) concerned. It shall act after consulting the European Parliament.

Article 79

(ex Article 63, points 3 and 4, TEC)

1. The Union shall develop a common immigration policy aimed at ensuring, at all stages, the efficient management of migration flows, fair treatment of third-country nationals residing legally in Member States, and the prevention of, and enhanced measures to combat, illegal immigration and trafficking in human beings.

2. For the purposes of paragraph 1, the European Parliament and the Council, acting in accordance with the ordinary legislative procedure, shall adopt measures in the following areas:

(a) the conditions of entry and residence, and standards on the issue by Member States of long-term visas and residence permits, including those for the purpose of family reunification;

(b) the definition of the rights of third-country nationals residing legally in a Member State, including the conditions governing freedom of movement and of residence in other Member States;

(c) illegal immigration and unauthorised residence, including removal and repatriation of persons residing without authorisation;

(d) combating trafficking in persons, in particular women and children.

3. The Union may conclude agreements with third countries for the readmission to their countries of origin or provenance of third-country nationals who do not or who no longer fulfil the conditions for entry, presence or residence in the territory of one of the Member States.

4. The European Parliament and the Council, acting in accordance with the ordinary legislative procedure, may establish measures to provide incentives and support for the action of Member States with a view to promoting the integration of third-country nationals residing legally in their territories, excluding any harmonisation of the laws and regulations of the Member States.

5. This Article shall not affect the right of Member States to determine volumes of admission of third-country nationals coming from third countries to their territory in order to seek work, whether employed or self-employed.

Article 151

(ex Article 136 TEC)

The Union and the Member States, having in mind fundamental social rights such as those set out in the European Social Charter signed at Turin on 18 October 1961 and in the 1989 Community Charter of the Fundamental Social Rights of Workers, shall have as their objectives the promotion of employment, improved living and working conditions, so as to make possible their harmonisation while the improvement is being maintained, proper social protection, dialogue between management and labour, the development of human resources with a view to lasting high employment and the combating of exclusion.

To this end the Union and the Member States shall implement measures which take account of the diverse forms of national practices, in particular in the field of contractual relations, and the need to maintain the competitiveness of the Union economy.

They believe that such a development will ensue not only from the functioning of the internal market, which will favour the harmonisation of social systems, but also from the procedures provided for in the Treaties and from the approximation of provisions laid down by law, regulation or administrative action.

Article 223

(ex Article 190(4) and (5) TEC)

1. The European Parliament shall draw up a proposal to lay down the provisions necessary for the election of its Members by direct universal suffrage in accordance with a uniform procedure in all Member States or in accordance with principles common to all Member States.

The Council, acting unanimously in accordance with a special legislative procedure and after obtaining the consent of the European Parliament, which shall act by a majority of its component Members, shall lay down the necessary provisions. These provisions shall enter into force following their approval by the Member States in accordance with their respective constitutional requirements.

2. The European Parliament, acting by means of regulations on its own initiative in accordance with a special legislative procedure after seeking an opinion from the Commission and with the approval of the Council, shall lay down the regulations and general conditions governing the performance of the duties of its Members. All rules or conditions relating to the taxation of Members or former Members shall require unanimity within the Council.

Article 227

(ex Article 194 TEC)

Any citizen of the Union, and any natural or legal person residing or having its registered office in a Member State, shall have the right to address, individually or in association with other citizens or persons, a petition to the European Parliament on a matter which comes within the Union's fields of activity and which affects him, her or it directly.

Article 228

(ex Article 195 TEC)

1. A European Ombudsman, elected by the European Parliament, shall be empowered to receive complaints from any citizen of the Union or any natural or legal person residing or having its registered office in a Member State concerning instances of maladministration in the activities of the Union institutions, bodies, offices or agencies, with the exception of the Court of Justice of the European Union acting in its judicial role. He or she shall examine such complaints and report on them.

In accordance with his duties, the Ombudsman shall conduct inquiries for which he finds grounds, either on his own initiative or on the basis of complaints submitted to him direct or through a Member of the European Parliament, except where the alleged facts are or have been the subject of legal proceedings. Where the Ombudsman establishes an instance of maladministration, he shall refer the matter to the institution, body, office or agency concerned, which shall have a period of three months in which to inform him of its views. The Ombudsman shall then forward a report to the European Parliament and the institution, body, office or agency concerned. The person lodging the complaint shall be informed of the outcome of such inquiries.

The Ombudsman shall submit an annual report to the European Parliament on the outcome of his inquiries.

2. The Ombudsman shall be elected after each election of the European Parliament for the duration of its term of office. The Ombudsman shall be eligible for reappointment.

The Ombudsman may be dismissed by the Court of Justice at the request of the European Parliament if he no longer fulfils the conditions required for the performance of his duties or if he is guilty of serious misconduct.

3. The Ombudsman shall be completely independent in the performance of his duties. In the performance of those duties he shall neither seek nor take instructions from any Government, institution, body, office or entity. The Ombudsman may not, during his term of office, engage in any other occupation, whether gainful or not.

4. The European Parliament acting by means of regulations on its own initiative in accordance with a special legislative procedure shall, after seeking an opinion from the Commission and with the approval of the Council, lay down the regulations and general conditions governing the performance of the Ombudsman's duties.

Article 238

(ex Article 205(1) and (2), TEC)

1. Where it is required to act by a simple majority, the Council shall act by a majority of its component members.

2. By way of derogation from Article 16(4) of the Treaty on European Union, as from 1 November 2014 and subject to the provisions laid down in the Protocol on transitional provisions, where the Council does not act on a proposal from the Commission or from the High Representative of the Union for Foreign Affairs and Security Policy, the qualified majority shall be defined as at least 72 % of the members of the Council, representing Member States comprising at least 65 % of the population of the Union.

3. As from 1 November 2014 and subject to the provisions laid down in the Protocol on transitional provisions, in cases where, under the Treaties, not all the members of the Council participate in voting, a qualified majority shall be defined as follows:

(a) A qualified majority shall be defined as at least 55 % of the members of the Council representing the participating Member States, comprising at least 65 % of the population of these States.

A blocking minority must include at least the minimum number of Council members representing more than 35 % of the population of the participating Member States, plus one member, failing which the qualified majority shall be deemed attained;

(b) By way of derogation from point (a), where the Council does not act on a proposal from the Commission or from the High Representative of the Union for Foreign Affairs and Security Policy, the qualified majority shall be defined as at least 72 % of the members of the Council representing the participating Member States, comprising at least 65 % of the population of these States.

4. Abstentions by Members present in person or represented shall not prevent the adoption by the Council of acts which require unanimity.

PROTOCOL (No 1)

ON THE ROLE OF NATIONAL PARLIAMENTS IN THE EUROPEAN UNION

THE HIGH CONTRACTING PARTIES,

RECALLING that the way in which national Parliaments scrutinise their governments in relation to the activities of the Union is a matter for the particular constitutional organisation and practice of each Member State,

DESIRING to encourage greater involvement of national Parliaments in the activities of the European Union and to enhance their ability to express their views on draft legislative acts of the Union as well as on other matters which may be of particular interest to them,

HAVE AGREED UPON the following provisions, which shall be annexed to the Treaty on European Union, to the Treaty on the Functioning of the European Union and to the Treaty establishing the European Atomic Energy Community:

TITLE I

INFORMATION FOR NATIONAL PARLIAMENTS

Article 1

Commission consultation documents (green and white papers and communications) shall be forwarded directly by the Commission to national Parliaments upon publication. The Commission shall also forward the annual legislative programme as well as any other instrument of legislative planning or policy to national Parliaments, at the same time as to the European Parliament and the Council.

Article 2

Draft legislative acts sent to the European Parliament and to the Council shall be forwarded to national Parliaments.

For the purposes of this Protocol, "draft legislative acts" shall mean proposals from the Commission, initiatives from a group of Member States, initiatives from the European Parliament, requests from the Court of Justice, recommendations from the European Central Bank and requests from the European Investment Bank for the adoption of a legislative act.

Draft legislative acts originating from the Commission shall be forwarded to national Parliaments directly by the Commission, at the same time as to the European Parliament and the Council.

Draft legislative acts originating from the European Parliament shall be forwarded to national Parliaments directly by the European Parliament.

Draft legislative acts originating from a group of Member States, the Court of Justice, the European Central Bank or the European Investment Bank shall be forwarded to national Parliaments by the Council.

Article 3

National Parliaments may send to the Presidents of the European Parliament, the Council and the Commission a reasoned opinion on whether a draft legislative act complies with the principle of subsidiarity, in accordance with the procedure laid down in the Protocol on the application of the principles of subsidiarity and proportionality.

If the draft legislative act originates from a group of Member States, the President of the Council shall forward the reasoned opinion or opinions to the governments of those Member States.

If the draft legislative act originates from the Court of Justice, the European Central Bank or the European Investment Bank, the President of the Council shall forward the reasoned opinion or opinions to the institution or body concerned.

Article 4

An eight-week period shall elapse between a draft legislative act being made available to national Parliaments in the official languages of the Union and the date when it is placed on a provisional agenda for the Council for its adoption or for adoption of a position under a legislative procedure. Exceptions shall be possible in cases of urgency, the reasons for which shall be stated in the act or position of the Council. Save in urgent cases for which due reasons have been given, no agreement may be reached on a draft legislative act during those eight weeks. Save in urgent cases for which due reasons have been given, a ten-day period shall elapse between the placing of a draft legislative act on the provisional agenda for the Council and the adoption of a position.

Article 5

The agendas for and the outcome of meetings of the Council, including the minutes of meetings where the Council is deliberating on draft legislative acts, shall be forwarded directly to national Parliaments, at the same time as to Member States' governments.

Article 6

When the European Council intends to make use of the first or second subparagraphs of Article 48(7) of the Treaty on European Union, national Parliaments shall be informed of the initiative of the European Council at least six months before any decision is adopted.

Article 7

The Court of Auditors shall forward its annual report to national Parliaments, for information, at the same time as to the European Parliament and to the Council.

Article 8

Where the national Parliamentary system is not unicameral, Articles 1 to 7 shall apply to the component chambers.

TITLE II

INTERPARLIAMENTARY COOPERATION

Article 9

The European Parliament and national Parliaments shall together determine the organisation and promotion of effective and regular interparliamentary cooperation within the Union.

Article 10

A conference of Parliamentary Committees for Union Affairs may submit any contribution it deems appropriate for the attention of the European Parliament, the Council and the Commission. That conference shall in addition promote the exchange of information and best practice between national Parliaments and the European Parliament, including their special committees. It may also organise interparliamentary conferences on specific topics, in particular to debate matters of common foreign and security policy, including common security and defence policy. Contributions from the conference shall not bind national Parliaments and shall not prejudge their positions.

Annex III

DIRECTIVE 2004/38/EC OF THE EUROPEAN PARLIAMENT AND OF THE COUNCIL of 29 April 2004

on the right of citizens of the Union and their family members to move and reside freely within the territory of the Member States amending Regulation (EEC) No 1612/68

and repealing Directives

64/221/EEC, 68/360/EEC, 72/194/EEC, 73/148/EEC, 75/34/EEC, 75/35/EEC, 90/364/EEC, 90/365/EEC and 93/96/EEC

(Text with EEA relevance)

(OJ L 229, 29.6.2004, p. 35)

THE EUROPEAN PARLIAMENT AND THE COUNCIL OF THE EUROPEAN UNION,

Having regard to the Treaty establishing the European Community, and in particular Articles 12, 18, 40, 44 and 52 thereof,

Having regard to the proposal from the Commission (¹),

Having regard to the opinion of the European Economic and Social Committee (²),

Having regard to the opinion of the Committee of the Regions (³),

Acting in accordance with the procedure laid down in Article 251 of the Treaty (⁴),

Whereas:

(1) Citizenship of the Union confers on every citizen of the Union a primary and individual right to move and reside freely within the territory of the Member States, subject to the limitations and conditions laid down in the Treaty and to the measures adopted to give it effect.

(2) The free movement of persons constitutes one of the fundamental freedoms of the internal market, which comprises an area without internal frontiers, in which freedom is ensured in accordance with the provisions of the Treaty.

(3) Union citizenship should be the fundamental status of nationals of the Member States when they exercise their right of free movement and residence. It is therefore necessary to codify and review the existing Community instruments dealing separately with workers, self-employed persons, as well as students and other inactive persons in order to simplify and strengthen the right of free movement and residence of all Union citizens.

(4) With a view to remedying this sector-by-sector, piecemeal approach to the right of free movement and residence and facilitating the exercise of this right, there needs to be a single legislative act to amend Council Regulation (EEC) No 1612/68 of 15 October 1968 on freedom of movement for workers within the Community (⁵), and to repeal the following acts: Council Directive 68/360/EEC of 15 October 1968 on the abolition of restrictions on movement and residence within the Community for workers of Member States and their families (⁶), Council Directive 73/148/EEC of 21 May 1973 on the abolition of restrictions on movement and residence within the Community for nationals of Member States with regard to establishment and

---

(¹) OJ C 270 E, 25.9.2001, p. 150.
(²) OJ C 149, 21.6.2002, p. 46.
(³) OJ C 192, 12.8.2002, p. 17.
(⁴) Opinion of the European Parliament of 11 February 2003 (OJ C 43 E, 19.2.2004, p. 42), Council Common Position of 5 December 2003 (OJ C 54 E, 2.3.2004, p. 12) and Position of the European Parliament of 10 March 2004 (not yet published in the Official Journal).
(⁵) OJ L 257, 19.10.1968, p. 2. Regulation as last amended by Regulation (EEC) No 2434/92 (OJ L 245, 26.8.1992, p. 1).
(⁶) OJ L 257, 19.10.1968, p. 13. Directive as last amended by the 2003 Act of Accession.

the provision of services (^{1}), Council Directive 90/364/EEC of 28 June 1990 on the right of residence (^{2}), Council Directive 90/365/EEC of 28 June 1990 on the right of residence for employees and self-employed persons who have ceased their occupational activity (^{3}) and Council Directive 93/96/EEC of 29 October 1993 on the right of residence for students (^{4}).

(5)   The right of all Union citizens to move and reside freely within the territory of the Member States should, if it is to be exercised under objective conditions of freedom and dignity, be also granted to their family members, irrespective of nationality. For the purposes of this Directive, the definition of 'family member' should also include the registered partner if the legislation of the host Member State treats registered partnership as equivalent to marriage.

(6)   In order to maintain the unity of the family in a broader sense and without prejudice to the prohibition of discrimination on grounds of nationality, the situation of those persons who are not included in the definition of family members under this Directive, and who therefore do not enjoy an automatic right of entry and residence in the host Member State, should be examined by the host Member State on the basis of its own national legislation, in order to decide whether entry and residence could be granted to such persons, taking into consideration their relationship with the Union citizen or any other circumstances, such as their financial or physical dependence on the Union citizen.

(7)   The formalities connected with the free movement of Union citizens within the territory of Member States should be clearly defined, without prejudice to the provisions applicable to national border controls.

(8)   With a view to facilitating the free movement of family members who are not nationals of a Member State, those who have already obtained a residence card should be exempted from the requirement to obtain an entry visa within the meaning of Council Regulation (EC) No 539/2001 of 15 March 2001 listing the third countries whose nationals must be in possession of visas when crossing the external borders and those whose nationals are exempt from that requirement (^{5}) or, where appropriate, of the applicable national legislation.

(9)   Union citizens should have the right of residence in the host Member State for a period not exceeding three months without being subject to any conditions or any formalities other than the requirement to hold a valid identity card or passport, without prejudice to a more favourable treatment applicable to job-seekers as recognised by the case-law of the Court of Justice.

(10)   Persons exercising their right of residence should not, however, become an unreasonable burden on the social assistance system of the host Member State during an initial period of residence. Therefore, the right of residence for Union citizens and their family members for periods in excess of three months should be subject to conditions.

(11)   The fundamental and personal right of residence in another Member State is conferred directly on Union citizens by the Treaty and is not dependent upon their having fulfilled administrative procedures.

(12)   For periods of residence of longer than three months, Member States should have the possibility to require Union citizens to

---

(^{1}) OJ L 172, 28.6.1973, p. 14.
(^{2}) OJ L 180, 13.7.1990, p. 26.
(^{3}) OJ L 180, 13.7.1990, p. 28.
(^{4}) OJ L 317, 18.12.1993, p. 59.
(^{5}) OJ L 81, 21.3.2001, p. 1. Regulation as last amended by Regulation (EC) No 453/2003 (OJ L 69, 13.3.2003, p. 10).

register with the competent authorities in the place of residence, attested by a registration certificate issued to that effect.

(13) The residence card requirement should be restricted to family members of Union citizens who are not nationals of a Member State for periods of residence of longer than three months.

(14) The supporting documents required by the competent authorities for the issuing of a registration certificate or of a residence card should be comprehensively specified in order to avoid divergent administrative practices or interpretations constituting an undue obstacle to the exercise of the right of residence by Union citizens and their family members.

(15) Family members should be legally safeguarded in the event of the death of the Union citizen, divorce, annulment of marriage or termination of a registered partnership. With due regard for family life and human dignity, and in certain conditions to guard against abuse, measures should therefore be taken to ensure that in such circumstances family members already residing within the territory of the host Member State retain their right of residence exclusively on a personal basis.

(16) As long as the beneficiaries of the right of residence do not become an unreasonable burden on the social assistance system of the host Member State they should not be expelled. Therefore, an expulsion measure should not be the automatic consequence of recourse to the social assistance system. The host Member State should examine whether it is a case of temporary difficulties and take into account the duration of residence, the personal circumstances and the amount of aid granted in order to consider whether the beneficiary has become an unreasonable burden on its social assistance system and to proceed to his expulsion. In no case should an expulsion measure be adopted against workers, self-employed persons or job-seekers as defined by the Court of Justice save on grounds of public policy or public security.

(17) Enjoyment of permanent residence by Union citizens who have chosen to settle long term in the host Member State would strengthen the feeling of Union citizenship and is a key element in promoting social cohesion, which is one of the fundamental objectives of the Union. A right of permanent residence should therefore be laid down for all Union citizens and their family members who have resided in the host Member State in compliance with the conditions laid down in this Directive during a continuous period of five years without becoming subject to an expulsion measure.

(18) In order to be a genuine vehicle for integration into the society of the host Member State in which the Union citizen resides, the right of permanent residence, once obtained, should not be subject to any conditions.

(19) Certain advantages specific to Union citizens who are workers or self-employed persons and to their family members, which may allow these persons to acquire a right of permanent residence before they have resided five years in the host Member State, should be maintained, as these constitute acquired rights, conferred by Commission Regulation (EEC) No 1251/70 of 29 June 1970 on the right of workers to remain in the territory of a Member State after having been employed in that State [1] and Council Directive 75/34/EEC of 17 December 1974 concerning the right of nationals of a Member State to remain in the territory of another Member State after having pursued therein an activity in a self-employed capacity [2].

(20) In accordance with the prohibition of discrimination on grounds of nationality, all Union citizens and their family members

---

[1] OJ L 142, 30.6.1970, p. 24.
[2] OJ L 14, 20.1.1975, p. 10.

residing in a Member State on the basis of this Directive should enjoy, in that Member State, equal treatment with nationals in areas covered by the Treaty, subject to such specific provisions as are expressly provided for in the Treaty and secondary law.

(21)   However, it should be left to the host Member State to decide whether it will grant social assistance during the first three months of residence, or for a longer period in the case of job-seekers, to Union citizens other than those who are workers or self-employed persons or who retain that status or their family members, or maintenance assistance for studies, including vocational training, prior to acquisition of the right of permanent residence, to these same persons.

(22)   The Treaty allows restrictions to be placed on the right of free movement and residence on grounds of public policy, public security or public health. In order to ensure a tighter definition of the circumstances and procedural safeguards subject to which Union citizens and their family members may be denied leave to enter or may be expelled, this Directive should replace Council Directive 64/221/EEC of 25 February 1964 on the coordination of special measures concerning the movement and residence of foreign nationals, which are justified on grounds of public policy, public security or public health (^{1}).

(23)   Expulsion of Union citizens and their family members on grounds of public policy or public security is a measure that can seriously harm persons who, having availed themselves of the rights and freedoms conferred on them by the Treaty, have become genuinely integrated into the host Member State. The scope for such measures should therefore be limited in accordance with the principle of proportionality to take account of the degree of integration of the persons concerned, the length of their residence in the host Member State, their age, state of health, family and economic situation and the links with their country of origin.

(24)   Accordingly, the greater the degree of integration of Union citizens and their family members in the host Member State, the greater the degree of protection against expulsion should be. Only in exceptional circumstances, where there are imperative grounds of public security, should an expulsion measure be taken against Union citizens who have resided for many years in the territory of the host Member State, in particular when they were born and have resided there throughout their life. In addition, such exceptional circumstances should also apply to an expulsion measure taken against minors, in order to protect their links with their family, in accordance with the United Nations Convention on the Rights of the Child, of 20 November 1989.

(25)   Procedural safeguards should also be specified in detail in order to ensure a high level of protection of the rights of Union citizens and their family members in the event of their being denied leave to enter or reside in another Member State, as well as to uphold the principle that any action taken by the authorities must be properly justified.

(26)   In all events, judicial redress procedures should be available to Union citizens and their family members who have been refused leave to enter or reside in another Member State.

(27)   In line with the case-law of the Court of Justice prohibiting Member States from issuing orders excluding for life persons covered by this Directive from their territory, the right of Union citizens and their family members who have been excluded from the territory of a Member State to submit a fresh application after a reasonable period, and in any event after a three year period

---

(^{1}) OJ 56, 4.4.1964, p. 850. Directive as last amended by Directive 75/35/EEC (OJ 14, 20.1.1975, p. 14).

from enforcement of the final exclusion order, should be confirmed.

(28) To guard against abuse of rights or fraud, notably marriages of convenience or any other form of relationships contracted for the sole purpose of enjoying the right of free movement and residence, Member States should have the possibility to adopt the necessary measures.

(29) This Directive should not affect more favourable national provisions.

(30) With a view to examining how further to facilitate the exercise of the right of free movement and residence, a report should be prepared by the Commission in order to evaluate the opportunity to present any necessary proposals to this effect, notably on the extension of the period of residence with no conditions.

(31) This Directive respects the fundamental rights and freedoms and observes the principles recognised in particular by the Charter of Fundamental Rights of the European Union. In accordance with the prohibition of discrimination contained in the Charter, Member States should implement this Directive without discrimination between the beneficiaries of this Directive on grounds such as sex, race, colour, ethnic or social origin, genetic characteristics, language, religion or beliefs, political or other opinion, membership of an ethnic minority, property, birth, disability, age or sexual orientation,

HAVE ADOPTED THIS DIRECTIVE:

CHAPTER I

GENERAL PROVISIONS

Article 1

Subject

This Directive lays down:

(a) the conditions governing the exercise of the right of free movement and residence within the territory of the Member States by Union citizens and their family members;

(b) the right of permanent residence in the territory of the Member States for Union citizens and their family members;

(c) the limits placed on the rights set out in (a) and (b) on grounds of public policy, public security or public health.

Article 2

Definitions

For the purposes of this Directive:

1. 'Union citizen' means any person having the nationality of a Member State;

2. 'family member' means:

   (a) the spouse;

   (b) the partner with whom the Union citizen has contracted a registered partnership, on the basis of the legislation of a Member State, if the legislation of the host Member State treats registered partnerships as equivalent to marriage and in accordance with the conditions laid down in the relevant legislation of the host Member State;

   (c) the direct descendants who are under the age of 21 or are dependants and those of the spouse or partner as defined in point (b);

(d) the dependent direct relatives in the ascending line and those of the spouse or partner as defined in point (b);

3. 'host Member State' means the Member State to which a Union citizen moves in order to exercise his/her right of free movement and residence.

Article 3

Beneficiaries

1.   This Directive shall apply to all Union citizens who move to or reside in a Member State other than that of which they are a national, and to their family members as defined in point 2 of Article 2 who accompany or join them.

2.   Without prejudice to any right to free movement and residence the persons concerned may have in their own right, the host Member State shall, in accordance with its national legislation, facilitate entry and residence for the following persons:

(a) any other family members, irrespective of their nationality, not falling under the definition in point 2 of Article 2 who, in the country from which they have come, are dependants or members of the household of the Union citizen having the primary right of residence, or where serious health grounds strictly require the personal care of the family member by the Union citizen;

(b) the partner with whom the Union citizen has a durable relationship, duly attested.

The host Member State shall undertake an extensive examination of the personal circumstances and shall justify any denial of entry or residence to these people.

CHAPTER II

RIGHT OF EXIT AND ENTRY

Article 4

Right of exit

1.   Without prejudice to the provisions on travel documents applicable to national border controls, all Union citizens with a valid identity card or passport and their family members who are not nationals of a Member State and who hold a valid passport shall have the right to leave the territory of a Member State to travel to another Member State.

2.   No exit visa or equivalent formality may be imposed on the persons to whom paragraph 1 applies.

3.   Member States shall, acting in accordance with their laws, issue to their own nationals, and renew, an identity card or passport stating their nationality.

4.   The passport shall be valid at least for all Member States and for countries through which the holder must pass when travelling between Member States. Where the law of a Member State does not provide for identity cards to be issued, the period of validity of any passport on being issued or renewed shall be not less than five years.

Article 5

Right of entry

1.   Without prejudice to the provisions on travel documents applicable to national border controls, Member States shall grant Union citizens leave to enter their territory with a valid identity card or passport and shall grant family members who are not nationals of a Member State leave to enter their territory with a valid passport.

No entry visa or equivalent formality may be imposed on Union citizens.

2.   Family members who are not nationals of a Member State shall only be required to have an entry visa in accordance with Regulation (EC) No 539/2001 or, where appropriate, with national law. For the purposes of this Directive, possession of the valid residence card referred to in Article 10 shall exempt such family members from the visa requirement.

Member States shall grant such persons every facility to obtain the necessary visas. Such visas shall be issued free of charge as soon as possible and on the basis of an accelerated procedure.

3.   The host Member State shall not place an entry or exit stamp in the passport of family members who are not nationals of a Member State provided that they present the residence card provided for in Article 10.

4.   Where a Union citizen, or a family member who is not a national of a Member State, does not have the necessary travel documents or, if required, the necessary visas, the Member State concerned shall, before turning them back, give such persons every reasonable opportunity to obtain the necessary documents or have them brought to them within a reasonable period of time or to corroborate or prove by other means that they are covered by the right of free movement and residence.

5.   The Member State may require the person concerned to report his/her presence within its territory within a reasonable and non-discriminatory period of time. Failure to comply with this requirement may make the person concerned liable to proportionate and non-discriminatory sanctions.

CHAPTER III

RIGHT OF RESIDENCE

Article 6

Right of residence for up to three months

1.   Union citizens shall have the right of residence on the territory of another Member State for a period of up to three months without any conditions or any formalities other than the requirement to hold a valid identity card or passport.

2.   The provisions of paragraph 1 shall also apply to family members in possession of a valid passport who are not nationals of a Member State, accompanying or joining the Union citizen.

Article 7

Right of residence for more than three months

1.   All Union citizens shall have the right of residence on the territory of another Member State for a period of longer than three months if they:

(a) are workers or self-employed persons in the host Member State; or

(b) have sufficient resources for themselves and their family members not to become a burden on the social assistance system of the host Member State during their period of residence and have comprehensive sickness insurance cover in the host Member State; or

(c) — are enrolled at a private or public establishment, accredited or financed by the host Member State on the basis of its legislation or administrative practice, for the principal purpose of following a course of study, including vocational training; and

— have comprehensive sickness insurance cover in the host Member State and assure the relevant national authority, by means of a declaration or by such equivalent means as they may choose, that they have sufficient resources for themselves and their family members not to become a burden on the social assistance system of the host Member State during their period of residence; or

(d) are family members accompanying or joining a Union citizen who satisfies the conditions referred to in points (a), (b) or (c).

2. The right of residence provided for in paragraph 1 shall extend to family members who are not nationals of a Member State, accompanying or joining the Union citizen in the host Member State, provided that such Union citizen satisfies the conditions referred to in paragraph 1(a), (b) or (c).

3. For the purposes of paragraph 1(a), a Union citizen who is no longer a worker or self-employed person shall retain the status of worker or self-employed person in the following circumstances:

(a) he/she is temporarily unable to work as the result of an illness or accident;

(b) he/she is in duly recorded involuntary unemployment after having been employed for more than one year and has registered as a job-seeker with the relevant employment office;

(c) he/she is in duly recorded involuntary unemployment after completing a fixed-term employment contract of less than a year or after having become involuntarily unemployed during the first twelve months and has registered as a job-seeker with the relevant employment office. In this case, the status of worker shall be retained for no less than six months;

(d) he/she embarks on vocational training. Unless he/she is involuntarily unemployed, the retention of the status of worker shall require the training to be related to the previous employment.

4. By way of derogation from paragraphs 1(d) and 2 above, only the spouse, the registered partner provided for in Article 2(2)(b) and dependent children shall have the right of residence as family members of a Union citizen meeting the conditions under 1(c) above. Article 3(2) shall apply to his/her dependent direct relatives in the ascending lines and those of his/her spouse or registered partner.

Article 8

Administrative formalities for Union citizens

1. Without prejudice to Article 5(5), for periods of residence longer than three months, the host Member State may require Union citizens to register with the relevant authorities.

2. The deadline for registration may not be less than three months from the date of arrival. A registration certificate shall be issued immediately, stating the name and address of the person registering and the date of the registration. Failure to comply with the registration requirement may render the person concerned liable to proportionate and non-discriminatory sanctions.

3. For the registration certificate to be issued, Member States may only require that

— Union citizens to whom point (a) of Article 7(1) applies present a valid identity card or passport, a confirmation of engagement from the employer or a certificate of employment, or proof that they are self-employed persons,

— Union citizens to whom point (b) of Article 7(1) applies present a valid identity card or passport and provide proof that they satisfy the conditions laid down therein,

— Union citizens to whom point (c) of Article 7(1) applies present a valid identity card or passport, provide proof of enrolment at an accredited establishment and of comprehensive sickness insurance cover and the declaration or equivalent means referred to in point (c) of Article 7(1). Member States may not require this declaration to refer to any specific amount of resources.

4. Member States may not lay down a fixed amount which they regard as 'sufficient resources', but they must take into account the personal situation of the person concerned. In all cases this amount

shall not be higher than the threshold below which nationals of the host Member State become eligible for social assistance, or, where this criterion is not applicable, higher than the minimum social security pension paid by the host Member State.

5.   For the registration certificate to be issued to family members of Union citizens, who are themselves Union citizens, Member States may require the following documents to be presented:

(a) a valid identity card or passport;

(b) a document attesting to the existence of a family relationship or of a registered partnership;

(c) where appropriate, the registration certificate of the Union citizen whom they are accompanying or joining;

(d) in cases falling under points (c) and (d) of Article 2(2), documentary evidence that the conditions laid down therein are met;

(e) in cases falling under Article 3(2)(a), a document issued by the relevant authority in the country of origin or country from which they are arriving certifying that they are dependants or members of the household of the Union citizen, or proof of the existence of serious health grounds which strictly require the personal care of the family member by the Union citizen;

(f) in cases falling under Article 3(2)(b), proof of the existence of a durable relationship with the Union citizen.

Article 9

Administrative formalities for family members who are not nationals of a Member State

1.   Member States shall issue a residence card to family members of a Union citizen who are not nationals of a Member State, where the planned period of residence is for more than three months.

2.   The deadline for submitting the residence card application may not be less than three months from the date of arrival.

3.   Failure to comply with the requirement to apply for a residence card may make the person concerned liable to proportionate and non-discriminatory sanctions.

Article 10

Issue of residence cards

1.   The right of residence of family members of a Union citizen who are not nationals of a Member State shall be evidenced by the issuing of a document called 'Residence card of a family member of a Union citizen' no later than six months from the date on which they submit the application. A certificate of application for the residence card shall be issued immediately.

2.   For the residence card to be issued, Member States shall require presentation of the following documents:

(a) a valid passport;

(b) a document attesting to the existence of a family relationship or of a registered partnership;

(c) the registration certificate or, in the absence of a registration system, any other proof of residence in the host Member State of the Union citizen whom they are accompanying or joining;

(d) in cases falling under points (c) and (d) of Article 2(2), documentary evidence that the conditions laid down therein are met;

(e) in cases falling under Article 3(2)(a), a document issued by the relevant authority in the country of origin or country from which they are arriving certifying that they are dependants or members of the household of the Union citizen, or proof of the existence of

serious health grounds which strictly require the personal care of the
family member by the Union citizen;

(f) in cases falling under Article 3(2)(b), proof of the existence of a
durable relationship with the Union citizen.

Article 11

Validity of the residence card

1.   The residence card provided for by Article 10(1) shall be valid for
five years from the date of issue or for the envisaged period of residence
of the Union citizen, if this period is less than five years.

2.   The validity of the residence card shall not be affected by
temporary absences not exceeding six months a year, or by absences of
a longer duration for compulsory military service or by one absence of a
maximum of 12 consecutive months for important reasons such as
pregnancy and childbirth, serious illness, study or vocational training,
or a posting in another Member State or a third country.

Article 12

Retention of the right of residence by family members in the event of death or departure of the Union citizen

1.   Without prejudice to the second subparagraph, the Union citizen's
death or departure from the host Member State shall not affect the right
of residence of his/her family members who are nationals of a Member
State.

Before acquiring the right of permanent residence, the persons
concerned must meet the conditions laid down in points (a), (b), (c) or
(d) of Article 7(1).

2.   Without prejudice to the second subparagraph, the Union citizen's
death shall not entail loss of the right of residence of his/her family
members who are not nationals of a Member State and who have been
residing in the host Member State as family members for at least one
year before the Union citizen's death.

Before acquiring the right of permanent residence, the right of residence
of the persons concerned shall remain subject to the requirement that
they are able to show that they are workers or self-employed persons
or that they have sufficient resources for themselves and their family
members not to become a burden on the social assistance system of
the host Member State during their period of residence and have
comprehensive sickness insurance cover in the host Member State, or
that they are members of the family, already constituted in the host
Member State, of a person satisfying these requirements. 'Sufficient
resources' shall be as defined in Article 8(4).

Such family members shall retain their right of residence exclusively on
a personal basis.

3.   The Union citizen's departure from the host Member State or his/
her death shall not entail loss of the right of residence of his/her
children or of the parent who has actual custody of the children, irrespective of nationality, if the children reside in the host Member State
and are enrolled at an educational establishment, for the purpose of
studying there, until the completion of their studies.

Article 13

Retention of the right of residence by family members in the event of divorce, annulment of marriage or termination of registered partnership

1.   Without prejudice to the second subparagraph, divorce, annulment
of the Union citizen's marriage or termination of his/her registered
partnership, as referred to in point 2(b) of Article 2 shall not affect the
right of residence of his/her family members who are nationals of a
Member State.

Before acquiring the right of permanent residence, the persons concerned must meet the conditions laid down in points (a), (b), (c) or (d) of Article 7(1).

2.   Without prejudice to the second subparagraph, divorce, annulment of marriage or termination of the registered partnership referred to in point 2(b) of Article 2 shall not entail loss of the right of residence of a Union citizen's family members who are not nationals of a Member State where:

(a) prior to initiation of the divorce or annulment proceedings or termination of the registered partnership referred to in point 2(b) of Article 2, the marriage or registered partnership has lasted at least three years, including one year in the host Member State; or

(b) by agreement between the spouses or the partners referred to in point 2(b) of Article 2 or by court order, the spouse or partner who is not a national of a Member State has custody of the Union citizen's children; or

(c) this is warranted by particularly difficult circumstances, such as having been a victim of domestic violence while the marriage or registered partnership was subsisting; or

(d) by agreement between the spouses or partners referred to in point 2 (b) of Article 2 or by court order, the spouse or partner who is not a national of a Member State has the right of access to a minor child, provided that the court has ruled that such access must be in the host Member State, and for as long as is required.

Before acquiring the right of permanent residence, the right of residence of the persons concerned shall remain subject to the requirement that they are able to show that they are workers or self-employed persons or that they have sufficient resources for themselves and their family members not to become a burden on the social assistance system of the host Member State during their period of residence and have comprehensive sickness insurance cover in the host Member State, or that they are members of the family, already constituted in the host Member State, of a person satisfying these requirements. 'Sufficient resources' shall be as defined in Article 8(4).

Such family members shall retain their right of residence exclusively on personal basis.

Article 14

Retention of the right of residence

1.   Union citizens and their family members shall have the right of residence provided for in Article 6, as long as they do not become an unreasonable burden on the social assistance system of the host Member State.

2.   Union citizens and their family members shall have the right of residence provided for in Articles 7, 12 and 13 as long as they meet the conditions set out therein.

In specific cases where there is a reasonable doubt as to whether a Union citizen or his/her family members satisfies the conditions set out in Articles 7, 12 and 13, Member States may verify if these conditions are fulfilled. This verification shall not be carried out systematically.

3.   An expulsion measure shall not be the automatic consequence of a Union citizen's or his or her family member's recourse to the social assistance system of the host Member State.

4.   By way of derogation from paragraphs 1 and 2 and without prejudice to the provisions of Chapter VI, an expulsion measure may in no case be adopted against Union citizens or their family members if:

(a) the Union citizens are workers or self-employed persons, or

(b) the Union citizens entered the territory of the host Member State in order to seek employment. In this case, the Union citizens and their family members may not be expelled for as long as the Union citizens can provide evidence that they are continuing to seek employment and that they have a genuine chance of being engaged.

Article 15

Procedural safeguards

1.   The procedures provided for by Articles 30 and 31 shall apply by analogy to all decisions restricting free movement of Union citizens and their family members on grounds other than public policy, public security or public health.

2.   Expiry of the identity card or passport on the basis of which the person concerned entered the host Member State and was issued with a registration certificate or residence card shall not constitute a ground for expulsion from the host Member State.

3.   The host Member State may not impose a ban on entry in the context of an expulsion decision to which paragraph 1 applies.

CHAPTER IV

RIGHT OF PERMANENT RESIDENCE

Section I

Eligibility

Article 16

General rule for Union citizens and their family members

1.   Union citizens who have resided legally for a continuous period of five years in the host Member State shall have the right of permanent residence there. This right shall not be subject to the conditions provided for in Chapter III.

2.   Paragraph 1 shall apply also to family members who are not nationals of a Member State and have legally resided with the Union citizen in the host Member State for a continuous period of five years.

3.   Continuity of residence shall not be affected by temporary absences not exceeding a total of six months a year, or by absences of a longer duration for compulsory military service, or by one absence of a maximum of 12 consecutive months for important reasons such as pregnancy and childbirth, serious illness, study or vocational training, or a posting in another Member State or a third country.

4.   Once acquired, the right of permanent residence shall be lost only through absence from the host Member State for a period exceeding two consecutive years.

Article 17

Exemptions for persons no longer working in the host Member State and their family members

1.   By way of derogation from Article 16, the right of permanent residence in the host Member State shall be enjoyed before completion of a continuous period of five years of residence by:

(a) workers or self-employed persons who, at the time they stop working, have reached the age laid down by the law of that Member State for entitlement to an old age pension or workers who cease paid employment to take early retirement, provided that they have been working in that Member State for at least the preceding twelve months and have resided there continuously for more than three years.

If the law of the host Member State does not grant the right to an old age pension to certain categories of self-employed persons, the age condition shall be deemed to have been met once the person concerned has reached the age of 60;

(b) workers or self-employed persons who have resided continuously in the host Member State for more than two years and stop working there as a result of permanent incapacity to work.

If such incapacity is the result of an accident at work or an occupational disease entitling the person concerned to a benefit payable in full or in part by an institution in the host Member State, no condition shall be imposed as to length of residence;

(c) workers or self-employed persons who, after three years of continuous employment and residence in the host Member State, work in an employed or self-employed capacity in another Member State, while retaining their place of residence in the host Member State, to which they return, as a rule, each day or at least once a week.

For the purposes of entitlement to the rights referred to in points (a) and (b), periods of employment spent in the Member State in which the person concerned is working shall be regarded as having been spent in the host Member State.

Periods of involuntary unemployment duly recorded by the relevant employment office, periods not worked for reasons not of the person's own making and absences from work or cessation of work due to illness or accident shall be regarded as periods of employment.

2.   The conditions as to length of residence and employment laid down in point (a) of paragraph 1 and the condition as to length of residence laid down in point (b) of paragraph 1 shall not apply if the worker's or the self-employed person's spouse or partner as referred to in point 2(b) of Article 2 is a national of the host Member State or has lost the nationality of that Member State by marriage to that worker or self-employed person.

3.   Irrespective of nationality, the family members of a worker or a self-employed person who are residing with him in the territory of the host Member State shall have the right of permanent residence in that Member State, if the worker or self-employed person has acquired himself the right of permanent residence in that Member State on the basis of paragraph 1.

4.   If, however, the worker or self-employed person dies while still working but before acquiring permanent residence status in the host Member State on the basis of paragraph 1, his family members who are residing with him in the host Member State shall acquire the right of permanent residence there, on condition that:

(a) the worker or self-employed person had, at the time of death, resided continuously on the territory of that Member State for two years; or

(b) the death resulted from an accident at work or an occupational disease; or

(c) the surviving spouse lost the nationality of that Member State following marriage to the worker or self-employed person.

Article 18

Acquisition of the right of permanent residence by certain family members who are not nationals of a Member State

Without prejudice to Article 17, the family members of a Union citizen to whom Articles 12(2) and 13(2) apply, who satisfy the conditions laid down therein, shall acquire the right of permanent residence after residing legally for a period of five consecutive years in the host Member State.

Section II

Administrative formalities

Article 19

Document certifying permanent residence for Union citizens

1.   Upon application Member States shall issue Union citizens entitled to permanent residence, after having verified duration of residence, with a document certifying permanent residence.

2.   The document certifying permanent residence shall be issued as soon as possible.

Article 20

Permanent residence card for family members who are not nationals of a Member State

1.   Member States shall issue family members who are not nationals of a Member State entitled to permanent residence with a permanent residence card within six months of the submission of the application. The permanent residence card shall be renewable automatically every 10 years.

2.   The application for a permanent residence card shall be submitted before the residence card expires. Failure to comply with the requirement to apply for a permanent residence card may render the person concerned liable to proportionate and non-discriminatory sanctions.

3.   Interruption in residence not exceeding two consecutive years shall not affect the validity of the permanent residence card.

Article 21

Continuity of residence

For the purposes of this Directive, continuity of residence may be attested by any means of proof in use in the host Member State. Continuity of residence is broken by any expulsion decision duly enforced against the person concerned.

CHAPTER V

PROVISIONS COMMON TO THE RIGHT OF RESIDENCE AND THE RIGHT OF PERMANENT RESIDENCE

Article 22

Territorial scope

The right of residence and the right of permanent residence shall cover the whole territory of the host Member State. Member States may impose territorial restrictions on the right of residence and the right of permanent residence only where the same restrictions apply to their own nationals.

Article 23

Related rights

Irrespective of nationality, the family members of a Union citizen who have the right of residence or the right of permanent residence in a Member State shall be entitled to take up employment or self-employment there.

Article 24

Equal treatment

1.   Subject to such specific provisions as are expressly provided for in the Treaty and secondary law, all Union citizens residing on the basis of

this Directive in the territory of the host Member State shall enjoy equal treatment with the nationals of that Member State within the scope of the Treaty. The benefit of this right shall be extended to family members who are not nationals of a Member State and who have the right of residence or permanent residence.

2. By way of derogation from paragraph 1, the host Member State shall not be obliged to confer entitlement to social assistance during the first three months of residence or, where appropriate, the longer period provided for in Article 14(4)(b), nor shall it be obliged, prior to acquisition of the right of permanent residence, to grant maintenance aid for studies, including vocational training, consisting in student grants or student loans to persons other than workers, self-employed persons, persons who retain such status and members of their families.

Article 25

General provisions concerning residence documents

1. Possession of a registration certificate as referred to in Article 8, of a document certifying permanent residence, of a certificate attesting submission of an application for a family member residence card, of a residence card or of a permanent residence card, may under no circumstances be made a precondition for the exercise of a right or the completion of an administrative formality, as entitlement to rights may be attested by any other means of proof.

2. All documents mentioned in paragraph 1 shall be issued free of charge or for a charge not exceeding that imposed on nationals for the issuing of similar documents.

Article 26

Checks

Member States may carry out checks on compliance with any requirement deriving from their national legislation for non-nationals always to carry their registration certificate or residence card, provided that the same requirement applies to their own nationals as regards their identity card. In the event of failure to comply with this requirement, Member States may impose the same sanctions as those imposed on their own nationals for failure to carry their identity card.

CHAPTER VI

RESTRICTIONS ON THE RIGHT OF ENTRY AND THE RIGHT OF RESIDENCE ON GROUNDS OF PUBLIC POLICY, PUBLIC SECURITY OR PUBLIC HEALTH

Article 27

General principles

1. Subject to the provisions of this Chapter, Member States may restrict the freedom of movement and residence of Union citizens and their family members, irrespective of nationality, on grounds of public policy, public security or public health. These grounds shall not be invoked to serve economic ends.

2. Measures taken on grounds of public policy or public security shall comply with the principle of proportionality and shall be based exclusively on the personal conduct of the individual concerned. Previous criminal convictions shall not in themselves constitute grounds for taking such measures.

The personal conduct of the individual concerned must represent a genuine, present and sufficiently serious threat affecting one of the fundamental interests of society. Justifications that are isolated from the particulars of the case or that rely on considerations of general prevention shall not be accepted.

3. In order to ascertain whether the person concerned represents a danger for public policy or public security, when issuing the registration

certificate or, in the absence of a registration system, not later than three months from the date of arrival of the person concerned on its territory or from the date of reporting his/her presence within the territory, as provided for in Article 5(5), or when issuing the residence card, the host Member State may, should it consider this essential, request the Member State of origin and, if need be, other Member States to provide information concerning any previous police record the person concerned may have. Such enquiries shall not be made as a matter of routine. The Member State consulted shall give its reply within two months.

4.   The Member State which issued the passport or identity card shall allow the holder of the document who has been expelled on grounds of public policy, public security, or public health from another Member State to re-enter its territory without any formality even if the document is no longer valid or the nationality of the holder is in dispute.

Article 28

Protection against expulsion

1.   Before taking an expulsion decision on grounds of public policy or public security, the host Member State shall take account of considerations such as how long the individual concerned has resided on its territory, his/her age, state of health, family and economic situation, social and cultural integration into the host Member State and the extent of his/her links with the country of origin.

2.   The host Member State may not take an expulsion decision against Union citizens or their family members, irrespective of nationality, who have the right of permanent residence on its territory, except on serious grounds of public policy or public security.

3.   An expulsion decision may not be taken against Union citizens, except if the decision is based on imperative grounds of public security, as defined by Member States, if they:

(a) have resided in the host Member State for the previous 10 years; or

(b) are a minor, except if the expulsion is necessary for the best interests of the child, as provided for in the United Nations Convention on the Rights of the Child of 20 November 1989.

Article 29

Public health

1.   The only diseases justifying measures restricting freedom of movement shall be the diseases with epidemic potential as defined by the relevant instruments of the World Health Organisation and other infectious diseases or contagious parasitic diseases if they are the subject of protection provisions applying to nationals of the host Member State.

2.   Diseases occurring after a three-month period from the date of arrival shall not constitute grounds for expulsion from the territory.

3.   Where there are serious indications that it is necessary, Member States may, within three months of the date of arrival, require persons entitled to the right of residence to undergo, free of charge, a medical examination to certify that they are not suffering from any of the conditions referred to in paragraph 1. Such medical examinations may not be required as a matter of routine.

Article 30

Notification of decisions

1.   The persons concerned shall be notified in writing of any decision taken under Article 27(1), in such a way that they are able to comprehend its content and the implications for them.

2.　The persons concerned shall be informed, precisely and in full, of the public policy, public security or public health grounds on which the decision taken in their case is based, unless this is contrary to the interests of State security.

3.　The notification shall specify the court or administrative authority with which the person concerned may lodge an appeal, the time limit for the appeal and, where applicable, the time allowed for the person to leave the territory of the Member State. Save in duly substantiated cases of urgency, the time allowed to leave the territory shall be not less than one month from the date of notification.

Article 31

Procedural safeguards

1.　The persons concerned shall have access to judicial and, where appropriate, administrative redress procedures in the host Member State to appeal against or seek review of any decision taken against them on the grounds of public policy, public security or public health.

2.　Where the application for appeal against or judicial review of the expulsion decision is accompanied by an application for an interim order to suspend enforcement of that decision, actual removal from the territory may not take place until such time as the decision on the interim order has been taken, except:

— where the expulsion decision is based on a previous judicial decision; or

— where the persons concerned have had previous access to judicial review; or

— where the expulsion decision is based on imperative grounds of public security under Article 28(3).

3.　The redress procedures shall allow for an examination of the legality of the decision, as well as of the facts and circumstances on which the proposed measure is based. They shall ensure that the decision is not disproportionate, particularly in view of the requirements laid down in Article 28.

4.　Member States may exclude the individual concerned from their territory pending the redress procedure, but they may not prevent the individual from submitting his/her defence in person, except when his/her appearance may cause serious troubles to public policy or public security or when the appeal or judicial review concerns a denial of entry to the territory.

Article 32

Duration of exclusion orders

1.　Persons excluded on grounds of public policy or public security may submit an application for lifting of the exclusion order after a reasonable period, depending on the circumstances, and in any event after three years from enforcement of the final exclusion order which has been validly adopted in accordance with Community law, by putting forward arguments to establish that there has been a material change in the circumstances which justified the decision ordering their exclusion.

The Member State concerned shall reach a decision on this application within six months of its submission.

2.　The persons referred to in paragraph 1 shall have no right of entry to the territory of the Member State concerned while their application is being considered.

Article 33

Expulsion as a penalty or legal consequence

1.   Expulsion orders may not be issued by the host Member State as a penalty or legal consequence of a custodial penalty, unless they conform to the requirements of Articles 27, 28 and 29.

2.   If an expulsion order, as provided for in paragraph 1, is enforced more than two years after it was issued, the Member State shall check that the individual concerned is currently and genuinely a threat to public policy or public security and shall assess whether there has been any material change in the circumstances since the expulsion order was issued.

CHAPTER VII

FINAL PROVISIONS

Article 34

Publicity

Member States shall disseminate information concerning the rights and obligations of Union citizens and their family members on the subjects covered by this Directive, particularly by means of awareness-raising campaigns conducted through national and local media and other means of communication.

Article 35

Abuse of rights

Member States may adopt the necessary measures to refuse, terminate or withdraw any right conferred by this Directive in the case of abuse of rights or fraud, such as marriages of convenience. Any such measure shall be proportionate and subject to the procedural safeguards provided for in Articles 30 and 31.

Article 36

Sanctions

Member States shall lay down provisions on the sanctions applicable to breaches of national rules adopted for the implementation of this Directive and shall take the measures required for their application. The sanctions laid down shall be effective and proportionate. Member States shall notify the Commission of these provisions not later than 30 April 2006 and as promptly as possible in the case of any subsequent changes.

Article 37

More favourable national provisions

The provisions of this Directive shall not affect any laws, regulations or administrative provisions laid down by a Member State which would be more favourable to the persons covered by this Directive.

Article 38

Repeals

1.   Articles 10 and 11 of Regulation (EEC) No 1612/68 shall be repealed with effect from 30 April 2006.

2.   Directives 64/221/EEC, 68/360/EEC, 72/194/EEC, 73/148/EEC, 75/34/EEC, 75/35/EEC, 90/364/EEC, 90/365/EEC and 93/96/EEC shall be repealed with effect from 30 April 2006.

3.   References made to the repealed provisions and Directives shall be construed as being made to this Directive.

Article 39

Report

No later than 30 April 2008   the Commission shall submit a report on the application of this Directive to the European Parliament and the Council, together with any necessary proposals, notably on the opportunity to extend the period of time during which Union citizens and their family members may reside in the territory of the host Member State without any conditions. The Member States shall provide the Commission with the information needed to produce the report.

Article 40

Transposition

1.   Member States shall bring into force the laws, regulations and administrative provisions necessary to comply with this Directive by 30 April 2006.

When Member States adopt those measures, they shall contain a reference to this Directive or shall be accompanied by such a reference on the occasion of their official publication. The methods of making such reference shall be laid down by the Member States.

2.   Member States shall communicate to the Commission the text of the provisions of national law which they adopt in the field covered by this Directive together with a table showing how the provisions of this Directive correspond to the national provisions adopted.

Article 41

Entry into force

This Directive shall enter into force on the day of its publication in the *Official Journal of the European Union*.

Article 42

Addressees

This Directive is addressed to the Member States.